REFUSING SETTLER DOMESTICITY

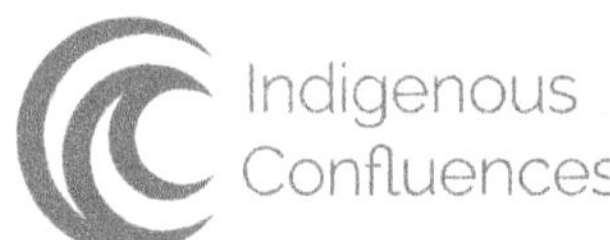

CHARLOTTE COTÉ AND COLL THRUSH *Series Editors*

CAITLIN KELIIAA

Refusing Settler Domesticity

Native Women's Labor and Resistance in the Bay Area Outing Program

University of Washington Press *Seattle*

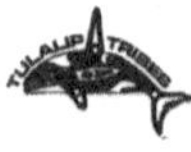

Refusing Settler Domesticity was made possible in part by a generous grant from the Tulalip Tribes Charitable Fund, which provides the opportunity for a sustainable and healthy community for all.

Design by Mindy Basinger Hill

Composed in Minion Pro

UNIVERSITY OF WASHINGTON PRESS / uwapress.uw.edu

LIBRARY OF CONGRESS CATALOGING-IN-PUBLICATION DATA

Names: Keliiaa, Caitlin, author.

Title: Refusing settler domesticity : native women's labor and resistance in the Bay Area Outing Program / Caitlin Keliiaa.

Description: Seattle : University of Washington Press, [2024] | Series: Indigenous confluences | Includes bibliographical references and index.

Identifiers: LCCN 2024022964 (print) | LCCN 2024022965 (ebook) | ISBN 9780295752983 (hardcover) | ISBN 9780295753003 (paperback) | ISBN 9780295752990 (ebook)

Subjects: LCSH: Indian girls—Social conditions—20th century. | Indian women—Social conditions—20th century. | Forced labor—California—San Francisco Bay Area—History—20th century. | Indians of North America—Cultural assimilation—California—San Francisco Bay Area—History—20th century. | San Francisco Bay Area (Calif.)—Social conditions—20th century.

Classification: LCC E78.C15 K455 2024 (print) | LCC E78.C15 (ebook) | DDC 979.4/610500497—dc23/eng/20240705

LC record available at https://lccn.loc.gov/2024022964

LC ebook record available at https://lccn.loc.gov/2024022965

♾ This paper meets the requirements of ANSI/NISO Z39.48-1992 (Permanence of Paper).

ABOUT THE COVER PHOTO: (*left to right*) Students Fomina Jackson and Agnes Dyer and teacher Helen Sheahan from Stewart Indian School. The photo ran with a piece titled "Indian Girls Rapidly Acquire Knowledge of Domestic Arts" that described an "experiment"—a precursor to the Bay Area Outing Program—to enable local housewives to acquire cheap Indian labor to "solve the servant problem." Dyer would later build her life in the San Francisco Bay Area.

Refusing Settler Domesticity: Native Women's Labor and Resistance in the Bay Area Outing Program is dedicated to the incredible women in my life who made me who I am today. To my grandma Margaret for being an unwavering cheerleader. To my grandma Helen, for her grounding assertiveness. And to my moo for giving me light and paving the way. You all made sacrifices for me, and I am eternally grateful.

For all the maternal figures in our lives who carry us, thank you.

Contents

Acknowledgments / *ix*

Preface / *xi*

Prologue / *xv*

Introduction / *1*

ONE / Domestic Labor in California, 1769–1940 / *22*

TWO / The Bay Area Outing Program: A Promise and a Predicament / *42*

THREE / "Indian Girls Prefer Park to Housework": Criminalization, Surveillance, and Runaways / *83*

FOUR / Breaking the Family: Outing Mothers and Indian Child Removal / *111*

FIVE / Containment, Sexual Surveillance, and Bodily Regulation / *147*

SIX / The Failure of Indian Health Care: A Negligent Privilege / *177*

Conclusion / *204*

Notes / *213*

Bibliography / *253*

Index / *267*

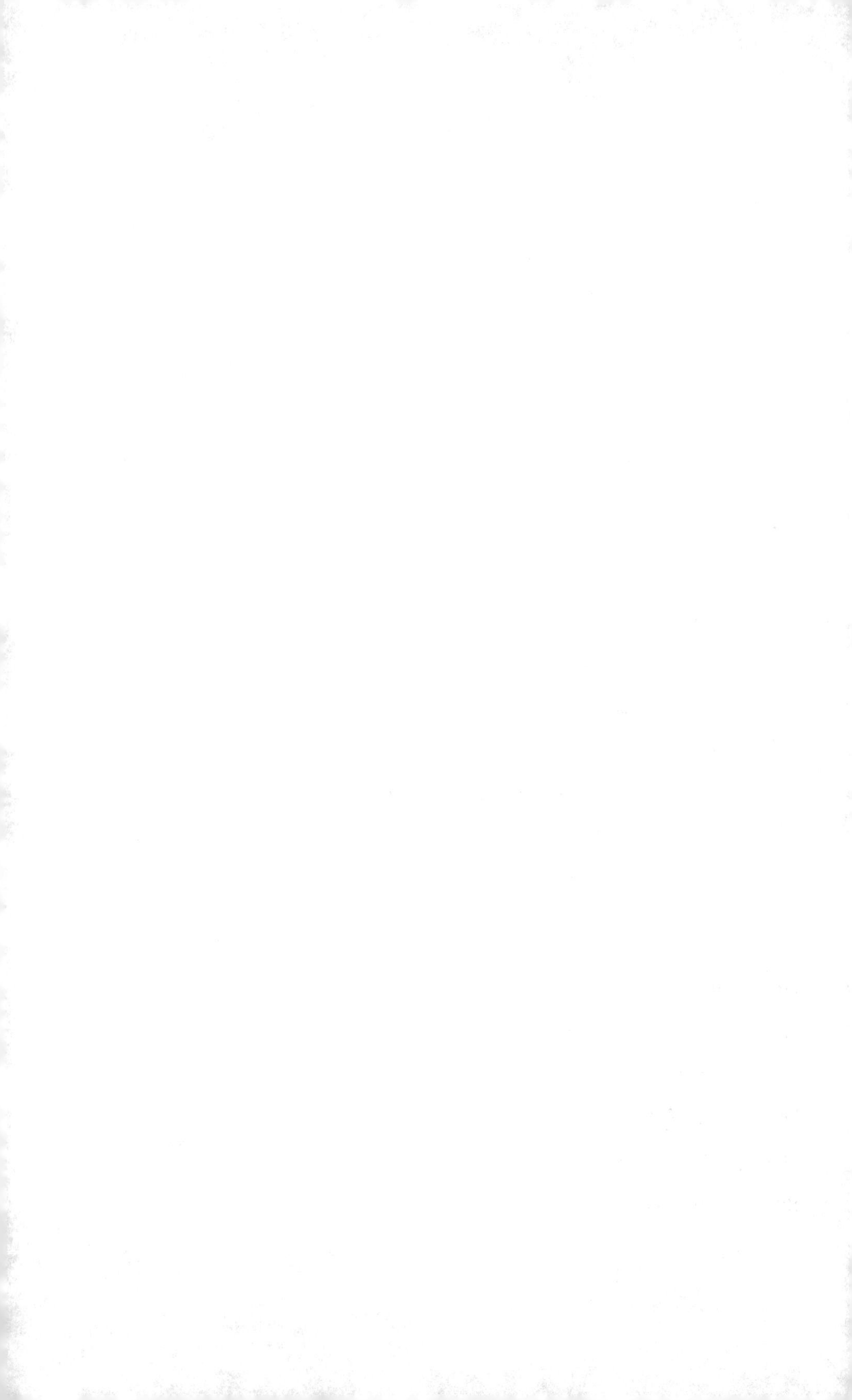

Acknowledgments

I HAVE MANY PEOPLE TO THANK for their love and support, which has made *Refusing Settler Domesticity* possible. I am grateful to my amazing committee for intellectually challenging me and supporting me: Shari Huhndorf, Tom Biolsi, Mark Brilliant, Evelyn Nakano Glenn, and Tsianina Lomawaima. To Deborah Lustig, Christine Trost, and David Minkus at the Institute for the Study of Societal Issues for uplifting my voice. I want to express my gratitude for my immensely supportive friends who offered guidance on this project: Kat Whiteley, Stephanie Lumsden, Olivia Chilcote, Ina Kelleher, Will Gow, and Jen Smith. The incredible Dana Linda Carballo was with me every step of the way. And I especially thank Dani Carrillo and Juliet Kunkel, who gave me strength when I needed it most.

Thank you to my friends and colleagues at UC Santa Cruz for encouraging me, Amy Lonetree, Judy Scott, Renya Ramirez, Felicity Amaya Schaeffer, and my IFN crew. To my book manuscript workshop dream team, William Bauer Jr., Mishuana Goeman, Margaret Jacobs, and Cutcha Risling Baldy. And to my editors at UW, Mike Baccam and Larin McLaughlin, and my copy editors, Hannah Archambault and Elizabeth Mathews. To my stellar undergraduate research assistants, Marina Cuneo, Daniella Dane, Bryce Lennan, and Sophia Grewell—a million thanks for your curiosity, talent, and dedication. Each of you brought something special to the project, and I am in awe of what we were able to accomplish. Thank you to all the librarians, archivists, and staff that made this research possible. I am also indebted to the unwavering support of the Bay Area Indian community and the Native community at UC Berkeley and UC Santa Cruz.

Refusing Settler Domesticity has been supported by generous grants from the American Council of Learned Societies, the Institute of American Cultures Visiting Research Scholar Fellowship, the Hellman Fellows, the Humanities Institute Faculty Research Fellowship, the Writing Fellows Program, the Ford Foundation, the Native Forward Scholars Fund, the Mellon/ACLS Dissertation Completion Fellowship, the Joseph A. Myers Center for Research on Native American Issues, the Graduate Fellows Program, the Institute for the Study of Societal Issues, the Center for Race and Gender, the Yerington Paiute Tribe, the Pinto-Fialon Graduate Fellowship, the Eugene V. Cota-Robles Fellowship, Koret Scholars Mentored Research, the Undergraduate Research Apprentice Program, and the Student Mentoring and Research Teams program.

And finally, thank you to my family for supporting my life as a perpetual student. In the difficult times and in the best, I am comforted by your love and laughter. To my husband, Donny, thank you for believing in me. I am eternally grateful for your love and couldn't ask for a better partner. Shout out to Jo Blow from Kokomo! And my godmother Shannon for cheering me on. Special thanks to Doo—my dad—for stepping up to the challenge of raising four loud girls. You are doing a *wonderful* job. *le ʔáŋawiʔ*! To my moo—*a minha querida mãezinha*—I hold your spirit and tenacity deep in my heart. Thank you for paving the way and fostering a love of education within me. *Amo-te para todo o sempre.* And to my grandma Helen—my *hutsi'i*—for inspiring this project. I am thankful for all that you did to bring me into this world.

Preface

I WRITE ON A GORGEOUS SEPTEMBER DAY, overlooking crystal-blue waters from my lakeside lodge at the Meeks Bay Resort. It's the first day of fall. I hear gentle waves lapping at the shoreline, the sun is out, and the air is crisp. In the late 1990s, then president Bill Clinton authorized a thirty-year agreement for the Washoe Tribe of Nevada and California to manage the resort and campground. Since then, my family has been coming to the lake annually and creating special memories on the shores of our ancestors.

daʔawʔá·gaʔ, or Lake Tahoe as it is known by many,[1] is the center of the Washoe universe. We have been coming to this lake for tens of thousands of years, since long before settlers arrived. It's a gathering place of great significance for Washoe people, where we have creation stories and sacred sites. And yet, the Washoe Tribe owns hardly a fraction of the land at Lake Tahoe. Across seventy-two miles of shoreline, not one mile belongs to our community. Few of the fifteen million tourists who visit the shores of *daʔawʔá·gaʔ* annually are even aware that they are visiting the ancestral homelands of the Washoe people. And so, when my family and I return here each year, we reconnect with a place whose soil, trees, and water run deep within our veins.

This recent history of *daʔawʔá·gaʔ* is a story of dispossession that is all too familiar for Native American communities, and it connects to the history of this book. *Refusing Settler Domesticity* reveals the unknown history of the Bay Area Outing Program. In the Bay Area, a place that is often considered a liberal bastion, Native American girls and women were funneled from Indian boarding schools to become live-in housemaids for elite and otherwise well-to-do white homeowners. The origins of this program are connected to Stewart Indian School in Carson City, Nevada. Built by the Office of Indian Affairs in 1890, Stewart was intended to assimilate Indian children. As the school was in the Great Basin, most students were Washoe, Paiute, and Shoshone from Nevada and California. Stewart and other Indian boarding schools attempted assimilation though vocational labor. Boys were taught trades such as masonry, carpentry, printing, and blacksmithing. Girls, however, were solely taught "domestic science," which effectively trained Indian girls to be maids. Indian children labored at schools like Stewart to gain "work experience" for the purposes of education. Outside of a typical school year, students were regularly contracted out to labor for local white farms and homes through the school's "outing" program. Native children regularly "outed" during summer and winter breaks when they should have been reunited with their families.

In the early 1900s, Stewart matrons wanted to put their students' training to use and thus placed Indian girls in homes throughout the Bay Area. This early iteration of outing was small and sparse. However, nearly two decades later, the Bay Area Outing Program became markedly more prolific. This independently run institution would funnel girls and women from not just Stewart but several other Indian boarding schools throughout the nation. Through outing programs such as this one, Native girls and women, from relatively matriarchal societies, were taught to be subservient and reproduce settler modes of domesticity.

I write this book as a Yerington Paiute and Washoe historian and an Urban Indian woman born and raised in Hayward, California. The Bay Area is home to a large Urban Indian population, including several community hubs and centers such as the American Indian Child Resource Center, Friendship House SF, the Intertribal Friendship House, the Native American Health Center, and the Indian Health Center of Santa Clara Valley. For generations, it has been home to major powwows, Indian sports leagues, schools, a Native film festival, and countless other culturally significant programming and events. Also, the Bay is connected to a deep history of Native activism, protest, and resistance. And for thousands of years, since long before this pan-Indian community came to the Bay Area, Ohlone people have called it home. We are all guests in their homelands. The Bay Area has always been a Native place and always will be.

Growing up in the Bay Area, I was regularly connected to this vibrant Native community, one that thrives to this day. And perhaps these are some of the unintended consequences of Indian policy. While Indian boarding schools and Indian Relocation were meant to assimilate, Native people used these federal projects to their own advantage. They embraced the city; they built community and have sustained generations. So while this story is one of dispossession, it also reveals a great deal of resistance and self-determination.

Prologue

TODAY, THE SAN FRANCISCO BAY AREA IS KNOWN for its mild coastal climate, diversity, liberal politics, expensive housing, and excellent food. It's the home of many tech booms and busts, top universities, and groundbreaking discoveries and inventions like the cable car, all-electric TV, and It's-It ice cream sandwiches. Bay Area streets have character and charm and exude a distinct culture. Across the stretch of nine counties, nearly eight million people call the Bay Area home. But one hundred years ago, when Native girls hopped off the train in Oakland, the Bay Area was a little different. Certainly, it was the home of commerce and invention, with its own version of industry moguls. In the mid-nineteenth century, with the advent of the transcontinental railroad and its terminus in Oakland, the East Bay became a well-connected and industrious region. Even then, it was considered diverse, with African American and Chinese enclaves, Native Americans of course, and an array of newly immigrated Europeans, including Portuguese and Italians. Many of these early residents were working-class and worked in factories, mills, and the railroad industry.[1]

As the new railroad tied California and the Bay Area more securely to the national economy, it brought in a flood of new residents, including the poor and destitute—among them, women and children. In turn, women in Oakland took steps to organize a new charitable landscape to deal with rapid urbanization and the feminization of poverty.[2] This new culture of charity was absolutely gendered. As one scholar notes, "White men counted on white women to provide poor relief for less fortunate women and children, and the female sex obliged in California as elsewhere in the nation."[3] These charitable women deferred to the notion of female dominion in philanthropy, especially for charity focused on women and children. They used their perceived moral authority and ties to religious and family life to establish charities and secure a space of their own.[4] For instance, the Ladies' Relief Society in Oakland, a charity that became well connected with the Bay Area Outing Program, was founded by wealthy, white, married women. Therefore, by the late nineteenth century, a culture of white women's charity was already present in the ever-expanding East Bay.

While San Francisco, the largest city in the West, may have initially eclipsed the East Bay, the latter region began to grow, especially after the 1906 earthquake. At 5:12 a.m. on April 18, 1906, a 7.7 magnitude earthquake rocked the Bay Area. Its epicenter was San Francisco. The quake ruptured 296 miles of Northern California's coastline and was felt from southern Oregon to south of Los Angeles and inland as far as central Nevada. As damaging as the earthquake and its aftershocks were, the subsequent three days of fires that spread throughout the city were far more destructive. In total, twenty-eight thousand buildings were destroyed, and more than three thousand lives were lost. San Francisco suffered the most fatalities.[5] When transportation across the bay resumed, thousands fled to the East Bay, especially Oakland. Between 1900 and 1910, Oakland's population ballooned 45 percent, to 150,000 residents.[6]

Postearthquake flight to the East Bay created a housing construction boom. The 1920s brought new real estate tracts like Piedmont, Montclair, and Trestle Glen, affluent neighborhoods that would become known for hiring Indian girls in the Bay Area Outing Program. By 1923, the Oakland region experienced a 900 percent increase in dwellings made over the past five years. While Oakland may have reflected a more working-class community in the nineteenth century, these newer tracts and neighborhoods were decidedly more upper-class. These new communities were praised for their fantastic views of the San Francisco Bay Area and their distance from the grime of the city. Residents in communities like Piedmont and Montclair found themselves, as one person put it, "far removed from the dirt and turmoil of the work-a-day world as though they have traveled fifty miles into the mountains."[7] Homes in these new districts were "restricted," meaning they were designed and sold with the prohibition of apartment houses, "freak houses," "shacks," and other undesirable or unsightly features. Unsurprisingly, many of these neighborhoods also adhered to racial covenants. For instance, a company developing in Lakeshore Highlands defined the following clause: "No person of African, Japanese, Chinese, or of any Mongolian descent, shall be allowed to purchase own or lease said property . . . or to live upon said property . . . except in the capacity of domestic servants of the occupant thereof."[8] The key exception here was domestic servants. So, while African American, Asian American, and therefore Native American people could not purchase or rent in these neighborhoods, they were allowed to live in these homes in the pursuit of domestic work.

And work they would. Homeowners in these newly established upper-class neighborhoods had the resources to hire help. And tapping into the feminization of charity, wealthy, white, married women were apt to hire the less fortunate; enter Native American girls. This phenomenon is best captured in a June 6, 1919, *Oakland Tribune* article. The front-page spread with an image of Indian girls announces, "27 Indian Girls from Reservation Welcomed by Oakland Housewives." The photo captures a large group of Washoe and Paiute girls, aged thirteen to twenty years old, adorned in their hats and coats, overflowing past the frame. Among the girls pictured are a few modest smiles but, overwhelmingly, concerned or indifferent faces, including that of one girl in a hat who looks forlorn. The corresponding article declares, "Shortage in Domestic Help Is Partly Received." The article maintains that the girls from the Carson Indian School in Stewart, Nevada, arrived to "help local housewives solve the problem of summer help" and that every girl was placed in a home within two hours of her arrival. The article professes, "Housewives breathed a sigh of relief at their coming" and notes that a second contingent of girls would be arriving the following week. The article cautions that a group of younger girls who could serve as nursemaids would be left in Stewart, "unless some eager women register" with the outing matron.[9] This front-page spread accomplished a great deal;

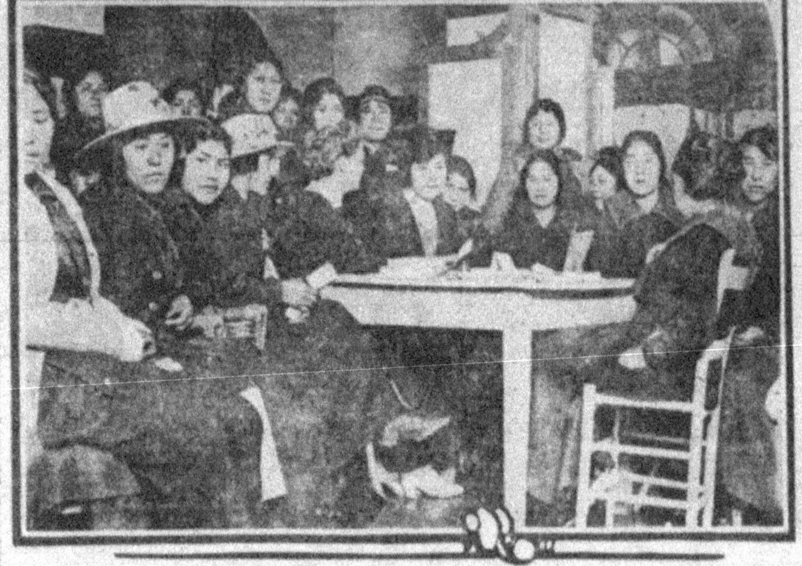

27 Indian Girls From Reservation Welcomed by Oakland Housewives

Oakland housewives are to have assistance in their work from twenty-seven Indian maids right from the reservation. Here are some of the twenty-seven, who arrived at the Y. W. C. A. today. They are all provided with places.

FIGURE 1. On June 6, 1919, the front page of the *Oakland Tribune* announced, "27 Indian Girls from Reservation Welcomed by Oakland Housewives." The photo, taken at the Oakland YWCA, captures a large group of Washoe and Paiute women and girls, adorned in their hats and coats before they are sent off their respective outing placements.

it established the local shortage and desire for live-in domestic workers, announced the arrival of Indian girls, and advertised the outing program for "eager women" who required the help of an Indian girl.

It must have been jarring for these young girls to have disembarked from the train in Oakland, be shuttled to this staged photo shoot at the Oakland YWCA, and then immediately be handed over to their new employers. It could not have been easy to be thrust into the city and then into a stranger's home where you would live and work for the next three months or longer. But the change of scenery that came with outing in the Bay Area must have felt like a reprieve from the monotony of rural boarding school life. Oakland, for instance, had three theaters to choose from, the Grand Lake Theatre, the Fox, and the Paramount. There, orchestras and famous touring concerts would delight crowds from all over the East Bay. In downtown Oakland, ballrooms and dance venues hosted famous musicians from across the nation.[10] Celebrated iconic sites like Lake Merritt, with its regatta boathouse and "necklace of lights," offered recreation. Downtown Oakland boasted architectural feats like City Hall, which was the first in the nation to be a designated skyscraper.[11] And across the city, Oakland had shops and department stores that Stewart, Nevada, could never compete with—stores where girls could spend their hard-earned monies on the latest fashions. While we cannot assume that all these amusements were available to the girls, on account of discrimination, the East Bay had much to offer. And with thorough and efficient Key System streetcars, girls were a quick ride away to basically every town in the East Bay as well as San Francisco.[12] The question would remain, if the wages, change of scenery, and the city lights were worth it.

REFUSING SETTLER DOMESTICITY

Introduction

ON TUESDAY, JUNE 7, 1927, the *Oakland Tribune* published an article in tall, prominent font announcing, "They Will Prove Studies in Housework." In the photo below the headline, five young Indian girls with short bobs surround a tall woman—Matron Bonnie Royce—featured front and center. One young girl, Ruby Wilder, looks up almost adoringly to Matron Royce. To her left, Delphine Holbrook smiles past. A lofty young girl, Belma Barber, stares off in the distance toward the camera.[1] A pair on the right—Rosie Pete and Ruby Paradice—smile as if just having exchanged a joke. The brief article declares, "Indian Girl Students Here" and reports,

> Forty Indian girls from the Carson Indian school at Stewart, Nevada will put their knowledge of domestic science to good use in Oakland during the vacation period. They arrived here today as the guests of the U.S. Indian Service and will do housework in various homes of this city to add to their practical knowledge along domestic science lines and to earn spending money for the next school term. Mrs. B. V. Royce, outing matron of the U.S. Indian Service, assisted in finding places for the Indian girls. The average age of the members of the group is 17 years, and they are completing their first year of high school work. Most of them belong to the Paiute or the Washoe tribe. They plan to return to the Carson school on September 1.

If they were yet unaware, locals learned that an Indian labor program was in their midst, one that would directly deliver young Native American girls

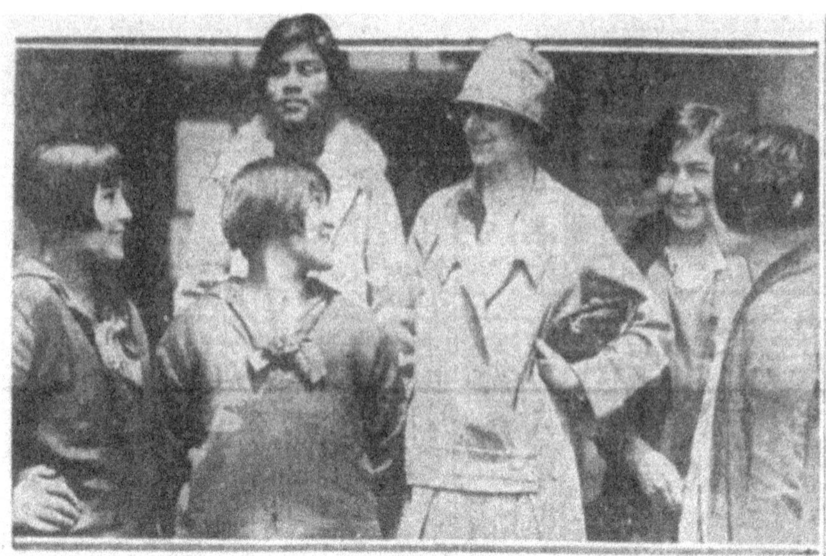

FIGURE 2. A June 7, 1927, *Oakland Tribune* article declared, "They Will Prove Studies in Housework." The included photo, which appears to be taken in front of the Oakland YWCA, shows an image of five young Indian girls and Outing Matron Bonnie V. Royce. *From left to right*: Delphine Holbrook, Belma Barber, Ruby Wilder, Matron Royce, Rosie Pete, and Ruby Paradice.

to their doorstep to work as live-in housemaids. Perhaps unbeknownst to some, this federal program was nearly a decade into operation by the time of the article's publication, and a similar placement program had existed prior. This article also put a face to this labor project, highlighting both the woman responsible for "placements" and the labor force in question—five young Indian women. For *Oakland Tribune* readers, Wilder, Holbrook, Barber, Pete, and Paradice are presented as the "after" product of Indian boarding school education. Their hairstyles, modern clothing, and laid-back attitudes in this urban backdrop reinforce a message of assimilation. Moreover, the image indicates their consenting participation in this "benevolent" project, a well-meaning mission intended to provide Indian girls with jobs, access to white American culture, and opportunity. Nonetheless, these girls would have relished in their fashionable haircuts and clothing and the prospect to—as Matron Royce often said—"make good" in the Bay Area.

This brief glimpse into San Francisco Bay Area history describes the Bay Area Regional Outing Program, a once-thriving project of government assimilation. From 1918 to roughly 1942, the Bay Area Outing Program coercively recruited over a thousand Native girls and women from US Indian boarding schools to work as live-in housemaids in homes across Berkeley, Oakland, and the greater Bay Area. In exchange for room, board, and meager pay, Native women and girls as young as twelve cooked, cleaned, and lived in the private homes of their employers. Indian labor programs, especially for students at boarding schools, were the prominent means of assimilation. In the late nineteenth and early twentieth centuries, this outing program was one of dozens that existed across the nation.

The *Oakland Tribune* article's particular choice of words such as "good use" and "guests" convey the outing program as a charitable act of goodwill. Young Indian girls were simply working to apply their "practical knowledge" toward earning spending money, and Matron Royce was simply "assisting" them. The truth was, however, these girls were not "guests" in the homes of their employers—they were child laborers. They were not under the compassionate "care" of Matron Royce—but under her wardship and surveillance. The Bay Area Regional Outing Program, though positioned as benign or beneficial, was coercive and exploitative. Ostensibly, domestic training worked to uplift Indian women's lives and create good, Americanized citizens. In reality, the outing program equated to labor exploitation and enforced servitude. And again, this was just one of many programs across the nation, programs that developed alongside Indian boarding schools.

At the end of the nineteenth century, reformers looked to a universalized, mandatory education system to solve the "Indian Problem." The government considered Native peoples' presence and culture as a hindrance to Euro-American settlement. One solution was a mandatory education system. The US government created Indian boarding schools to separate Indian children from their families and culture and mold them into Christianized, patriarchal, thrifty laborers. These institutions were gendered in nature and operated on the labor of Indian children. Indian boys built school dormitories, while Indian girls cleaned them.

And whereas boarding schools separated Indian children from their families during the school year, outing programs that stemmed from these schools kept children during the summer and winter breaks. Generally, each boarding school operated its own outing program and through it contracted out student labor to local white farms and homes. Though Indian boys might labor as farmhands, masons, or blacksmiths, Indian girls labored solely as domestics. Both on- and off-school labor was peddled as "work experience" for the purpose of "education."

"Outing," coined by Richard Henry Pratt, was a means to transfer Indian children "out" of their communities to work in white homes, farms, and businesses. Pratt believed white contact was the "supreme Americanizer."[2] In 1878, Pratt, conducted his first outing experiment on Indian prisoners of war at Fort Marion in Florida. Freed from their chains, these prisoners were sent to labor for local whites and earned a small wage. The perceived success of outing inspired Pratt to continue his experiment in 1879 at the first US off-reservation boarding school—the Carlisle Institute in Pennsylvania. Pratt's "civilization" program consisted of a half day of basic education, reading, and math and a half day of manual labor in white households through his outing program. His curriculum became the standard for Indian education, and outing became the cornerstone of nineteenth- and twentieth-century Indian policy.

Roughly forty years later, the Bay Area Outing Program emulated the same principles. However, it operated independently from Indian boarding schools. Instead, it funneled Native women's labor from western-based schools, including Chemawa Indian School in Salem, Oregon; Sherman Institute in Riverside, California; and Stewart Indian School in Carson City, Nevada, among others. Whereas Carlisle and other Indian boarding schools "outed" both boys and girls, the Bay Area program was exclusively for girls and women. The program was intertribal, with a majority of women from California, the Pacific Northwest, and the Southwest. Once in the Bay Area, outing matrons, who managed the program, placed girls in homes throughout the Bay Area, particularly the East Bay, and especially in the affluent city of Piedmont. Some girls outed for short stints during seasonal breaks, while others worked for the same family for years. Although some women outed in their early twenties and thirties, most were adolescents, roughly fourteen to nineteen years old. For about two decades, the Bay Area Outing Program was part of the federal government's "civilizing mission," establishing a ready pool of exploitable Native labor for white residents for the purpose of assimilation.

This book focuses on outing in the San Francisco Bay Area and draws on more than four thousand outing-related archival documents. I detail the personal lives of Native women and girls who outed in the 1920s, '30s, and '40s. My analysis focuses on their working conditions and the ways in which they resisted the confines of domestic labor and the outing program as a whole. I center Native women's localized resistance to federal policy and illuminate a longer history of Indigenous servitude in the region, for the Bay Area Outing Program capitalized upon California's long history of statewide Indian labor exploitation. Native domestic workers negotiated and, at times, frustrated the program's oppressive conditions. They fought for their wages, their autonomy, and their families, and they ultimately helped create the Bay Area Indian community as we know it today. Despite the oppressive structures within which they worked, Native women managed to forge social connections and establish relationships with the program's white female supervisors, known as "matrons," and their domestic employers. In doing so, they unsettled a program meant to "domesticate" them. While this book focuses on the lives of Native domestic workers, the profession of domestic work does not exist in a vacuum. Today, it is commonly found among immigrant and marginalized women globally. Native women's labor is therefore connected to the history of this global labor force.

Historically Connecting Domestic Workers' Lives

From the United States to Europe to Korea, domestic workers span the globe, performing a double load of physical and emotional labor. Scholars have carefully documented the lives and histories of Latina, Filipina, and Japanese domestic workers in the United States.[3] These domestic workers, especially live-in workers, experience similar tensions: laboring almost invisibly from dawn until dusk, managing an entire home, a whole family, and the demands thereof. They typically do so for little pay. Rarely, if ever, do they receive commensurate wages. This workforce is primarily made up of women of color and immigrant women. While scholars have documented domestic work among migrant or immigrant women, few have illuminated the labor of Native American domestic workers. These women and girls mostly labored within the confines of US-based "outing" programs beginning in the late nineteenth century and continuing into the mid-twentieth century. These women also faced labor exploitation as well as physical and emotional abuse and surveillance, all under the auspices of the federal government's Indian assimilation efforts.

The Nature of Domestic Work

Historical and contemporary studies establish that domestic work is a gendered, racialized profession made more complicated for immigrant and migrant women and women of color.[4] From the mid-nineteenth century until 1930, domestic service was the largest field of paid employment for all women in the United States.[5] Following these years, the percentage of nonimmigrant white women performing this work declined as they turned to other jobs in factories and schools. Women of color and immigrant women, however, remained relegated to the profession. Domestic labor was, and remains, an underregulated, often underground economy. Many women of color gravitate toward domestic work because it provides entry into the urban labor market and because there is less competition from white women domestics.

Because factors of gender, class, race, and ethnicity shape the social organization of care, women—especially marginalized women—are assumed to be its natural providers. In consequence, care is historically coerced from marginalized communities.[6] Moreover, domestic work reproduces and intensifies racial hierarchies. Indeed, among privileged, typically white women employers, subordination prevails. Pierette Hondagneu-Sotelo argues that "by subcontracting to private domestic workers, these women purchase release from their domestic responsibilities to other women who are distinct and subordinate by race and class, and now also made subordinate through language, nationality, and citizenship status."[7] Unsurprisingly, in colonial contexts, domestic labor fulfilled a crucial role in maintaining colonial rule.[8]

While a profession in and of itself, domestic labor also attempted to "domesticate," a fact that was especially prominent in colonial and settler colonial contexts.[9] Whether through reform among women prisoners or through Americanization programs for the newly immigrated, settlers designed domestic labor to indoctrinate. Domestic work attempted to conform marginalized women to middle-class standards of femininity and to pacify and control them while asserting an Anglo-American social order. Evelyn Nakano Glenn asserts that "the domestication of subaltern women operated as an essential element in larger projects for incorporating potentially disruptive groups into a stratified social order."[10] Ultimately, whatever its form, in the United States domestic service stratifies our society both racially and ethnically.[11] This is a fact that Native women knew very well and yet found domestic work was one of the only options available to them in the early twentieth century. It was therefore common for Native women and girls to "out" multiple times. One Native woman in search of wages and an education did just that.

On Thursday, June 9, 1932, twenty-one-year-old Ivora Nelson arrived in Oakland, California, on the 2:50 p.m. Western Pacific train. She was accompanied by another outing participant named Marie Penrose. Along the Feather River route, the two traveled through the Sierra Nevada Mountains into Sacramento. And as they traversed into the Bay Area, they saw miles of vast orchards in Hayward and San Leandro before taking in Oakland's bustling harbor. While the sights may have been incredible, they were familiar for Nelson—she had made this trip before.

Her outing story began three years prior, in the summer of 1929. Nelson was a recent graduate of Sherman Institute in Riverside, California. Built by the Office of Indian Affairs in 1903, the Indian boarding school was intended to assimilate Indian children, especially through vocational labor. For Native girls like Nelson, this meant an education in "domestic science," which effectively trained Indian girls to be maids. Recent graduates and current students requested or were coerced into outing labor. Nelson was one of the women who requested an outing position and a place in a local nursing program. At Sherman, she was in the Nurse Corps for two years, so the transition to school was natural. On behalf of herself and her good friend Thana Thompson, Nelson requested outing homes near each other, training in the same hospital with the highest wages possible.

That summer of 1929, Nelson, Thompson, and two other Sherman graduates arrived to start nurses' training in Bay Area hospitals. The small cohort was not the first of its kind, but it was a less common occurrence in the outing program. Upon Nelson's request, she and Thompson began their studies together at Children's Hospital San Francisco. Nelson was placed two miles away from Thompson in a newly built four-bedroom home in the Trestle Glen neighborhood in Oakland, where she earned forty-five dollars a month. On top of domestic outing work, Nelson was engaged in practical training at the hospital across the bay. The schedule, however, was intense, and managing live-in domestic work on top of nurses' training was impossible. By September of 1929, Nelson quit the program and left the Bay Area. In fact, of the original cohort, none completed nurses' training. Nelson eventually returned a few months later to continue outing work. Not to be deterred, Nelson continued her education and graduated with an associate degree from Haskell Institute in Lawrence, Kansas. In fact, her journey to Oakland on the Western Pacific began in Kansas. Nelson worked in a total of seven East Bay homes until the fall of 1933. During her time in the outing program, her younger sisters Bernice and Winifred also outed. The three girls came to the outing by way of three different Indian boarding schools: Sherman, Haskell, and Chemawa respectively.

The Nelson sisters, like other Native women in the Bay Area Outing Program, experienced racialized and gendered barriers in live-in work. These women and girls were constantly at the beck and call of their employers while working extremely long days. Although menial, this labor was physically and emotionally demanding—especially for those who cared for children. Further, in the outing home, racial dynamics were tangible. A Native woman serving a white, middle-class family reinforced hierarchies long established in California—that Native peoples, and especially Native women, were subservient and subordinate to settlers. It also normalized domestic work for Native women. Further, because racial hierarchies and divisions are reproduced and intensified through domestic work, the outing home maintained settler colonial rule. Therefore, Native women and girls serving settlers reinforced settler hierarchies. Predictably, domestic service is a consistent feature of colonialism. Accordingly, for Indigenous women, domestic servitude is not simply an occupation but also a site of control and exploitation. These Native women from nearly a century ago were bound to an entrenched system.

Settler Colonialism, Gender, and Labor

In order to address the Native women's stories that form the core of this book—their struggles under the exploitative and controlling institution of "outing" in the early twentieth century—it is imperative to outline foundational concepts. Central among these is the idea of settler colonialism, a term that has received a great deal of attention in recent literature and on which my project relies. Connected with this term are key questions of land, gender, and labor—issues of pressing concern in the history of the region we now know as California. In the scope of this book, the term "settler colonialism" is broadly defined as the erasure of Native peoples and their cultural values or the supplanting of these values with those of Euro-American origin. As I will discuss in a later chapter, Patrick Wolfe succinctly asserts, "Settler colonialism destroys to replace."[12] Whereas Wolfe and others address settler colonialism as a form of elimination and erasure, I use the work of Cutcha Risling Baldy, Maile Arvin, Eve Tuck, and Angela Morrill to expand the analysis to include Indigenous feminist readings of settler colonialism and heteropatriarchy. Further, I employ Margaret Jacobs's settler colonial analysis to consider Indigenous child removal as another form of elimination in a cultural and biological sense. In the West, outing capitalized on preexisting practices of Indian labor exploitation. I therefore consider outing a vital element of settler colonialism. My intervention reframes the argument that the Native relation to settlers is one of *solely* land theft. Instead, I demonstrate that Indigenous people's relationship to settler colonizers is one of both land *and* labor.

Urban Indians

To tell the story of the Bay Area Outing Program is to tell the story of Urban Indians and labor. Contrary to popular belief, most Native American people in the United States live in urban areas and not on reservations. Urban Indians, or "City Indians," are Native peoples who call the city or the suburb home, and countless have done so for generations. The scholarship on Urban Indians is limited but diverse, examining Native communities across the United States, in Seattle, Los Angeles, Chicago, and the San Francisco Bay Area, to name a few.[13] While some survey mid-twentieth century Indian Relocation and beyond, others take up the histories of local Indigenous tribes as well as the early pan-Indian migrants. In these earlier communities, wage labor was a common catalyst that brought Native peoples to the city. Indeed, in cities like Los Angeles, domestic workers were some of the earliest Native migrants and came by way of local Indian boarding schools. While their paths may not have crossed, they too would have worked alongside local California Indian laborers across the city.[14]

As Native populations grew, so did Native organizing. Chicago, for instance, was the birthplace of the Indian Fellowship League, an organization that advocated for Native rights, including citizenship. In Los Angeles, the American Indian Progressive Association was founded in 1924 and the Los Angeles Indian Center in 1935. Native organizing in both cities before World War II demonstrates early Urban Indian communities prior to federal Indian Relocation. Indeed, a survey of former Flandreau Indian School students found that boarding school graduates preferred urban employment.[15] While, certainly, Native people experienced challenges and discrimination in the city, opportunity was vital.

Statistics demonstrate this phenomenon. In 1900, the total percentage of Native American people living in urban areas was less than 1 percent. By 1950, Native Americans in urban areas grew to over 13 percent.[16] This spike coincided with the start of the federal Indian Relocation. On January 1, 1952, the BIA launched its Voluntary Relocation Program.[17] Through it, Native Americans on reservations could move to major cities like Denver, Chicago, Los Angeles, Cleveland, and Seattle. The program aided in securing temporary housing and employment for relocatees. From 1952 to 1972, the Voluntary Relocation Program moved over one hundred thousand Native American people from reservations into urban areas.[18] Ho-Chunk scholar Renya Ramirez asserts the clear goal of Indian Relocation was assimilation. She argues, "Government officials hoped that these urban migrants would adjust to the cities and assimilate, the reservation system would end, and the government could then get out of the Indian business."[19] Despite these goals, as Douglas Miller notes, when Native people developed Urban Indian communities, "they did not necessarily do so with the expense of loyalty to the tribal economies, cultures, and communities."[20] Indeed, as the literature on Urban Indians demonstrates, Native people continued to have ties to their communities and maintain culture in urban settings, and for some, urban mobility allowed them greater control of their socioeconomic circumstances.

The Project

Refusing Settler Domesticity articulates Native women's localized resistance to gendered assimilative labor. I uncover how Native women navigated the challenges and opportunities of the Bay Area Outing Program during the early twentieth century. I do so in the context of an enduring history of colonial labor policies directed at Native communities. My project asks the overarching question, Within the confines of domestic labor, how did Native women comply with, resist, and negotiate their circumstances? Specifically, I investigate how Native domestic workers managed and frustrated the oppressive conditions of the outing program and how the program left an enduring legacy in the Bay Area Indian community.

My analysis of domestic labor focuses on the Bay Area Outing Program for its insight into gendered, racialized labor. The US federal government established the Bay Area–based iteration of outing as an extension of boarding school policy. In practice, it contracted Native women and girls to work as domestic laborers in private homes—thus shirking federal responsibilities and placing them in the hands of white homeowners. A focus on the Bay Area enables us to consider the ways in which outing—not tied to any institution—brought increasing numbers of Native women into the labor market and city well before Indian Relocation. Because the Bay Area Outing Program lasted for two decades, into the 1940s, it also highlights the lack of practical change afforded by major Indian policy shifts such as the 1928 Meriam Report or the 1934 Indian Reorganization Act (IRA). Meriam, officially named *The Problem of Indian Administration*, critiqued Indian Affairs, including outing, stating, "Whatever it may have been in the past, at the present the outing system is mainly a plan for hiring out boys for odd jobs and girls for domestic service, seldom a plan for providing real vocational training."[21] Six years later, the IRA pushed to uphold tribal sovereignty and undo the work of cultural assimilation. Despite critique and policy change, Indian women and girls in the Bay Area continued to clean other people's homes, care for their children, and receive no vocational training. Moreover, the Bay Area Outing Program is a crucial element in the history of Indigenous labor in California. In the West, this institution capitalized on preexisting processes of Indian labor exploitation. My project examines the long history of labor policies directed at Native communities while considering settlement not as only place-taking but also place-making. I thus illustrate the *longue durée* of settler colonization. Furthermore, analysis of this particular program reveals the ways in which Native American women negotiated oppressive labor conditions. Finally, outing in the Bay Area provides insight into the creation of the intertribal Bay Area Indian community.

A substantial body of research on Indian boarding schools interrogates the schools themselves but rarely the off-campus labor programs that proliferated around these institutions. The origin and history of outing is neglected. A close analysis of outing uncovers the reach of federal Indian boarding schools—how even hundreds or thousands of miles away from school, Native children and young adults were still subject to its rules and regulations. It also reveals how federal programs extended structures of domesticity, gender, labor, and settler colonialism. In the context of my project, outing research especially explores the paternalistic and maternalistic relationship—manifested by the role of matrons—between the government, Native women, and their families. I also interrogate how women navigate the systemic effects of entrenched gendered domestic labor.

Not until recently have scholars taken up the study of these regional and school-based programs. Few have examined the San Francisco Bay Area, and only two have examined outing at manuscript length.[22] My project departs from these studies by centering Native women's experiences and demonstrating a prolific outing program that continued well into the 1940s. Abigail Markwyn and Margaret Jacobs offer meaningful and significant contributions regarding maternalism, agency, and community in the Bay Area Outing Program.[23] Their work opens up important questions about runaways, carcerality, detention, sexual surveillance, and health, which I pursue here. I build upon their work and develop a deeper understanding of the Bay Area Outing Program.

Recent scholarship on the Bay Area Outing Program or "Outing Center" has considered a portion of the archival data available.[24] By investigating the whole body of outing records, including previously restricted materials, I consider crucial yet unanalyzed documents that demonstrate the material consequences of outing on Native women's health, safety, and well-being. In my analysis, I have also interrogated surveillance of Native women's sexuality and bodies and the ways in which outing matrons, employers, and local officials criminalized and incarcerated women in the outing program. Scholars have considered the carceral elements of boarding school life: the presence of "jails" at schools; military atmosphere; harsh forms of discipline, including corporeal punishment; and constant surveillance and confinement.[25] Yet, the carcerality of outing programs remains largely unexplored. This analytical shift changes our understanding of assimilation-oriented labor policies as a whole. Understanding outing as a form of carcerality highlights how Indian girls and young women continued to be contained by the government even in their "independence" as laborers.[26]

I situate my analysis of the Bay Area Outing Program within a longer history of Indian servitude and exploitation in California. My work is founded in a recognition of the deep roots of Indian child labor in California's history and of the state's role in establishing and cultivating those labor markets. There is a clear connection between nineteenth-century Indian labor practices and twentieth-century outing programs. Most California histories begin with the eighteenth-century arrival of Spanish missionaries in Southern California and skip the Indian labor policies in the American period that grew from both Spanish and Mexican practices of Indian labor exploitation and enslavement. This omission overlooks the traces of history that give rise to Indian labor policies—especially Indian child labor—that proliferated in the state. This book advances existing work on Indian boarding schools and Urban Indians and contributes to the history of Native California. Overall, my project expands the scholarship on labor in US colonization and documents the essential and understudied intersection of gender and labor in the assimilationist project. My study provides a woman-centered history of outing in the San Francisco Bay Area—expanding gender-specific knowledge of Urban Indians prior to midcentury Indian Relocation. By considering the contemporary Bay Area Indian community, my project reveals the long-lasting effects of outing. *Refusing Settler Domesticity* deepens the outing story.

At the heart of my study are Native women's voices uncovered from the archive. I use qualitative data analysis software to examine more than four thousand outing-related documents. My study draws upon Bureau of Indian Affairs records at NARA San Bruno, NARA Washington, DC, and special collections at the UC Berkeley Bancroft Library. These archives include letters from concerned parents of outing girls, women contesting adoption, and women advocating for commensurate wages. The Bay Area Outing Program files are archived in a series of records catalogued as "Relocation, Education and Employment Assistance Case Files, 1926–1946," and "Case Records of Relocation, Training and Employment Assistance, 1928–1951." The former account for the majority of outing-specific files—fourteen boxes in total—while some are also found in the latter—one box total.

This rich data set of government files reveals the program's larger structural framework and captures a complicated network of local organizations, social services agencies, and institutions affiliated with the Bay Area Outing Program. These records also trace changes of administration over time, including Matron Van Every's transition from outing to "social work." The latter cases continue to document Native women's labor in the Bay Area and impacts on the Indian family. In large measure, the same women who participated in outing are present in social work case files, which demonstrates change—or lack thereof—over time. Indian women found it difficult to venture into new industries even under this change.

Among the bulk of outing records are rich "employee" files that reference Native women's places of employment, respective wages, tribal affiliation, blood quantum, and other such details that illuminate their circumstances and conditions. Federal forms also reveal how outing matrons quantified the lives of Native women, commenting on individuals' training, characteristics, and morals and whether they might be "good," "attractive," or "big-headed." Aside from these documents, the archive contains letters from concerned parents of outing girls as well as from women who advocated for commensurate wages, appealed to the matron for assistance, or refused the doctrine of the outing program. Overwhelmingly, these records demonstrate the government's detailed day-to-day management and exploitation of women in the outing program—but most importantly, Native women's resistance to it. While certainly rife with correspondence *about* Native women from matrons, employers, and BIA officials, these files also include Native girls' and women's testimony. Even where testimony is less available, I highlight Native women's agency accordingly. I excavated this partial view into the archive from thousands of federal documents with the help of a team of undergraduate research assistants. I highlight these firsthand accounts to uncover Native women's crucial agency and autonomy. I thus reveal Native women's subtle and overt forms of resistance to domesticity and assimilation.

While the archive is certainly revealing, it does not capture the full weight of the outing program. For example, only in rare cases are girls' letters to family and friends present in the archive—and largely because they were confiscated. Outside of this, we will never fully know what they personally revealed to relatives and confidants. Likewise, unless mentioned in correspondence, we do not know the extent of relationships women forged in the Bay Area—whether professional, amicable, or romantic—or their personal reflections on city life. Ultimately, unless the information is revealed in these formal government documents, we will not know the stories that women chose not to share. Conversely, there are certainly issues in the archive that women may have meant to conceal from their relatives, such as an unplanned pregnancy or incarceration. Such events are often painstakingly detailed in federal letters and reveal much more than Native women may have intended. Nonetheless, the deficiencies prompt Michel-Rolph Trouillot's notion of the "absences in the archive."[27] These silences are laden with power and speak to the fact that certain histories are privileged and upheld while others are obscured. Amid the silences and the privilege are stories that remain outside of the historical record. It must also be said that much of this data was created by outing matrons and other officials. Undoubtedly, their predispositions imbue the data. Nonetheless, the archive offers a glimpse into the complex lives of Native women.

Because the breadth of Native women's experiences is not adequately represented in the archive, I also draw from a few select interviews. At the start of this project, I planned to interview a larger group of Native women elders who experienced outing firsthand. However, many of the women I had hoped to interview passed away; others chose not to be interviewed. Instead, I relied on one-on-one semistructured interviews with my late great-aunt, Esther Wasson. As a young student, Wasson labored on the grounds at Stewart Indian School and also participated in outing. She later worked as a domestic throughout California and Nevada. In fall 2013 through fall 2016, I conducted interviews with her at her home in the Portola District of San Francisco. In these interviews, Wasson gave a partial view of her experience at Stewart—much of it scrubbing on her hands and knees. She recollected Matron Van Every as someone who got Indian women jobs, and she recounted how she managed domestic work among other side jobs to provide for her family. Because the Bay Area Outing Program stems from Stewart administration and a network of Indian schools that relied upon and produced Indian laborers, Wasson's story is representative of the experiences of thousands of other Native girls and young women placed in the program. Moreover, her experience directly illuminates the pre-Relocation Urban Indian community in the Bay Area.

In writing *Refusing Settler Domesticity*, I tried to divorce myself from the stories of the women I encountered in the archive. However, it became harder to be simply "objective" in the facts of their lives as detailed by outing matrons from nearly one hundred years ago. Indeed, the women in these files were much like my grandmother, my great-aunt, and so many relatives before them. In fact, my paternal great-grandmother, my great-uncle, and distant relatives were found in this archive. So as much as I would have liked to separate myself from these histories, they are indeed intertwined with my own. In her intimate study of the Hupa women's flower dance in Northern California, Cutcha Risling Baldy states, "The research here is interpersonal—necessarily interpersonal."[28] One cannot separate oneself and one's experience from one's research. Therefore, I delve into this intimate history, and I do so with the knowledge that my own life story intersects with the legacy of outing. And perhaps this reality is what has made me choose to use outing participants' full names and fully fleshed out lives as guideposts throughout the book. While it is certainly a risky choice, I want the descendants of these women to know what our government did to them. I want them to know what their aunts and grandmothers and great-grandmothers endured to give them the lives they have today. These vivacious, complex, and sometimes heartbreaking stories are necessary. Telling truth is necessary. And as these truths have been hidden for nearly a century, it is time for them to be told.[29]

In addition to these intimate sources, I analyze further archival documents, including California Indian indenture policy, Indian boarding school curricula, and early twentieth-century Bay Area newspaper articles. My sources reveal that Native women challenged their liminal standing and resisted outing in various ways: they fought for wages, ran away, and battled to keep their children. The chapters of this book chronicle a history of gendered, racialized labor and its effects on Native women and their families. I show how Native women navigated a system of oppression and reworked potential and possibility into this system.

The Chapters

Chapter 1 sets the foundation of understanding Indian labor and domesticity in a California context. I begin with the contention that the field of settler colonial studies has argued that the Native relation to settlers is one of *solely* land theft. This chapter asks the foundational question, What if Indigenous people's relationship to settler colonizers is one of both land *and* labor? Then I begin to unpack the arc of domestic labor in California. While scholars have examined domestic work in the scope of national Indian assimilation policy, they have yet to examine the overarching connections between these policies and early colonial practices in the West. This chapter traces gendered Indian labor practices and policies enacted in colonial California and into the mid-twentieth century. I link these labor systems and argue that outing in California emerged from both a long history of statewide Indian labor practices and national federal Indian policy.

Chapter 2 brings the reader into the world of the outing program, detailing the history of the program in the Bay Area and Native women's experiences in it. I trace the good and the bad—subpar working conditions, surveillance, low wages, and grueling schedules, but also women's vibrant social lives in the diverse Bay Area and its growing Indian community. This chapter asks, What were Native women's conditions in the outing system? What choices did they have, and how did they respond? Whereas the previous chapter focuses on Indian labor as a form of control, this chapter begins to consider wage labor as crucial to the survival of Native communities. I explore the first iteration of outing in the San Francisco Bay Area as documented in twentieth-century newspapers. I then examine the process through which Native women were recruited and the ways they were policed and surveilled by their employers and outing matrons. In my analysis, I consider forms of coercion and the fact that few Native women could find jobs outside of domestic work. Ultimately, I argue that outing presented a predicament—the promise of wages and public schooling, bound to the likelihood of undesirable conditions, surveillance, and lack of agency.

Chapter 3 uncovers Native women's discontent and criminalization by tracing runaways and those incarcerated in detention homes. This chapter asks, How did Native women frustrate the outing system while exhibiting agency and autonomy? What were the circumstances that created runaways? How were runaways treated? The first section is informed by early twentieth-century Bay Area newspaper articles. I observe how localized rhetoric sought to convey the charity of the outing program while justifying control of Native women. In the second section, I closely examine powerful stories of women and girls who expressed their dissatisfaction, ran away, stayed out past curfew, and wound up in Bay Area detention homes. While some women left permanently, others would return to the Bay Area to work in outing homes, using the professional training that boarding schools had given them—in domestic labor. Ultimately, I show that Native women refused to perform and reproduce social and sexual norms mandated by matrons, their employers, and the outing program as a whole.

Chapter 4 expands the focus to the Indian family and analyzes how mothers who worked in the outing program and their relatives fought the program's practice of Indian child removal. This chapter asks, How did the Bay Area Outing Program affect the Indian family? How did Native women fight against Indian child removal? What were the circumstances and challenges for Indian children of outing mothers? Because outing women were live-in servants, their children were seen as a barrier to employment, and outing matrons made it their duty to intervene. Matrons' assumptions about "unfit" Indian mothers and Indian families informed their regular interventions. I therefore closely examine the painful stories of Native women involved with the outing program who had children, were thought to be sexually active, or became pregnant in the Bay Area. Ultimately, I describe outing matrons' three central methods of removal: boarding infant children, enrolling children into a federal Indian boarding school, and finally, attempting, and at times succeeding in, the fostering or adoption of Native children.

Chapter 5 investigates the program's policing of Native women's sexuality through "health clearances" and carceral institutions. This chapter addresses the overarching questions, How did sexual surveillance in the Bay Area Outing Program affect Native women? How does the centering of Native women in these sexual histories open new ways of thinking more broadly about settler forms of containment? The analysis reveals how outing matrons and local agencies and authorities attempted to contain and sexually surveil outing women. To this end, I highlight how efforts to combat venereal disease targeted the "immoral" woman, thus fusing the notion of female delinquency and sexually transmitted infections. I connect this history to sexual surveillance within the Bay Area Outing Program and the criminalization of Native women. Through close analysis of case files, I trace various "scales of containment" Native women experienced, first in boarding schools and then in outing homes followed by various Bay Area institutions, such as juvenile detention centers. Through these intimate stories, I demonstrate the ways in which the settler state attempted to control, and at times succeeded in controlling, Native women.

Chapter 6 focuses on Native women's health and the Bay Area Outing Program's response to cases of tuberculosis—a disease that ravaged Indian country well into the mid-twentieth century. This chapter addresses two overarching questions: How did the Bay Area Outing Program affect Native women's access to health care? In turn, how did it affect Native women's bodies? In my analysis, I demonstrate the difficulties Native women experienced in accessing health care and especially tubercular care. I show how the fickle benevolence of the outing program's leadership intersected with federal negligence. This, paired with the dangerous inadequacies of Indian health care services, cost Native women's lives. I therefore examine the state of Indian health through the nineteenth and early twentieth centuries, providing a context of federal negligence and rampant disease. As I trace the federal response—or lack thereof—to Indian health care and wellness, I closely analyze three cases of outing women who became critically ill while in the Bay Area. Ultimately, I uncover state violence shrouded under the cover of federal neglect.

This history of the Bay Area Outing Program hits very close to home. My Paiute grandmother and Washoe grandfather both attended Stewart in the 1930s and 1940s. Both of their lives were deeply shaped by the school, where they spent their childhood, adolescence, and young adulthood. Boys like my grandpa Marvin were able to learn skills that would help them build lifelong careers. But girls like my grandma Helen received an education in domestic work, which trained her, her sister, and her peers to be maids. These gendered labor roles formed very specific life experiences for my grandparents and thousands of other Native children who came before and after them.

Refusing Settler Domesticity was inspired by women like my grandma Helen, who was raised in a system invested in her dispossession—a system that she would struggle against. After years of outing through Stewart Indian School in Nevada, my grandmother briefly worked at a laundry in Yosemite. There, Native women were a majority of the workforce. World War II brought her and my grandpa Marvin to the Bay Area, where they became involved with the Four Winds Club, one of the first pan-Indian organizations in the Bay Area. Before the war came to an end, they had their first child, my father. After some years living outside of California, they returned and set roots in the East Bay.

Throughout her life in the Bay Area, my grandmother continued domestic service but on her own terms. She worked independent of any outing or employment placement program and instead secured live-out positions. Her insistence on refusing any kind of placement program meant that she was free of any matron's discretion or rules. She could select her employers, set her own wages, and exhibit more agency than outing women. I learned that my grandmother was also successful in securing employment for several other Native women, among them her sister, Esther Wasson, and their cousins and friends. One family my grandmother worked for was very well off and likely paid competitive wages and treated their employees well. These instances remind me that Native women often find stability in even the most precarious of situations. Despite the "education" she received at Stewart, my grandmother worked hard to create new possibilities for her children. Raising them in the Bay Area meant they were not forced into boarding schools or domestic work. Instead, they attended newly built schools in Hayward and went on to attain college degrees and raise families of their own in the Bay Area. I attended those same schools and benefited from the sacrifices she made.

ONE
Domestic Labor in California, 1769–1940

For Native families in California, the institutionalization of domestic labor is well known. Ancestors from the recent and distant past, especially women, are remembered for their work as laundry workers, housekeepers, hotel maids, and other domestic laborers. This collective memory reveals the remnants of settler practices and federal policy that created a vibrant Indian labor market—especially of domestic labor for Native women. In the West, long histories of colonialism established a gendered division of labor among California Indian communities. Across the Spanish, Mexican, and American eras, settlers put Native peoples to work. They were forced to labor in an entrenched system that continued to thrive into the twentieth century. Settlers used Native peoples for the purpose of settlement on the California frontier and into the burgeoning California metropolis. Throughout this process, among varying colonial systems, labor served as a means to "domesticate" Native peoples. Whether in 1769, 1850, or 1930, Native labor in all its forms was integral to the settler colonial project in the state we now call California. Indigenous servitude was a fact of Native life.[1]

Ohlone families, descendants of the original peoples of the San Francisco Bay Area, recollect their grandmothers and great-grandmothers who served as housekeepers in affluent Bay Area homes. Renowned Washoe basket maker Dat So La Lee's skills were said to have been discovered by her employer when she was a domestic worker for the Cohn family. While some women remember being treated as members of the family, others were treated poorly and left domestic work with a sense of aversion.[2] The concept of a Native woman working as a live-in domestic laborer for a white middle- to upper-class home is not remotely foreign. Indian servitude became a feature of settler colonial California.

While scholars have examined such domestic work in the scope of national Indian assimilation policy, they have yet to examine the overarching connections between these policies and early colonial practices in regions such as California and the Southwest.[3] In these areas, colonial Indian labor practices thrived at least a century before federal Indian assimilation labor policies existed. To overlook these connections renders an incomplete picture of Indian labor and colonial labor for that matter. Certainly, domestic and "outing" labor as it is understood in the late nineteenth and twentieth centuries was essential to creating an entrenched national policy of domestic servitude for Indian women, but it was not solely responsible. Therefore, to consider Indian outing labor in California as a product of the twentieth century or even the late nineteenth century eclipses the region's long-standing reliance on and exploitation of Indian labor—especially domestic labor of Native women.

This chapter traces gendered Indian labor practices and policies enacted in colonial California and nationally in the United States. I link the overarching connections between these labor systems, and I argue that outing in California arose from a combination of statewide Indian labor practices and national federal Indian policy. Further, I contend that outing is an extension of labor policies designed to "domesticate" Indian people and Native women in particular. Largely, this chapter analyzes California-based Indian labor policies and practices within a framework of settler colonialism. I provide a brief survey of California Indian labor history throughout three colonial systems: the Spanish, Mexican, and American periods. Within this section I examine forms of labor practices such as enslavement and Indian child indenture.[4] Second, I analyze twentieth-century Indian education policy as an extension of that history. This chapter asks, How did colonial labor systems operate in California? How were these policies gendered? How did boarding school education extend historical labor policies, especially in California?

Settler Colonialism

To consider the history of the United States, the West, and California is to consider the institution of settler colonialism. Settler colonialism is broadly defined as the replacement and/or erasure of Native peoples and values, including, but not limited to, traditional home and familial practices, gender roles, language, identity, and sovereignty, and their displacement by Euro-American values. As Patrick Wolfe succinctly asserts, "Settler colonialism destroys to replace."[5] Wolfe continues, "It erects a new colonial society on the expropriated land base—as I put it, settler colonizers come to stay: invasion is a structure not an event."[6] That is to say that the effect of settler colonialism is enduring. In this chapter, I lay out the nature of this new colonial society, founded upon genocide and the exploitation of Indian laborers. I focus particularly on settlers' extraction and exploitation of Indian labor, often disguising enslavement as indenture programs.

From this broader definition of settler colonialism, predicated on the replacement or transformation of Native peoples, settler colonialism encompasses a multitude of aims, including the removal, relocation, or containment of Native peoples; their assimilation and transformation; and elimination and genocide. Unsurprisingly, violence is a major facet of settler colonialism. In fact, the American brand of settler colonialism is, as one scholar argues, the "most violent."[7] It extended widely and outlasted colonialism and European imperialism.[8] These acts of violence can come in many forms, such a policies and practices that are tools of settler colonialism. Therefore, extermination campaigns and the removal or expulsion of Native peoples from their homelands are all facets of settler colonialism. Further, while not outright murder or genocide, assimilation programs like Indian boarding schools and outing programs, for that matter, are tools of settler colonialism—technologies meant enact cultural genocide and to transform Native peoples.

Reiterating Wolfe, settlers "come to stay." And as settlers colonize and build their homes on another's land, they strive to maintain a mythology of benevolence or a practice of misremembrance. Although settler projects are inevitably violent, Lorenzo Veracini argues, the settler psyche needs to disavow this foundational violence.[9] Settlers thus embrace denial and seek a clean conscience. Indeed, as Kaitlin Reed argues, the genocide and violence that founded California is erased from state curricula and settler consciousness,[10] thus allowing the myth of settler benevolence to proliferate. Accordingly, if you, reader, have never learned or heard of the history chronicled in this book, that is not a mistake, but rather intentional.

Aside from settler narratives of disavowal and technologies of extermination or assimilation, settler colonialism has been and continues to be a gendered process. In their treatise for pushing what feminism could mean for all peoples, Maile Arvin, Eve Tuck, and Angela Morrill maintain that heteropatriarchy and heteropaternalism are part and parcel of settler colonialism. Heteropatriarchy is an imposed social system in which heterosexuality and patriarchy are perceived as natural, while the contrary is unacceptable. Heteropaternalism maintains nuclear domestic arrangements with a male figure at the center. These models adhere to a narrow male/female binary and presume men are strong and capable while women are weak and incompetent. Indeed, as the chapters of this book describe, through settler projects like the outing program, Native women were forced into heteropaternal structures.[11]

To further contextualize the gendered elements of settler colonialism is to demonstrate how Native women are targeted. In her study on a young women's coming-of-age ceremony, Cutcha Risling Baldy describes the tradition of Native women's power and autonomy prior to settler colonial invasion and how that autonomy was perceived. She writes, "In these cultures, and societies, where women exercised autonomy—could serve as leaders, could marry, divorce, and own property—and menstruation was venerated and celebrated, Native societies were conceptualized as not only primitive but oppressive to men."[12] Because settler colonial systems continuously reinforce heteropatriarchal social norms, women and their ceremonies became targets, for they demonstrated the power to resist settler ideals of domesticity and assimilation. As Risling Baldy describes the indiscriminate violence California Indian peoples experienced at the hands of settlers, she argues, "The types of gender violence experienced by California Native women during this time illustrate how the colonial project viewed the subjugation of

Native women as essential to the subjugation of Native societies and Native land."[13] Therefore, settler colonial society needed to eradicate challenges to heteronormative order and thus targeted Native women.

Subjugation, however, did not stop at Native women. This chapter will reveal how settler colonialism has historically targeted the Indigenous child. In her comparative study, historian Margaret Jacobs argues that Indigenous child removal—literally the theft of Native children from their families—"constituted another crucial way to eliminate indigenous people, both in a cultural and biological sense."[14] Removing Native children from their families made US boarding schools "instruments of violence, punishment and control, and in fact, often more effective ones than military conquest alone."[15] Moreover, forced removal practices were often tricky, brutal, and traumatizing. Jacobs maintains that although "government officials and reformers touted *assimilation* in the United States . . . as compassionate policies designed to lift indigenous children out of poverty and give them greater opportunity, the approach by which they set out to accomplish this goal undermined their claims of benevolence."[16] Even in the act of ripping children from their families, the settler is still interested in maintaining their innocence.

Amid these definitions of settler colonialism, I contend that gendered labor is a major component of settler colonialism. Later, I will show how early California settlers adopted policies and practices to build empires at the expense of California Indian peoples and their exploited labor. Before Wolfe's now famous assertion that invasion is a structure not an event, he articulated settler colonialism's role in establishing structures of race. Wolfe's argument is seated in the context of Australia's, the United States', and Brazil's struggles concerning land, labor, culture, and power. Wolfe argues that Native American and Aboriginal peoples' relationship with their colonizers is "centered on land." In contrast, African Americans' relationship with their colonizers is "centered on labor."[17] To put it plainly, Native American peoples' relationship to settlers was one of land, and African Americans' relationship was one of labor.[18] But what happens when Indigenous people's relationship to settler colonizers is one of both land *and* labor? What happens when colonizers seek to both replace Natives on their land and extract their “surplus value” through exploitative labor? What if the subordinated labor force is Native? California colonialism enacted a distinct brand of Indian indenture and servitude that capitalized on Indian labor and built it into the fabric of the state. Settlers stole Indian land and forced Native people to labor on their stolen land—farming, cultivating, and expanding white settlement. The theft of Indian land and the laboring of Indian bodies worked to “domesticate” Indian people.

Domestication, Empire, and Household as Nation

The labor practices of settlers in California were based on the idea of *domesticating* the Native population. In practice, Indian labor indenture intended to domesticate and make compliant Indian people. Evelyn Nakano Glenn’s research on elite women’s public caring in the late nineteenth century reveals that “domesticating” projects meant to “produce subjects who willingly undertook their gender-assigned duties and obligations.”[19] In short, domestication, especially through caring labor, was also gendered.[20] Amy Kaplan’s literary research on empire underscores the power dynamics of domestication. Kaplan asserts that domestication “entails conquering and taming the wild, the natural and the alien. Domestication in this sense is related to the imperial project of civilizing, and the conditions of domesticity often become markers that distinguish civilization from savagery.”[21] Kaplan’s argument stems from understanding the domestic as both household and nation, therefore imbricating what is “foreign.” In the interest of theorizing settler colonial studies, Kaplan examines domesticity and race as “structural to the institutional and discursive processes of national expansion and empire building.”[22] If Wolfe maintains that settler colonialism is structural, then Kaplan might agree that domesticating labor is embedded in settler colonial expansion. Overwhelmingly, domestication in settler California took place in the home.

To further unpack the domesticating role of the home, interdisciplinary scholars provide insight. Margaret Jacobs identifies domestic space between Indigenous children servants and white families as “domestic frontiers,” where “colonial relationships continue to play themselves out.”[23] This frontier, she argues, was meant not merely to reflect the "new colonial order imposed upon Indian peoples but also to reproduce and perform it in a kind of long-running theatrical production."[24] This *long-running* production is at the heart of this book, considering the enduring structure of settler colonial labor practices in California.

Victoria Haskins argues the home was a historically significant "space for a white woman's intervention in and negotiation with colonization . . . both symbolic and literal."[25] Haskins's research on half-caste Aboriginal domestics in Australia illuminates how white women galvanized to "domesticate the frontier" through their work with Aboriginals. Amid the power struggles and efforts at "absorb[ing]" "hybrid women," the home had become a "battle ground."[26] This battleground is what Ann Laura Stoler calls the "domains of the intimate," the places and spaces within which one can identify and locate colonial politics and colonial rule.[27]

Mary Louise Pratt considers such spaces as "contact zones," where cultures grapple with one other, often in contexts of asymmetrical relations of power, such as colonialism and enslavement.[28] Amid certain violence on the "frontier," the settler home itself was a colonial space. Liz Conor builds upon Pratt's notion with "imperial contact zones," arguing that "colonial thresholds—doorways, stoops, verandas, and gates—were contact zones where exclusions and inclusions were enacted and enforced."[29] The settler domicile itself was a contact zone. Haskins argues that the domestic service experience is quintessentially a site of colonial encounter.[30] In the context of Aboriginal domestic labor in Australia, Haskins maintains that "the private households of well-to-do suburban women can be regarded as a colonising 'contact zone' if we consider an ongoing process of colonisation in the encapsulation of female Aboriginal bodies by state direction."[31] Whether in the nineteenth century or the twentieth century, these Californian "domestic frontiers" were not simply neutral spaces but political grounds, productions of colonial rule and maternalist regulation—long-running extensions of the settler colonial domesticating project. These domesticating spaces played a part in establishing and maintaining this new settler colonial society. In settler California, this brand of colonialism takes on a distinct character throughout three historical eras: the Spanish, Mexican, and US periods.

Enslavement and Domesticity in California

Spanish missions were carceral spaces that established an entrenched system of Indian enslavement. Indian laborers at the mission were the foundation for California's economy. Neophytes—that is, converted California Indian peoples who resided in a mission—constructed buildings, herded cattle, worked fields, and performed all the labor that contributed to the Spanish crown and the proliferation of the mission system.[32] Labor at the mission was seasonal. Mission Indians planted and harvested crops, sheared sheep, slaughtered livestock, and manufactured woolen and leather goods. Cattle were key to the mission system, and through the hide and tallow trade, the commodities produced by California's Indian labor entered the international economy.[33] The gendered division of labor at Franciscan missions meant that men were trained in and performed work in trades like masonry, carpentry, leatherwork, or manual labor in the fields. Women, on the other hand, performed domestic tasks such as sewing, washing, culling wheat, and grinding pinole. This division of labor essentially kept Indian women inside the mission compound. They could not be vaqueros or field hands.[34] Within this division of labor, children were especially targeted, for they could be "taught with ease and without violence."[35] This understanding continued into the Mexican and American periods.

In 1821, when Mexico achieved independence from Spain, the once thriving mission economy would eventually become available to settlers, namely "Californios," through a process called secularization.[36] From roughly 1834–36, secularization dismantled the twenty-one missions that dotted the California coastline and released vast mission properties and the resources thereof into the hands of private citizens. This process thrust roughly twenty thousand mission Indians into the uncertain California frontier. For many California Indians, this instated a new era of labor exploitation.[37] Those born and raised in the mission system were especially affected. Therefore, Mexican California established a kind of palimpsest, an exploitation of California Indian labor that capitalized on mission Indians who were raised and trained in the mission system. While scholars argue that Indians possessed more freedom in postsecularization California,[38] Mexican policy further divested Indians of their land and rights. Edward Castillo maintains that this "hacienda-peon" society continued and developed into the Mexican rancho system, which ranged from coercion to enslavement.[39] The most notable feature of Mexican California was its rancho system. Born after Mexican independence, the rancho period peaked fifteen years after the 1834 secularization.[40] Because secularization dispossessed California Indian land and labor for the benefit of Californios, Mexican ranchos continued to rely on Indian domestic servants and agricultural laborers.[41] While much labor was seasonal, household servants worked year-round. These would have been ex-neophytes who had training in domestic tasks and would have been considered trustworthy.[42]

Many well-known Californios built their empires on the backs of Indian laborers. For example, in 1834, military commander Mariano Guadalupe Vallejo was granted the lands and resources of Mission San Francisco de Solano, including former mission Indians. These ex-neophytes had little choice but to labor for authorities like Vallejo, who had control of the greater Sonoma and Napa Valleys and Santa Rosa region.[43] No other Californio had access to as many Indians as he, and none were as wealthy.[44]

At Vallejo's home in Sonoma and at his 66,000-acre Rancho Petaluma, Vallejo retained numerous California Indian servants—more than any other rancho. Vallejo's rancho was diverse, including various tribes from the region and at least four different ethnolinguistic groups. Rancho Petaluma was the largest rancho in Alta California and conducted a business in hides, tallow, agricultural products, and manufactured goods such as blankets, candles, and shoes.[45] The booming business matched the production of the wealthiest missions. During missionization, no rancho could compete with mission production of hide and tallow, but after secularization, ranchos were free to capitalize on Indian labor and land.

Life at Rancho Petaluma strongly resembled life at Franciscan missions. Native workers started their day at sunrise. After roll call, they would have had a breakfast of atole and labored until their midday meal, followed by a siesta. They continued to work until early evening or dusk. The rancho emulated a gendered division of labor found in missions. Women generally performed cooking, cleaning, grain processing, weaving, basket making, and hide working. Men plowed fields, herded, butchered livestock, and cared for horses. Similar to mission life, both men and women constructed adobe buildings and corrals, worked the crop fields, processed hides, and rendered tallow. In exchange for labor, most received goods rather than money, including beads, tools, alcohol, and items manufactured at the rancho, such as blankets.[46] Rancho labor was largely debt peonage.[47] However, when in need of more labor, Vallejo and other Californios carried out seasonal expeditions to seize and kidnap local Indians as slaves. By the 1830s, these slave-raiding expeditions were a common means to meet labor demands on Mexican ranchos and regularly resulted in manslaughter.[48]

Five years after Vallejo gained control of the Sonoma and Napa Valleys, his contemporary and rival gained access to the Sacramento Valley. In 1839, Governor Juan Alvarado permitted Swiss John A. Sutter to "colonize" the Sacramento Valley.[49] Sutter's fort outside Sacramento, California, became the destination for overland immigrants to settle in the Mexican state. In the same way as Vallejo, under the Mexican republic, John Sutter forged Indian alliances, exploited Indian labor, and displaced California Indians from their land.[50] Sutter's labor camp and rancho, known as "New Helvetia," developed into a mill and fort based on Indian labor and exploitation. Workers at the rancho wore necklaces with disks marked with chads indicating each day of labor. Indians could then exchange this form of currency for clothing or other goods.

With this debt credit system, Sutter controlled Indian wages, prices for goods, and Indian trade.[51] The self-proclaimed patriarch maintained that Indians needed to be kept "strictly under fear."[52] While some Indians under Sutter were volunteer workers, Sutter, just like Vallejo, regularly raided local Indian communities to acquire enslaved labor. Sutter is also known for trafficking Indian children with an implied "sexual dimension."[53] He captured children during attacks on Indian communities and sold or leased them to other ranchers. Also, Sutter and his contemporaries had Indian mistresses, as was commonplace on the frontier.[54]

Though conditions for California Indians under Mexican rule were challenging and exploitive, Anglo-American rule enacted a more dangerous brand of servitude. As the California climate quickly changed with the influx of more American immigrants, hostilities that had developed between Californios and Anglos intensified in May 1846, when the United States went to war with Mexico.[55] The incoming Gold Rush, the flux of immigrants with it, and American militia campaigns brought forth a malicious force throughout California.[56] On February 2, 1848, Mexico signed the Treaty of Guadalupe Hidalgo, thus ceding the land of California and northern territory to the United States. The shift to Anglo-American rule enacted a dangerous, exploitative frontier for Native peoples within the soon-to-be US state.[57] As Anglo settlers quickly occupied and seized Indian land, they pined for legal access to Indian labor.

In the first session of the California legislature—five months before statehood—officials passed the 1850 Act for the Government and Protection of Indians. Lawmakers understood that California Indian labor had long benefited both Anglo and Hispano settlers in the state.[58] Moreover, during the Gold Rush, the immense demand for Indian labor reflected the scarcity of white wageworkers.[59] In its operation, the new Anglo-American law legalized the enslavement of California Indian people. Under the act, white settlers had exclusive right to petition Indian wards from local courts.[60] In turn, they gained the custody, control, and earnings of Indian children and vagrants. Settler use of Indian servants became widespread in homes throughout the state.[61] As the act effectively gave white settlers the freedom to control Native bodies, enslavement and sex trafficking were part and parcel of this law and its 1860 amendment. Settlers indentured young Indian women for purposes of both "labor and lust" and paid higher prices for a "likely young girl."[62] Because settlers considered Native women profitable, they targeted them and stole them from their communities. Starvation, war, and sexual assault shaped their lives.[63]

While this policy directly affected Native women, it also created a demand for domestic labor performed by Indian children. Across the state, Indian children waited on white settlers and their families: cooking, washing, doing laundry, and caring for other children. Indeed, married white women settlers played a major role in the demand for bound Indian labor. In exchange for total control of Indian bodies, the policy required settlers treat their "Indians humanely and . . . properly clothe and feed them."[64] However, the act lacked provisions to establish legal rights for Indians and thereby made the stipulation of humane treatment hardly enforceable. Throughout Northern California, Indian child labor was especially prominent.[65] Colusa County records reveal that some children were indentured as young as three years old and contracted until maturity at twenty-one. Moreover, in light of age limits, petitioners had a strong incentive to underestimate the ages of their would-be wards to keep them longer.[66] The practice of "apprenticing" Indian children was incredibly common, and California settlers from all likes were eager to acquire free enslaved labor.

In 1855, Colusa County settler Henry Bailey and his wife, Harriet, eagerly acquired Lopez, an Indian boy of seven or eight years old. Apparently, his guardians were "only too glad" to surrender the boy, and Bailey happily reflected, "We went home an Indian richer."[67] Lopez was responsible for both domestic household chores and assisting Bailey in the fields. Bailey found the "experiment" of binding Indian children to domestic labor a success. In retrospect, he conceded that boys like Lopez usually protested household drudgery but that "young servants" "lightened the burdens of the women of the house."[68] The labor of Lopez and other Indian children allowed white women settlers to free themselves of domestic duties.[69] Not surprisingly, but to Bailey's frustration, these captive child laborers remained unwilling and discontented servants. Upon maturity—"manhood" or "womanhood," as Bailey explained—nothing could encourage them to remain bound. In fact, within two years, Lopez ran away back to his rancheria. Though Bailey whipped the boy into submission, Lopez escaped for good just a few days later.[70] Where Indian boy domestics were somewhat typical, Indian girl servants were more common.

In 1864, the Chase family in San Francisco acquired an eight-year-old Diegueño, or Kumeyaay, girl they called Emma. The family procured Emma from a friend after seven years of back-and-forth letters on the topic.[71] A few months before her arrival, Chase wrote to his friend, "When do you think the Indian girl will be ready for shipment?"[72] Though Chase regarded Emma as similar to a piece of merchandise in his wholesale business, the family believed they were undertaking a charitable act. After some time with Emma, Mr. Chase wrote, "I am very glad I heeded your advice in taking her, not only because of the assistance I receive from her (for she has been also a great care) but because I find her worthy to be redeemed from the life of degradation which she would have led with her own people."[73] Though the Chase family benefited from Emma's labor, the family believed that by contracting her from her father, they were saving her from ills of her own community. Much like maternalists—or paternalists for that matter—the Chase family felt that they were literally parenting their Indian servant. The family insisted on her indenture until the age of eighteen under contract. During that time, Emma washed dishes, sewed, and performed domestic housework while Mrs. Chase taught her reading and arithmetic.

Though the family acquired Emma under the 1850 act and its 1860 amendment, the notion that they participated in a form of bondage was completely lost upon the family. In April of 1865, as Confederate Robert E. Lee surrendered, Mr. Chase wrote, "Glory Hallelujah. . . . The people are free."[74] California may have entered the United States as a "free" state, but Chase and other settlers like him thrived upon the enslaved, exploited labor of Indian men, women, and children. By touting California exceptionalism and ignoring the hypocrisy in their own homes, California settlers ignored and denied their part in enslavement.

Well after the state repealed the act, Native children remained entrenched in an enduring system of domestic child labor. Decades later, Indian boarding schools in the western states carried on these traditions. The "outing" labor programs developed at the schools continued to fill the region's long-established labor demands. Outing in California—and the Bay Area in particular—emerged from a long history of statewide Indian labor practices as well as national federal Indian policy.

Outing and Indian Boarding Schools

"Outing," coined by Richard Henry Pratt, was a means to get Native people "out" of their communities to work in white homes.[75] Pratt believed that white contact was the "supreme Americanizer." In 1878, Pratt conducted his first outing experiment on Indian prisoners of war at Fort Marion in St. Augustine, Florida. From their chains, Pratt sent these prisoners to labor for local whites, where they earned a small wage. He later brought some of these same prisoners to the Hampton Institute in Virginia, where they received instruction among African American students. The perceived success of these experiments inspired Pratt to lobby for his own school. Shortly thereafter, he was granted the use of unused military barracks and authorized to recruit 125 students.[76] In the fall of 1879, Pratt opened the first US off-reservation boarding school—Carlisle Indian Industrial School in Pennsylvania.[77] There, Pratt implemented his "civilization" program on Indian children and adults. Carlisle was highly regimented. Students followed Pratt's half-day plan: a half day of basic education and a half day of manual labor. Pratt's plan would become the model for subsequent Indian boarding schools as they developed across the nation.[78]

Pratt's experiments did not operate in a vacuum—he had the support of those who had seen his "progress" firsthand and, importantly, government reformers invested in solving the "Indian Problem." The US government designed Indian boarding schools as a universalized, mandatory education system to assimilate Indian children. Contrary to Indian war policy, schools, as David Wallace Adams put it, could "civilize in record time," and it was "less expensive to educate Indians than to kill them."[79] A recent study finds that the United States operated over 523 Indian boarding schools across thirty-eight states from 1801 to present.[80] By 1900, nearly eighteen thousand Native children attended Indian boarding schools.[81] By 1926, nearly 83 percent of school-age Indian children were enrolled in boarding schools.[82]

In practice these "schools" separated Indian children from their families and culture to mold them into Christianized, patriarchal, thrifty laborers. These civilizing institutions were designed to *transform* Native children and therefore enrolled children as young as five years old.[83] Civilization, or "Americanization," required "transformation of nations and individuals."[84] More specifically, this meant the replacement of Native heritage languages with English, "paganism" with Christianity, and the replacement of economic, political, and social institutions.[85] While each boarding school was different, schools attempted to assimilate Native children's cultural identity in several ways. Upon arrival, Indian boys had their long hair cut short, and all students were given uniforms to assert homogeneity and emulate

Euro-American standards of dress. Students were also given new names, sometimes poor translations of their tribal names.

In the late nineteenth century, school facilities were often in poor and unsafe conditions. And throughout the nineteenth and twentieth centuries, students were grossly underfed and often went to bed hungry. At school, students experienced relentless regimentation, surveillance, and control. Every aspect of every single day was scheduled, and students had to be quick to respond to a demanding bugle or bell. Indian boarding schools were militaristic, and in some ways, students were treated as inmates.[86] Indeed, the presence of on-campus jails is telling. While school resources varied over the years, and across locations, schools were largely deficient. In 1928, the Meriam Report found that Indian boarding schools were severely inadequate, leading to malnourished children, overcrowded dorms, and unsanitary living conditions. In addition to these issues, the report also found that the use of student labor was nothing more than "production work" performed to maintain the institution.[87]

At the creation of Indian boarding schools, many federal officials did not believe that Native people were capable of higher education or an advanced career. In fact, many Indian boarding schools did not go past the sixth grade, and the curriculum focused on manual labor.[88] Young men often received training in a variety of trades, such as masonry, blacksmithing, roofing, or electrical work. However, young women were exclusively taught in domestic science. In 1901, former superintendent of Indian Schools Estelle Reel declared in her school curriculum manual, "When the Indian children shall have acquired a taste for study and a love for work, the day of their redemption will be at hand."[89]

Unsurprisingly, child labor was a crucial element of Indian boarding schools. So much so that Native children were integral to the upkeep of the schools. At one school in Michigan, girl students performed much of the routine cleaning and produced most of the school's clothing and linens—in one year making over $2,600 of products.[90] At another school in California, a commissioner of Indian Affairs celebrated the students for their recent construction of school buildings. The commissioner called it "remarkably efficient construction work" and boasted that the students saved them about two-thirds the cost of labor on the open market.[91] That same school operated on a demanding daily schedule, starting at 5:30 a.m. and ending at 9:00 p.m.[92] Indian boarding schools were gendered in nature and operated on child labor. Indian boys built school dormitories, while Indian girls cleaned them. The Meriam Report later revealed that in-school labor at some school sites was in violation of state child labor laws.[93]

Despite constant surveillance, regimentation, and poor conditions, Native students had a multitude of experiences in boarding school. Some alumni reflected on their boarding school years in a positive light, for they were able to shape their experiences to fit their needs. They created their own communities and resisted acculturation.[94] At one school, Hopi students "turned the power" of boarding school aims and used the school to preserve and protect their cultural ways. And when they returned home, they used their new skills to give back to their community.[95] Native children were incredibly adaptive and used the tools gained at school to represent themselves and challenge assimilation policy.[96] Nonetheless, these same precarious policies extended past the walls of the boarding school into outing programs.

Whereas boarding schools separated Indian children from their families during the school year, outing programs kept children away during seasonal breaks. Each boarding school typically operated its own outing program and contracted out student labor to local white farms and homes. Whereas Indian boys might labor as farmhands or blacksmiths, Indian girls labored solely as domestics. Officials peddled on- and off-school labor as "work experience" for the purpose of "education." This practical training secured Indians' social status as America's laboring class.[97] Nonetheless, outing was complex. On the one hand, outing exploited and infantilized. On the other, some students sought out employment in the system as a means of achieving some modicum of autonomy in their personal finances and choices.[98] That being said, Pratt's experiments were a catalyst to an enduring shift in Indian policy. Pratt set a standard, and however complicated, outing became the cornerstone of nineteenth- and twentieth-century Indian education.

As the Office of Indian Affairs introduced outing programs in the western states, they continued patterns of labor exploitation developed in the East, but with a key difference. For Pratt, outing was a means to expand students' experiences of white, Euro-American ways beyond the school grounds.[99] Carlisle officials carefully selected outing homes to ensure that outing employers treated students like family members rather than servants—and unannounced site visits ensured children's welfare. In the West, however, outing focused less on cultural incorporation into settler society and more on labor extraction.[100] This led to less supervision of outing placements and more wholesale employment. For instance, the Phoenix Indian School's outing program located an onyx factory on campus to appease the demands of a local businessman.[101] And in Sherman Institute's prolific outing program, hundreds of outing students lived and labored as farmworkers.[102] Indeed, school officials strategically positioned both institutions to provide local businesses with cheap Indian child labor. Similarly, Stewart Indian School's local outing program served to bolster support from the nearby community. The school petitioned residents' help in apprehending unenrolled Native children. In exchange, the institution promised "trained help for your field, shops, and kitchens."[103] Tucson's outing program was similar to the Bay Area Outing Program in that it operated independently from boarding schools and placed solely Indian girls and women. This western-based domestic labor program entrenched racial hierarchies in the region while regulating the lives of Native women. Given the history of Indian enslavement and indenture in the West, local settlers may have been more inclined to embrace outing labor in this fashion.[104]

Outing Programs and Labor Assimilation Context

In recent decades, scholars have taken up the question of Indigenous child labor at global and national levels.[105] These scholars argue that Indian child labor in and out of boarding schools was damaging, exploitative, and yet vital to the upkeep of the federal institution. Encoded in boarding schools and particularly in outing programs were regulations of control and surveillance aimed at Indian children, especially Native girls and women. Officials generally granted boys more freedom in their attire and work details. And where boys could delve into blacksmithing, printing, carpentry, masonry, and more, Native girls were limited to domestic work. Gendered notions of

Victorian morality paired with the cult of domesticity or true womanhood underpinned both boarding school curriculum and outing programs.[106] Victorian ideals emphasized industrial work ethic, personal improvement, morality, and chastity. They required Indian children to adhere to strict codes of conduct, discipline, and order. The cult of domesticity enforced Euro-American notions of femininity among Native girls and women, emphasizing domesticity, piety, submissiveness, and male authority.

Indeed, school administrators and outing matrons upheld these notions in their management of Native women. Program matrons were agents of state surveillance and control. The Tucson program worked to override Indian interests and was "designed to constrain indigenous power and autonomy."[107] However, Tucson's outing matrons were "complicated and refracted in their role,"[108] torn between carrying out policies and practices that controlled Native women and simultaneously expressing the needs of these women to their superiors. Nonetheless, while power dynamics functioned in multiple capacities, matrons certainly exhibited great authority over Native women. In the Phoenix outing program, for example, Matron Chingren had the power to place, punish, or jail outing women—including those from adjacent reservations.[109] It is true that non-Native women were subjected to the rigid standards of the time. Yet for Native women, discipline was unevenly applied on the basis of race as well as gender. From a young age, federal institutions actively trained these young women for labor exploitation. This federal assimilation tactic normalized domestic work among generations of Native women and served as a disciplinary method.

Margaret Jacobs's study on the Bay Area Outing Program reveals various forms of exploitation and surveillance. Because women boarded in private homes, their employers and matrons subjected them to rules and morals. They also suffered conditions consistent with modern-day live-in domestics—loneliness, abuse, exploitation, and long hours but low wages. In this way, the Bureau of Indian Affairs continued its long-established wardship over Indian people, producing what Beth Piatote calls "unnatural children"—an invention of the state with material consequences. According to Piatote, federal policies treated Native Americans as if they were children in two ways. First, the government's racial classification system labeled them as "wards," assuming they were childlike and simple. Second, Native American "wards" were not allowed to become independent adults but were kept under government control.[110] This idea influenced the national outing programs and reinforced settler power while benefiting the local labor market.

Local businesses that were keen to secure cheap Indian labor supported the Phoenix Indian School from its inception. Local orchards capitalized on superintendents who quickly met labor demands. Whereas Pratt's program in Pennsylvania had retained educational and assimilationist ideals, Phoenix's outing program was solely for labor. Indeed, Superintendent Harwood Hall admitted, "The hiring of an Indian youth is not looked upon by the people of the valley from a philanthropist standpoint. It is simply a matter of business."[111] Business it certainly was; Native domestics were certainly not treated "like family." Phoenicians so relied upon Indian child labor that as many as four hundred children outed per year. In 1909, for example, thirty-seven girls employed as domestics grossed five thousand dollars in wages. Having an Indian girl servant in the house was fashionable. Over the decades, the program experienced its ups and downs, including scandalous "wild" girls, gambling, drinking, and "moral delinquency" that led to compulsory marriages, and locals did not treat students well. Ultimately, the program proved much too large to manage.

Sherman Indian School had a remarkably similar start to Phoenix. Superintendent Harwood Hall was likewise invested in gaining local support with the promise of Indian labor. In an attempt to relocate the school from Perris, California, to Riverside, he flooded the citrus-growing community with low-wage outing laborers. Hall's idea worked, and Sherman's outing program grew to sustain the burgeoning agricultural industry. Many young men labored on local orchards as farmworkers. Women exclusively engaged in domestic work. At Sherman, school officials considered Indian women superior representatives of the school and yet traded them as commodities. Indian girls between the ages of ten and thirteen worked for as little as one dollar a month. As Superintendent Hall assured one labor recipient, "If the girl is not satisfactory, you may return her at once."[112] It seems clear that western patrons of outing were concerned not with education but rather with cheap labor, and western-based Indian boarding schools delivered.

In the context of this exploitative and coercive environment, Native women resisted officials attempts to mold, shape, and control them. In these spaces, policymakers worked to discipline Native children's minds and bodies. Focusing on "bloomer stories," K. Tsianina Lomawaima uncovers Native girls' subtle and collective resistance to boarding school uniforms and dress policy. By means of complex networks, bonds, and friendships, young Indian women united to outwit school matrons and frustrate stifling boarding school regulations.[113] Lomawaima maintains that in these instances, students "successfully exercised their own power in their resistance."[114] Indeed, in the face of boarding school and outing institutions, Indian children rejected, refused, and frustrated these imposed labor structures.

This chapter has traced gendered Indian labor practices and policies enacted in colonial California and nationally in the United States. Through analysis of these labor systems, I argue that outing in California emerged from a long history of statewide Indian labor practices as well as national federal Indian policy. Therefore, outing in California was not solely a product of federal assimilation policy but also a consequence of the region's persistent exploitation of Indian labor. In the mission compound, on the Californio rancho, or in the Anglo settler home, domestic labor was thrust upon Native people. In these intimate spaces, domestic work played a part in establishing and maintaining a new settler colonial society. Boarding schools enforced Euro-American ideals of domestic space through labor. These institutions targeted Native women, stripped them of their power and agency, and made servants of them. Not unlike California Indian labor policy, domestic science assimilation curricula turned young girls into labor commodities, readily available for consumption. These inextricable, reverberating policies established regimes of domination and control over Indian people, uniquely affecting Native women. Colonial California Indian labor policy was a unique brand of bondage and, when paired with federal Indian policy, targeted Native communities, exploited their labor, and through "domestication," attempted to dispossess Native women. Indeed, Native people's relationship to settler colonizers is one of both land and labor.

TWO

The Bay Area Outing Program

A Promise and a Predicament

IN THE SUMMER OF 1928, Stella Healey, a Shoshone student from Stewart Indian School, arrived in the Bay Area for work. She was just thirteen years old. Built by the Office of Indian Affairs in 1890, Stewart, like other Indian boarding schools, was intended to assimilate Indian children especially though vocational labor. For Native girls like Healey, this meant an education in "domestic science," which effectively trained Indian girls to be maids. Recent graduates of Indian boarding schools and current students requested or were coerced into outing labor. Healey's records do not show that she requested an outing position, suggesting that she was assigned the placement. At thirteen years old, she was one of the youngest outing participants in the entirety of the program. She began her first placement five days shy of her fourteenth birthday and celebrated the milestone working in her employer's home. Healey's Outing Certificate from Stewart indicated that she made "good rolls" and was an "excellent worker and is very anxious to please."[1] Over the course of several years, Healey worked at nine outing placements in Oakland, Berkeley, San Mateo, Richmond, San Anselmo, and San Francisco.

Though Stella Healey was raised at Stewart, her mother and stepfather lived in Elko, Nevada, in a two-bedroom main house with no modern conveniences. A government agent described the front of the home as "very attractive," with vines, flowers, and a few small trees. Though adjacent to the newly established Elko "colony," or reservation, the home was within city limits. Stella's mother, Alice, labored in town doing domestic work—washing, ironing, and scrubbing. Alice's husband, Bill, collected and sold wood for five dollars a load. When not working, Alice could be found enjoying a round of handgame, a traditional guessing game.[2] In the fall, Alice and Bill practiced traditional subsistence with an annual pine nut harvest. Unless granted leave from work or school, their children were unable to partake. Together the couple relied on a mix of domestic work, menial labor, and subsistence methods to make ends meet. Compared to many outing families, who officials deemed "indigent" or who had no means of income, Stella's parents were well-off. Their eldest son worked for the Civil Works Administration in Utah. And Stella's older sisters Virginia and Pauline were also at Stewart. The eldest daughter, Dorothy, who was the first of the girls to participate in outing, lived in the Bay Area. Like Stella, Dorothy started at a young age. She was just twelve years old when she started outing in 1926—three months shy of her thirteenth birthday. Bay Area outing participants regularly consisted of sisters, cousins, and whole families.

Healey's first outing placement was a short summer stint at fifteen dollars a month. In late August, just before she returned to school, Healey was eager to receive her first wages. No doubt she would have liked to do some back-to-school shopping. She wrote to Carson administration and requested twelve dollars of her own earnings. The assistant superintendent responded, "Mrs. Royce will let you have as much money as she thinks is best."[3] For schoolgirls like Healey, one-third of her wages was transferred to a bank account under Matron Royce's custodianship. The remaining two-thirds was sent back to her respective boarding school. Girls could not access their wages without the direct approval of federal officials. That first summer, Healey earned roughly forty-five dollars—or the equivalent of nine loads of wood her stepfather sold in Elko, Nevada. At just fourteen years old, Healey could be considered a breadwinner for her family. And yet, gaining access to her wages was no small feat. After that first outing placement, Healey continued to out during the summer. But later, at the request of her employer, her placement was permanent. In 1931, with only one year left at Stewart, she enrolled in a local school and began outing full-time.[4]

Healey was one of over a thousand young Native women who outed in the Bay Area. In 1916, the Office of Indian Affairs authorized the Bay Area

Outing Program, and it officially gained traction in 1918.[5] Outing in the Bay Area complemented and tapped into California's long history of Indian indenture. It operated independently from Indian boarding schools and funneled Native women's labor from western-based schools. The program's sole purpose was to contract Native girls and women to work as live-in housemaids in homes across the San Francisco Bay Area region. "Outing," a term coined by Richard Henry Pratt, founder of the Carlisle Indian School, transferred Indian children "out" of their communities to work in white homes. Federal officials designed this system so that Indian boarding school students would abandon their Native practices and embrace "civility," which included, as Superintendent Estelle Reel later articulated, a "love of manual labor."[6] Through these systems, federal officials, in the form of outing matrons or placement officers, sent boys to work on farms and ranches and girls to work domestic service. Pratt's curriculum was the standard for Indian education, and "outing" became the cornerstone of nineteenth- and twentieth-century Indian policy.[7]

This chapter turns to an analysis of the Bay Area Outing Program. The program operated as an Indian labor agency, developing upon California's long-standing culture of Indian indenture. The Bay Area Outing Program is unique in its ability to provide insight into gendered labor in colonization. This women-run program started in the San Francisco Bay Area, tapping into a large network of reform organizations. Through outing matrons, the Bay Area's growing nonprofit and social services arm sought to oversee and sanction Native women placed in the outing program. Moreover, the Bay Area Outing Program endured long after many outing operations based in boarding schools. Whereas some campus-based programs ended in the 1920s and 1930s, the Bay Area Outing Program continued long past the Great Depression and into World War II. And while the program staff morphed into a social services agency, women continued domestic outing work well into the 1940s. I uncover a prolific outing regime that existed well beyond the ostensible end of the assimilation era.[8] In doing so, I expand scholarship that argues such labor programs dissolved after the 1934 Indian Reorganization Act, also known as the Indian "New Deal." Overall, this labor program speaks to the feminization of settler colonialism in the West and its effects on

Native women and their families. Finally, my research departs from existing outing scholarship, which has focused on the 1930s era and white women outing matrons.[9] Instead, I situate the program within a longer history of Indian servitude in California, centering Native women's experiences.

In this chapter, I answer the following questions: What is the history of the Bay Area Outing Program? What were Native women's conditions in the outing system? How were their bodies policed and surveilled? What choices did they have, and how did they respond? To this end, I closely examine the Bureau of Indian Affairs' (BIA) Relocation, Training, and Employment Assistance records. These rich files illuminate Native women's circumstances and conditions, allowing me to analyze powerful and painful stories of women and girls who labored in the Bay Area Outing Program. First, I discuss Indian labor historically, then I turn to the first iteration of outing in the San Francisco Bay Area as documented in twentieth-century newspapers. From this framework, I delve into my analysis of the Bay Area Outing Program. I examine the process through which outing matrons recruited Native women and the ways both matrons and employers policed and surveilled outing participants. In my analysis, I consider forms of coercion and the fact that few Native women could find jobs outside of domestic work. I also describe the contracts that Native women were required to sign in the early 1930s and provide an in-depth analysis of outing labor, wages, and Native women's organizing through an organization called the Four Winds Club. Ultimately, I find that even under coercion, Native women challenged their liminal standing and frustrated the Bay Area Outing Program.

Outing Labor and Indian Education

At the late nineteenth- and twentieth-century, acculturation and assimilation ideologies dominated Indian policy. Therefore, officials designed outing to transform Indian children and thus Indian people into hardworking, thrifty individuals who operated within the capitalistic nation-state.[10] While Native children performed outing labor in city homes and rural farms, they also provided in-school labor on campus. Cheap (and in many cases, essentially free) student labor was a regular practice at Indian boarding schools and provided budget relief. In fact, Indian child labor sustained the national boarding school system. At Midwest-based boarding schools, young women manufactured their own dresses, uniforms, and cloaks.[11] Girls performed much of the routine cleaning of the facilities and produced much of the schools' clothing and linens. These same women would have labored in school kitchens, laundries, and on-site practice cottages.[12] Women in schools in western states largely performed the same kind of labor. At Sherman Institute in Southern California, young men learning masonry, roofing, or electrical work were expected to perform these tasks on campus. In fact, these same young men were largely responsible for building the majority of campus structures, including expansion projects as the school grew.[13] At boarding schools, Indian boys constructed the dormitories, and Indian girls cleaned them. Such gendered labor persisted in outing.

Following Pratt's 1878 outing experiment, outing programs were commonplace. By 1900, at least a dozen outing programs developed across the nation—at Haskell Institute in Kansas, Sherman Institute in Southern California, Stewart Indian School in Nevada, Fiske Institute in New Mexico, Phoenix Indian School and Fort Mojave Indian School in Arizona, and Genoa Industrial School in Nebraska.[14] Schools located close to their students' tribal communities, like Chilocco in Oklahoma, had comparatively minor outing programs because students often went home during break.[15] Outing programs also operated through lesser known schools such as Grand Junction Indian School in Colorado, Seger Indian Training School in Oklahoma, and the on-reservation Mescalero Indian Boarding School.[16] The Bay Area Outing Program emulated the same outing principles established in these schools. Whereas Carlisle and other off-reservation boarding schools operated their own outing programs for boys and girls, however, the Bay Area Outing program was *exclusively* for girls and women. Moreover, this program was entirely independently run by the Office of Indian Affairs and was not affiliated with any particular Indian boarding school.

Indian Labor Historically

Labor as a concept was inherent to Native peoples long before settlers arrived. In Northern California, among the Yuki and Maidu, creation stories described "creation as an act of work and labor, the complementary social ties between Native Californians and the land and Native California labor."[17] These stories not only served as original instructions but emphasized the labor necessary to form the world. Therefore, for many Native communities, labor was an integral part of an Indigenous worldview. Nonetheless, Native American labor is often overlooked. As William Bauer Jr. notes, "Until recently, scholars have rarely included American Indians in studies of American labor history. Partly, this results from the view that the American Indian story has been one of unemployment. . . . Additionally, many people view American Indians as 'antimodern' and as victims of historical and economic change."[18] Indeed, the literature on Native labor tells a different story.

David Beck shows how Native Americans at the 1893 World's Columbian Exposition in Chicago worked to support their families, control their labor, and create new economic pathways.[19] Brenda Child's family history demonstrates how in the face of few opportunities for work, Ojibwe families adapted to new ways and pieced together various sources of income.[20] Brian Hosmer similarly highlights Native Americans' adaptive resilience in the turn-of-the-century market economy. In their edited collection, Hosmer and Colleen O'Neill show how Native peoples integrated work and economic development, demonstrating how these adaptations strengthened rather than erased Native cultural identity.[21] O'Neill's study on Navajo laborers also emphasizes Native agency and choice. She shows how Navajos chose to engage in part-time labor as a means to stay connected to their community and culture. In short, they engaged in wage labor on their own terms.[22] Paige Raibmon chronicles a history of Indigenous laborers from Washington, British Columbia, and Alaska who labored as hop pickers in the Puget Sound. There, Native individuals and families picked hops from sunup to sundown, and quickly became a local tourist attraction. The workers adapted to their audience by becoming hunting and fishing guides for tourists and selling woven baskets or mats and other curios.[23] Bauer's study on Round

Valley Reservation labor reveals how Indians used wage labor to create and maintain a sense of community. Through agricultural jobs like picking hops and shearing sheep, Round Valley Indians adapted to their environment to both survive and persist into the twentieth century.[24]

Indian wage labor has existed for centuries and has been integral to the survival of Native individuals, families, and communities. While the previous chapter highlighted the ways Indian labor was enforced as a form of control, into the nineteenth century, wage labor became a means of survival. Native American wage labor participation during the nineteenth century was largely self-motivated.[25] However, coercion occurred, such as when Indian agents threatened to revoke rations to coerce Indians into labor. While an essential part of Native life, wage labor, and the commodification of labor itself, is an adaptation to settler colonialism.[26] Consequently, labor practices are gendered and conform to Euro-American standards. Throughout the nineteenth and twentieth centuries, Native men performed wage labor in farmwork, lumber, mining, rail construction, and a myriad of projects. However, Native women primarily engaged in domestic work and occasionally harvest or agricultural work. Land and resource theft and extraction motivated Native peoples to adapt to wage labor. As they were driven from their homelands, they were forced into wage labor to survive.[27]

Because survival was integral, whole families labored. For instance, in the Great Basin, Paiute families regularly subsisted as family units, so when they pursued off-reservation labor, they did so as a whole family.[28] This meant that Native laborers traveled—sometimes long distances—for work. High mobility was so common that it affected student enrollment at boarding schools and reservation populations. In Nevada, Indian agents attempted to lure Paiute families back to the reservation with the promise of wages. But government wages were insufficient compared to wages one could earn on local settler farms and ranches. In Moapa, alfalfa farming on a two-and-a-half-acre allotment could produce seventy-five dollars for a season's work. But a whole family could pick cantaloupes in the valley and earn the same amount in two weeks.[29] Native people willingly followed the higher wages.

While Native individuals and families engaged deeply in wage work, they did so with the knowledge that they experienced wage discrimination—even from the Office of Indian Affairs. In 1865, Indian workers earned $1.00 a day for farm labor and up to $2.50 a day for mining work. In 1870, Paiutes earned 75 percent less than white laborers did. And well into the 1920s, Southern Paiute wages were frequently one-third to one-half of those paid to non-Indians. While settlers preferred white labor, there was simply not enough. Further, white workers wanted room and board and a steady job. In contrast, Indian workers did not have the same demands and could work for a season.[30] Seasonal wage labor complemented traditional subsistence practices such as pine nut harvesting, which was common throughout the Great Basin. Therefore, Native individuals and families survived on a mix of wage labor, traditional subsistence, reservation work, rations, and other forms of income.

Throughout the nineteenth century, gendered labor continued in the same established pattern: Native men performed various types of manual labor, while Native women largely engaged in domestic work. In fact, by the end of the nineteenth century, Native women's steady employment in household domestic work was far more reliable than Native men's ad hoc labor. So much so that some Native women earned more than their husbands.[31] Unlike Euro-American women, Native women were accustomed to labor and socialized to support their families from a young age. Like Native men, they participated in wage labor early but, because of the nature of domestic work, perhaps more often than their male counterparts. Ultimately, throughout the nineteenth century, Indian wage labor was decidedly rural and characterized as unskilled, manual, with low prestige, low pay, and without promotion.[32]

Culturally speaking, gender roles themselves were not a foreign concept for Native American women. Prior to settler arrival, and even after, Native communities had established gender roles, particularly in the division of labor. For instance, among Southern Paiute women in the Great Basin, traditionally, women were the primary harvesters of plants. But this division of labor was not rigid. Women could also hunt and set traps for small animals. Within the division of labor, women worked with other women and were not under the direction of men. Overall, women provided a substantial portion of subsistence with the tools they made and controlled the products of their labor. All of this they did well beyond the parameters of the "household." It was not until the arrival of settlers that Native women were thrust into "women's work." Euro-American employers hired Native American women in sexually stereotyped labor such as laundry and housecleaning. Nonetheless within this work, Native women gained their own income and controlled it exactly as they pleased.[33]

Similarly, among Pomo women in California, the gendered division of labor, where men would hunt and women would gather, was not a reflection of status or a power hierarchy. These different duties and roles were necessary to each other and required cooperation. Therefore, unlike Euro-American "women's work," Native gendered labor patterns were complementary and not subservient nor hierarchical. However, as gender roles changed after contact, Native women took on new roles. Pomo women increasingly became heads of households and successfully maintained their families because of domestic work positions. Meanwhile, each harvest season, whole families gathered to pick grapes, prunes, and hops. Even Pomo women working as domestics in the Bay Area always returned home for the "hops." Over time, with the new authority accrued from their economic advantage, Pomo women became powerful religious leaders. So, while they performed backbreaking work in white homes, Pomo women nonetheless gained autonomy within their own homes.[34]

By the 1920s, Indian employment became significantly urban, particularly because few jobs were available in rural communities. Further, the conditions were gendered; existing jobs were reserved for male ranch hands or construction workers. Few jobs existed for Native women outside of domestic work.[35] Native women, anxious to work, followed the jobs. In the 1920s, Indian women were "economically active." The US Census indicates that Native women serving in private household service increased from 13.4 percent in 1900 to 22.5 percent in 1930.[36] The interwar years shifted urban employment, especially during the Depression. Jobs were particularly scarce in remote reservation communities. For many, urban employment was the only opportunity. This shift only increased during World War II. Ultimately, in the early twentieth century, Indian labor was still seasonal and short-term, and it relied on high mobility. In this way, outing labor was compatible with the overall Indian labor market and was a viable option for Native women and their families.

Early Traces of Bay Area Outing

Federal Indian outing in the Bay Area began nearly a decade before the Bay Area Outing Program. This early iteration ran through Stewart Indian School, also known as Carson Indian School, in Carson City, Nevada—the same Indian boarding school Stella Healey attended. Matrons at the school managed the placement of Native women students as live-in domestics in the San Francisco Bay Area. Because this early version was the product of and administered by an Indian boarding school, it was characteristic of most national outing programs. During these early years, the student body at Stewart was the sole workforce for the school's outing program. The majority of students were Washoe, Paiute, and Shoshone from the Great Basin region of Nevada and California. However, while most school-based outing programs were coed, this early iteration of the program was still solely for Indian girls and would remain so for the next two decades.[37] Early twentieth-century Bay Area newspaper articles reveal Native women's on-the-ground experiences. One of the first documented articles chronicles the story of a runaway.

In September 1911, the *San Francisco Call* reported that Minnie Rook, a student from Stewart Indian School, was employed in Oakland as a domestic worker.[38] That year, Rook ran away from Stewart Indian School with two other girls. She fled to an Oakland home, where she worked as a domestic. The police arrested Rook and turned her over to Mrs. S. Barnes of Stewart, who sent her back to the school. The article reported that the two other girls were still at large. A year later, in August 1912, the same paper reported that a cohort of twenty-five girls from Stewart Indian School worked as domestics for families in the "bay cities," earning their railroad fare.[39] That summer, T. T. Waterman, professor of anthropology at UC Berkeley, arranged for the girls to meet Ishi, a Yana man who had been captured a year prior and extensively researched by the academics.[40] At the reception, Ishi exchanged songs with the Shoshone, Washoe, and Paiute girls.

Further inspection of Bay Area newspapers also uncovers a number of "situation wanted" ads in the classified sections initiated by a matron at Stewart Indian school. One advertisement, for example, ran for a week in the summer of 1913 and read, "Wanted—Positions as general help in house for a number of Indian girls from Carson school, Nev., in private homes; ages 12–18; wages $10–$20 per month."[41] Interestingly, these advertisements were printed alongside ads seeking Japanese domestics and day workers, which at the time were commonplace in the region.[42] Subsequent references to this early iteration of the Bay Area Outing Program surfaced in classified ads and articles. All mentions of the outing girls referred to them as residents of the "Carson Indian Reservation" or students from the Stewart Indian School.[43]

The Bay Area Outing Program

The Bay Area Outing Program officially launched in 1916 and gained traction in 1918. In the early years, cohorts were small; about sixty students labored during the summers. Over time, the program grew to include school-aged students who worked into the school year. The outing matron was responsible for arranging young women's transportation to the Bay Area and securing live-in positions in a local home. Boarding Native women within the home facilitated a "perfect" form of discipline and released the program from having to secure women's housing.

In 1918, the program was headquartered at a home on Prince Street in the "streetcar suburb" of Elmwood in Berkeley, California.[44] This inaugural location was roughly a mile south of the UC Berkeley campus and central to local reformer organizations, including the Indian Defense Association of Central and Northern California and the highly active Young Women's Christian Association (YWCA) centers in Berkeley and Oakland. The Salvation Army and Catholic Charities were also in close proximity and, through the outing program, became entangled with the lives of Native women. Importantly, the home was adjacent to a number of middle- and upper-class neighborhoods where outing matrons could secure positions for Native women. As indicated in the maps on pages 54–55, positions went as far as the North Bay, the South Bay, and the peninsula, but they were highly concentrated in the East Bay, especially Piedmont, Oakland, Berkeley, and Alameda.[45]

Outing matrons and other federal officials funneled student labor from Indian boarding schools in the greater Pacific Northwest region, including Chemawa Indian School in Salem, Oregon; Sherman Institute in Riverside, California; and Stewart Indian School in Carson City, Nevada. From its inception, federal officials designed the program to domesticate Indian girls and women through housework in white homes. Outing stemmed from the long-standing belief that laboring Indians—especially Indian women in domestic work—would eventually solve the "Indian problem." In sum, the program established a far-reaching, regional outing system.

The Bay Area Outing Program began with a "disgruntled" employee—Bonnie V. Royce—the same Matron Royce from the introduction of this book. Royce worked alongside her superintendent husband at Stewart as a field matron. Apparently dissatisfied with the position, Royce and her husband advocated for her to work in the decidedly more cosmopolitan Bay Area. One federal official backed her selection for the newly created outing matron position. In September 1918, Commissioner of Indian Affairs Cato Sells declared that Royce was to

> give special attention to procuring [employment in] homes for Indian girls after they have left school or for any other Indian women of Nevada and Northern California . . . in order that they may be protected from the degrading moral conditions which are found in the small mining towns of Nevada and the country adjacent thereto.[46]

Sells clarified further that as outing matron, Royce should "ascertain the character and reputation of the parties wishing Indian help and make regular visits to the homes where such employment is given so that no mistake may be made in placing these girls in homes only where helpful influences are radicated." He had full confidence that Royce could "give the girls the motherly advice and encouragement which will prove an uplift to those placed in her care."[47]

Commissioner Sells's final words epitomized the goals of the Bay Area

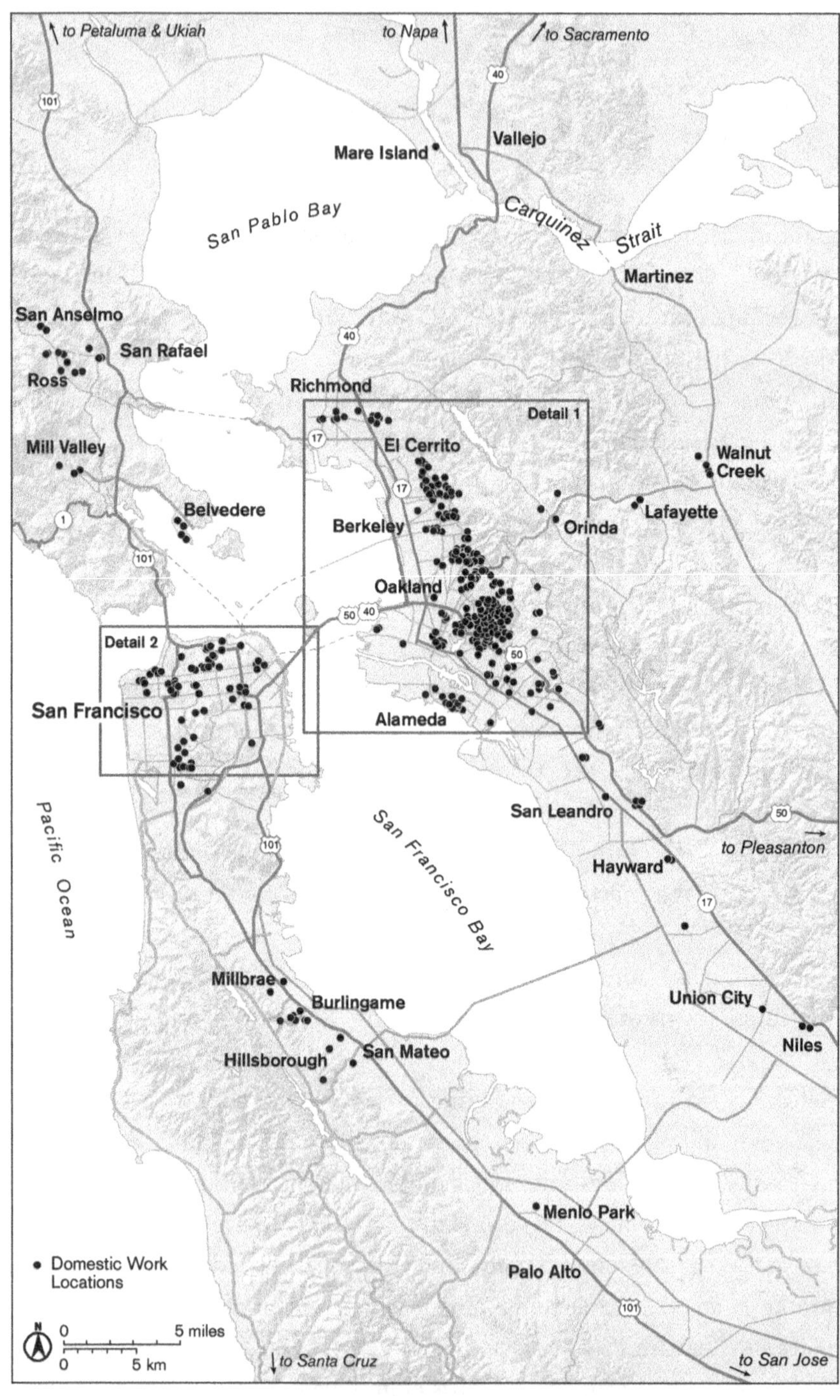

This map, visualizing over seven hundred outing placements in the San Francisco Bay Area, indicates hundreds of Native women's and girls' multiple employment locations throughout their outing careers. Due to missing data within the archive and undercounting, this map is not a complete representation of the Bay Area Outing Program.

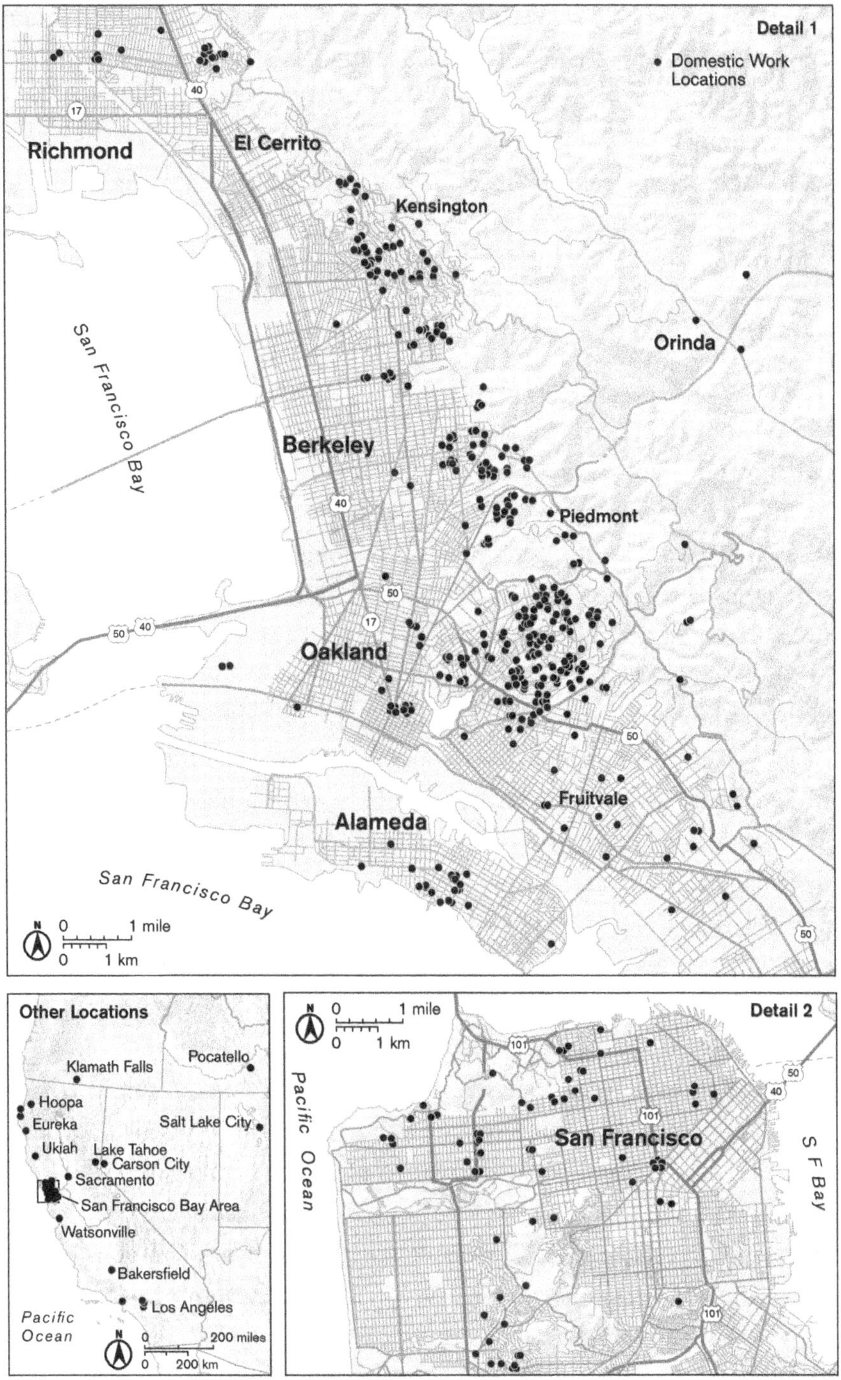

Detail 1

Domestic Work Locations

Richmond

El Cerrito

Kensington

Orinda

San Francisco Bay

Berkeley

Piedmont

Oakland

Fruitvale

Alameda

San Francisco Bay

0 1 mile

0 1 km

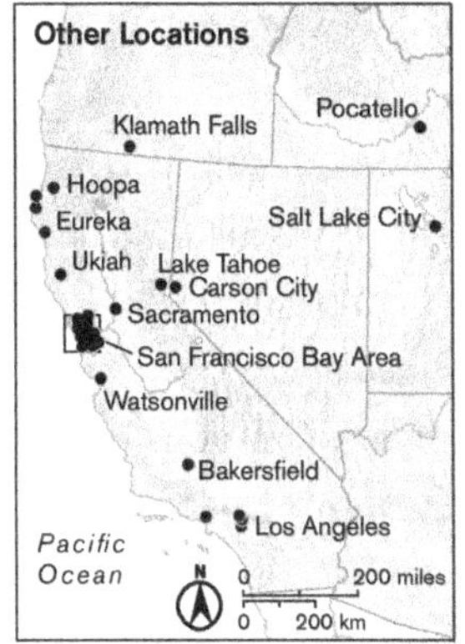

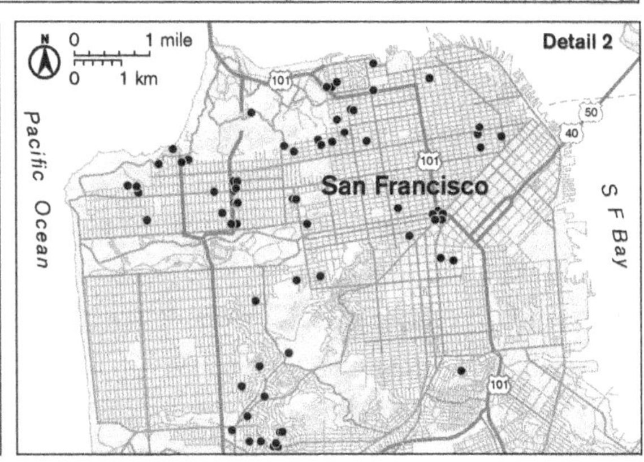

Outing Program. Native women, especially those from "degrading moral conditions," needed protection, helpful influences, motherly advice, and encouragement. Certainly, these aims also reveal that federal officials believed Indian families were incapable of providing such support. So "out" and away from their families and their tragic conditions, Native women could be uplifted by the promise of interaction with whites and domestic wage labor.

Outing Matrons

Federal officials like Sells believed that outing matrons and white women employers were capable of inculcating Native women with decidedly civilized, "American" values. These matrons were middle-class women who strongly identified as wives and mothers and intended to pass down their own "civilized" norms to Native girls and women. In doing so, they entangled notions of nationhood, civilization, and domesticity. Indeed, federal policy intended to create a "new" kind of Indian. For Indian girls, this transformation meant "a process of civilization derived from the Victorian model of middle-class white domesticity."[48] Patriarchal domesticity underpinned the notion of American civilization, and white women were central to the project.

Though largely marginalized from politics in the nineteenth and twentieth centuries, white women reformers throughout the United States found their calling in Indian reform. Through their own activism and political participation, these women sought to gain public legitimacy and authority while simultaneously undermining Indigenous communities. Whereas the state became the "father" to Indigenous children, white women imagined raising these children—and in many cases adults—as surrogate "mothers."[49] Maternalists eagerly campaigned for greater roles in Indigenous policy issues, often serving as matrons facilitating Indian removal practices or as schoolteachers responsible for socializing and assimilating Native children. Jacobs posits that while the state was the legal or imagined guardian of Indigenous children, it nonetheless "subcontracted" "guardianship responsibilities . . . education, discipline, punishment, affection and emotional support to white women."[50] White women maternalists were thus deeply woven into the fabric of the settler colonial project.

Throughout the history of the Bay Area Outing Program, two outing matrons and one assistant controlled operations. Bonnie V. Royce served as outing matron until the early 1930s, during which time she relied on the assistance of Jeannette Traxler. In 1934, Mildred Van Every entered as the final outing matron.[51] In the outing system, white women viewed their matronly duties as a charitable and necessary effort in addressing the "Indian problem." In their maternalist positions of power, they wielded much control over Native women's lives. For example, matrons embraced Victorian ideals, lauded sexual restraint (chastity), and maintained strict codes of conduct. Though mid- to late nineteenth-century Victorian ideals were somewhat passé by the early twentieth century, matrons and federal officials regarded them as useful tools for controlling and shaping Native women. Through these values, matrons commended individualism and personal improvement. Victorian gender ideologies were intended to give girls purpose, ambition, and drive. In return, Native girls and women were meant to gain "civilization" through their work in American homes.[52]

In her own words, inaugural outing matron Royce desired girls to "make good" while in the program. Overwhelmingly, this meant sticking to the aforementioned standards. In one case, Royce pleaded with a young woman who left nurses' training: "I am so interested in you and know there is a great deal to you and with the proper incouragement [*sic*] you can make something of yourself. Do'nt [*sic*] allow your school training to be wasted."[53] In typical situations, Royce claimed, "I will always do all I can for her or any other Indian girl," but more often than not, "all she could" was limited to the constraints of the program—Americanization, civilization, and above all, domestication. Presented as compassionate, benevolent, charitable work, the outing program disguised its oppressive nature. Outing matrons were agents of state surveillance and control.

"When I Graduated . . . I Could Not Get Any Other Job but as a Housekeeper"

Because the program was based in Berkeley, California, and not tied to a specific school, all Indian women—students or not—were considered for employment.[54] However, among these cohorts, young girls in schools had less of a choice about whether or not they would participate in the program, and their integration into the Bay Area Outing Program—especially in its early years—was coercive. In contrast, women who had previously graduated Indian schools had the opportunity to decide whether or not to apply for work through the outing program. Nonetheless, many women found that domestic outing work was all for which they were qualified. In August of 1933, Irene Tungate wrote directly to then commissioner of Indian Affairs John Collier to express her frustrations about her education and inability to find work outside of the domestic sphere. Tungate wrote from her employer's home in West Hollywood, "I am an Indian girl and a graduate from Sherman Institute, Riverside, California. I was sent out to that school to get an education. When I graduated, I found I could not get any other job but as a housekeeper. Any girl knows how to do that sort of work, I'm sure. My four years wasted. I found I could have accomplished more if I had attended a regular public high school."[55] In fact, public school curricula were geared to keep women out of the job market. Indian boarding school curricula pushed them into it.[56]

Discontent among boarding school graduates was not uncommon. For instance, a 1929 survey among Stewart Indian School graduates found dissatisfied students. Rose Pete was a domestic worker but felt she did not receive adequate nor efficient training. Lydia Holbrook felt her education at Stewart taught her "nothing."[57] While Native women had difficulty getting work outside of domestic labor, they also experienced racial discrimination. In fall of 1942, outing participant Lois Godawa wrote Van Every in search of government work in Oakland's factories. Godawa had little luck finding work in Beatty, Oregon, saying, "You see they are pretty strict around here with the jobs. They only hire the white women. It's pretty hard to explain."[58] Many women who outed briefly had little choice but to return to the BIA-run program for employment.

Further, the Bay Area's population boom in the early twentieth century made for a diverse labor force and racialized labor conditions. Among thousands of recently arrived Southern and Eastern Europeans, Mexicans,

Asians, and African Americans, outing girls, like Japanese women, were relegated to domestic work. Native-born white women held higher-status and better-paid jobs in offices, department stores, and factories. Women of color were typically excluded from these positions.[59] Also, California had the greatest shortage of household workers, so women of color filled domestic jobs native-born workers rejected.[60] Coercion colored most Native women's employment experience.

Outing Process

Native women learned of and engaged in the Bay Area Outing Program in three main ways: through referrals from boarding school or reservation officials, through recruitment efforts by outing matrons, and finally through word of mouth. Recruitment through boarding schools and word of mouth were the most common. In addition to these methods, parents or relatives who likely learned of the program through local Indian agents or field nurses referred their daughters to the outing program. In the fall of 1940, Harry H. Meyers wrote Mildred Van Every in search of employment for his seventeen-year-old daughter, Dorothy. Dorothy had just returned from the Albertinum Convent, a boarding school and orphanage in Ukiah. He hoped to find her work in a private home caring for children. The family of six lived in a "dilapidated" two-bedroom apartment in San Francisco, so the household would certainly benefit from her wages.[61]

For those coming by way of boarding school, the Bay Area Outing Program was affiliated with mostly western-based schools such as the Stewart Indian School in Carson City, Nevada; the Sherman Institute in Riverside, California; and the Chemawa Indian School in Salem, Oregon. However, girls also ventured from Haskell Institute in Lawrence, Kansas, and other Midwest Indian boarding schools. Matron Mildred Van Every conducted recruitment trips to Sherman Indian School every summer. In general, matrons kept regular contact with boarding school staff and superintendents for recruitment purposes.[62] Their presence was seen and efforts well-known. In 1939, Helen Kibby, a young Hoopa woman, wrote Van Every in search of childcare or housekeeping work: "I am the girl you spoke to at Stewart last spring. About a job in Oakland or elsewhere. I would like very much to have a job about the middle of November."[63]

By the 1930s, Indian girls and women knew of outing programs and how to contact outing matrons for work. Girls often referenced the kind of placement they desired and occasionally set pay rates. Adult women well out of boarding school were more vocal in asserting commensurate wages.[64] In 1936, for example, twenty-six-year-old Freda Eleck, a Pomo woman from Potter Valley, wrote to Matron Van Every in search of domestic employment, "Will you please try and secure employment for me. I have very little experience. It has been a long time since I worked for families. I would like to do housekeeping of some sort, take care of babies and I can do a little cooking. Will you write me to the above address if you find a place?"[65]

A month later, Eleck established her salary, stating, "I am willing to start at either $20 or $25 a month. I will get my report as to my physical condition and general health on February 15. I would rather not go down there until I know for certain there is a job for me. Please let me know when you find a job. Then I will let you know the day I will arrive."[66] Eleck's mention of a health report references a post-1930 requirement that women and girls submit a health clearance before placement. Once in the outing system with health clearance, girls were prompted to formally "apply" for work. Forms like Application to Bay Region Employment Agencies for Employment or Application for Older Girls gathered relevant data about the young Native woman in question—her education, years in public school or at Indian schools, weight, height, and skills.[67] In particular, this form calculated her abilities and training in home economics, nursing, and practical experience, especially regarding housekeeping, cooking, serving a table, and answering a doorbell. Such documents also gauged the applicant's personal appearance, her "neatness," "alertness," and "cheerfulness." Throughout similar assessment forms, matrons sometimes took liberties to expand further on their praise or disdain of said young woman. In short, outing matrons monitored and policed Native women, scrutinized their general appearance and emotional state, and surveilled Native women's sexuality.

"I Would Like a Thirty Dollar Girl"

On the other side of the outing program, employers had a much simpler process for applying for "girls." At the height of the program in the 1930s, an official United States Indian Field Service form from the Department of the Interior, titled Application for Girls, facilitated the placement process. In February 1936, Mrs. W. A. Henderson of Oakland applied for a Native girl to do general housework in her one-story home. At the time, Henderson was seven months pregnant and had a little girl in need of caretaking.[68] Because Freda Eleck indicated that she was good with children, Matron Mildred Van Every arranged for her to work in the home. Eleck worked for the Hendersons for about five months that summer. Overall, matrons facilitated the placement process, which was to some extent haphazard, though a few guiding principles seem to have been adopted. If girls noted they wanted to work with small children, the matron often placed them in a home with children. If they requested not to work with children, matrons regularly honored that as well. In general, the matron served as an intermediary between the employers and these Native women; in this arrangement, employers' desires were typically placed above girls' needs. Although Indian girls' application forms collected minute details about their skills and abilities, applications for homeowners did not. Matrons did not require homeowners to respond to the suitability of their home or their ability to care for Indian girls. In some cases, the matron conducted an interview with prospective employers.[69] However, records reveal that aside from rare cases, matrons did not perform site visits to ensure the safety of outing girls and women.

Moreover, within the structure, many girls were regarded as disposable labor commodities. For example, Hazel Emm periodically engaged in outing work in Berkeley, Oakland, San Mateo, and Richmond until 1935. Matron Van Every commended Emm as "one of the best girls with children."[70] In November of 1933, during her first stint in the program, Emm decided to leave her placement on account of loneliness. A concerned Dorris C. Taft, in whose house Emm was working, wrote to the girls' placement officer, Mrs. Traxler. Taft explained that Emm expressed loneliness working in San Mateo, far away from other outing girls in the East Bay. Taft wrote that "she would rather work in Oakland where she knows someone . . . she said her good girl friends had gone home and that seemed to upset her a bit." She continued, "I am dreadfully disappointed; she is an excellent girl, as clean and neat as possible, very capable and apparently well trained. . . . Would it be possible for me to get another Indian girl as good as Hazel?"[71]

Employees similarly coveted Kathryn Jones, a Paiute and Shoshone girl from Owyhee, Nevada. Jones was fourteen years old when she started outing, and she worked at six homes intermittently from 1926 to 1935 in Alameda, Berkeley, Oakland, Piedmont, and San Francisco. According to her record notes, Jones was "very dependable and an excellent worker."[72] In the summer of 1930, Jones worked for Lettie Holland in Brookdale, California, and had to leave to return to Stewart Indian School. In August, Holland wrote to Matron Royce, explaining that she was sad she could not keep Jones through the summer: "I am hoping you will bring me a nice girl as a helper for the three more months we expect to remain down here after we return to Oakland. I would like a thirty dollar girl if possible."[73] As girls transferred homes and left to return to school, they were often treated as material goods—replaceable and exchangeable.

Having secured a position of employment, women were responsible for reimbursing their transportation to the Bay Area. This was especially true for women who were of age. In a February 1932 letter, Superintendent McNeilly from the Western Shoshone Indian Agency wrote to Matron Royce regarding funds he had loaned two outing women, Josephine Marsh and Lucy Egan. The superintendent explained that he let Marsh borrow money from his accounts to travel from Elko to California to get work. He wrote, "Since she did not have money for her transportation I furnished it." He continued, "In December I took Lucy Egan out for the same purpose and let her have $15, which was to be returned in the same manner. . . . These girls could not get work here and they had no way to pay their expense unless someone advance the money, so I felt it was justified."[74] McNeilly's letter reveals two things: that few jobs existed in rural tribal communities and that Native women, especially those of age, would have had to furnish their own transportation to the Bay Area for outing work. Considering the figures the superintendent referenced—fifteen dollars and twenty dollars—Native women would have had to spend and in some cases reimburse at least half a month's wage on transportation to the Bay Area.

The Nature of Outing Labor

Though the outing program offered no training to young women, in all Indian boarding schools, women were instructed in "domestic science": basic household skills, cooking, ironing, and laundry. At Stewart and regional boarding schools, girls and young women received daily training, some of it thematically. In 1935, Mondays focused on sewing, mending, and learning the cost and durability of fabrics. Girls learned arithmetic by way of measuring fabric and grammar by learning to spell the names of fabrics. Wednesdays were devoted to handicrafts. Fridays focused on food—how to purchase groceries, cook inexpensive cuts of meat, and prepare and serve food. Since its inception, Stewart maintained a robust domestic training program, which expanded in 1936. The change required female students enroll in six years of domestic training.[75] This gendered curriculum rooted in Victorian ideals emphasized industrial work ethic, personal improvement, morality, and chastity.[76] It established Euro-American notions of femininity, emphasizing domesticity, piety, submissiveness, and male authority.

These all-encompassing gendered labor dynamics were a daily reality for Indian girl students at boarding schools. So much so that many would argue that it was all they learned. Esther Wasson, a Yerington Paiute woman from Smith Valley, Nevada, attended Stewart Indian School in the 1930s and '40s. In her youth, she was employed in domestic work, and she later settled in the San Francisco Bay Area. At Stewart, Wasson recollected, her education was divided equally between classroom time and industrial work—known as the "half-day plan."[77] Considering the labor-intensive schooling Wasson received at Stewart, she believed the boarding school prepared her for future domestic work. Even with a ninth- or tenth-grade education from a boarding school like Stewart, women were more experienced in labor activities than formal schooling. And many, like Wasson, felt that the need for employment superseded any scholastic ambitions. Wasson states, "My reading [or spelling] was never [very] good . . . so I figured I might as well go work."[78]

Indian boarding school curricula forced Native women into domestic work, a particularly demanding kind of labor. Significantly, the crucial element of live-in domestic work is the "on call" nature of employment. Even during breaks and off time, live-in domestics were expected to respond to employers' needs as they arose. Further, Margaret Jacobs's study on the Bay Area Outing Program reveals various forms of exploitation and surveillance. Because women boarded in private homes, their employers and matrons subjected them to rules and morals. They also suffered conditions consistent with modern-day live-in domestics—loneliness, abuse, exploitation, and long hours but low wages.

The nature of outing positions varied from employer to employer, but Native women were generally required to clean house, cook, do laundry by hand, and take care of any children within the home. In the pre-automated home, these were physically demanding tasks. Further, employers scrutinized the quality of the work; if an outing girl singed a tablecloth while ironing, her employer would dock her wages. Live-in positions required work at nearly all hours of the day. One girl labored from 6:30 a.m. to 9:30 p.m., averaging about ninety hours a week. Outing women had hardly any downtime and only one day off a week—usually Thursdays. On average, Native women worked in modest three- and four-bedroom homes. However, some worked in large, eleven-bedroom mansions that were doubtless challenging to clean.

While separated from their families—including sometimes their own children—some outing women and girls were responsible for raising their employers' children. Some liked the idea of caring for children and specifically sought homes with youngsters. Others complained of disobedient children and requested transfers when they could no longer tolerate it. Indeed, some women outright requested homes without children, for they found the work so demanding. While not all outing participants agreed on this point, it was a common feature in most positions. Further, because outing positions were typically short-term, it seems less likely that women maintained intimate long-term relationships with the children they raised.

Generic outing forms show that outing applicants were surveyed about their "special capabilities" related to domestic work, including care of children, cooking, ironing, answering the doorbell, answering the telephone, and serving the table.[79] Earlier forms from the 1930s, called "outing certificates," delved into more specific details.[80] Matrons and boarding school home economics teachers were required to indicate the applicant's ability in regard to domestic tasks. This thorough assessment covered a great deal, indicating that in the home, Native girls and young women would have been charged with an abundance of responsibilities, including bathing, entertaining, and putting children to bed; vacuuming; dusting; bed making; laundry; cooking; baking bread, cakes, and pies; planning, organizing, and serving meals throughout the day; dishwashing; sewing; and mending as necessary.

This kind of manual domestic labor was considered imperative for an Indian girl's transformation into a "thorough housewife." Federal officials touted "domestic science" as a means to inculcate Native women and girls in Euro-American standards. With these skills they would better emulate their white counterparts. Superintendent of Indian Education Estelle Reel was especially adamant that girls be trained in the "practical everyday life of the household."[81] The ability to cook, clean, serve, sew, and wash would unravel her tribal teachings and prove a Native woman's "domestication." Reel declared, "The art of housekeeping, as learned in the home under the mother's eye is what we want to teach our Indian girls, assuring them that because our grandmothers did things in a certain way is no reason why we should do the same."[82] Reel's emphasis on the "dignity" of labor as "practical training" was hinged upon her belief that the Indian race was intellectually deficient. Above all, therefore, labor was imperative for Indian children's "redemption," and boarding school curricula and outing programs reflected this.[83]

While not all homes demanded the full range of domestic tasks, outing women were regularly forthcoming with their needs and experience. For example, in March of 1932, twenty-four-year-old Harriet Cleveland wrote Matron Royce requesting a position for sixty-five dollars or more a month. She specifically requested no child work and indicated she was a "good plain cook" and a "good housekeeper."[84] Unfortunately, the scarcity of jobs during the Depression meant that Cleveland had no choice but to accept a job with children.[85] In April, she started at a remote home three miles outside of Napa. Cleveland tolerated the job for about two months. In June of 1932, she wrote to Royce to explain her departure and air her grievances:

> I'm leaving my place the 11th of June—I do not like it here. She will not let me have a day off or one Sunday a month even. The work is too much for the money she pays me. I also sleep in the same room as the baby and I'm up all hours of the night—I never get through with my work till 9:30 in the night. So if you have any place in view by the 11th would you call me at the telephone number in the city? I will be there after I leave here.

As promised, Cleveland left Napa on the eleventh. Records show that she did not return to the outing program until two years later, when she worked at a home in San Francisco. There, she earned a whopping eighty dollars a month, or over three times the average outing wage.[86] Native women like Cleveland knew their value and rarely suffered through difficult outing conditions. While some had very demanding tasks, other positions were more lenient. For example, in February of 1941, Van Every—then a social worker—wrote to Helen Williams to explain the details of an available position. The household had two adults and one eight-year-old child who was "not spoiled" and "able to look out for herself." The duties included general housework, preparation of vegetables and evening meals, and childcare. The housework was "simple," with light laundry and no entertaining. Apparently, the last Indian girl in the home had no practical experience, but Mrs. Krieger was "patient."[87] The position was fairly easygoing with a tolerable employer. Williams, who desperately needed a job for herself and "the ones that . . . depend[ed]" on her, happily accepted.[88]

Native women who worked in the Bay Area Outing Program often did so on short stints. Teenage girls outed mostly during the summer and occasionally during winter breaks from their respective boarding schools. Some adolescents were able to continue outing throughout the school year, only with officials' permission and usually at the behest of their employers. For instance, in August of 1925, a Mrs. Alice Davies Endriss of Oakland desired to "retain" her domestic worker, Ruby Paradice—the same Ruby from the

Oakland Tribune article that introduced this book. While officials were often open to students staying throughout the school year, Assistant Superintendent Beahm at Stewart Indian School was not sympathetic. On August 17, 1925, he wrote to Endriss, declaring, "This arrangement would not be at all satisfactory for us. Ruby is one of our very bright students and is really a leader amongst our student body and is a girl whom we believe has a future before her if she will continue school. . . . It will not be satisfactory for Ruby to drop out of school at this time."[89] Teenage girls who did work throughout the year usually enrolled at a Bay Area–based high school. These young women typically attended Oakland High School or Alameda High School.

Among all ages, outing positions could be as short as a few days and more regularly lasted at least a few months. It was not uncommon for women to have several outing positions over a few years. While some women and girls remained throughout the school year, none appeared to stay in the same home for much longer than a year or so. In fact, it was very uncommon to find women who worked in the same home for two or three years. Outside of outing, Native women engaged in seasonal labor such as hop picking with family and selling Indian baskets through the outing matron. During and after outing positions, some women obtained domestic work on their own accord, laboring independently of the matron's authority. Some transitioned to work in local canneries; during wartime, they ventured into local shipyards. Ultimately, those who transitioned away from outing sought more permanent, lucrative work elsewhere.

Contractual Surveillance and Obedience

In a brief example from the archives, we learn of further surveillance of Native women and their forms of agency through outing contracts. In the Bay Area Outing Program files, these contracts were especially common in the 1930s. In 1930 and 1931, Josephine Natchez, a seventeen-year-old Pyramid Lake Paiute student at Stewart Indian School, worked for the outing program for two summers. In June of 1930, upon starting the program, Natchez signed a contract between herself, the outing matron, and her employer for the summer. The contract declared four main points regarding wages, how young women would be monitored and checked for disobedience, and the program's gendered and supposedly "educational" intentions.

In exchange for her paid services, Natchez was offered "suitable quarters," and the contract stated that the employer would "extend proper interest in the advancement, welfare, and safeguarding of the pupil."[90] The contract also established that "at no time will the pupil be allowed to leave the homes of the employer at night without proper escort." Importantly, the contract included disobedience clauses threatening the removal of Indian women if they did not abide by the rules of the program: "Disobedience, or misconduct on . . . the part of the pupil, or absence without permission will be promptly reported to the matron in charge who may return the girl to the school." While the contract asserts surveillance of Native girls and the permission and approval they required from matrons and homeowners,[91] it extensively affirms young women as "pupils"—students at their respective Indian boarding schools. This seemingly insignificant language demonstrates how outing was ostensibly educational and yet clearly oriented for labor exploitation.

Contracts further decreed the outing program's civilizing, gendered intentions. Natchez's contract states that "it is also agreed and understood that the pupil will at all times conduct herself in a ladylike manner and always endeavor to improve herself in every possible way and earnestly endeavor to make a good record for herself."[92] In this way, contracts establish the goals of the outing program as an assimilationist "improvement" tool. Simple words such as "ladylike," "improve," and "good" accentuate a feminine form of inculcation. Moreover, these words highlight the patriarchal underpinnings of outing derived from preceding policies. In concert with policies like Allotment and Indian boarding schools, outing intended to rework Native communities into heteropatriarchal nuclear families that then subjugated and subordinated Native women. Purportedly, outing was for the benefit of Indian girls. Yet woven through the program was what Lomawaima would call "training in dispossession."[93] Bay Area Outing Program contracts make this goal visible.

Aside from daily surveillance and gendered intentions, contracts also established pay rates. Natchez, for example, agreed to twenty-five dollars a month for services with room and board and free time on Sunday and Thursday afternoons. However, women saw only one-third of their actual monthly pay. Two-thirds of this amount was paid "through" the superintendent of one's boarding school. The operative word "through" stressed that the outing program funneled Indian children's wages back into the schools that sent them.[94] Ostensibly, this safeguarded students' earnings and cultivated thrift. However, at the heart of this arrangement was the assumed incompetency of Indian students. Victoria Haskins argues that this structure, which was common nationally, "made a symbolic statement about their inability, as Indian girls, to be entrusted with their own finances."[95] Furthermore, the remaining third of funds that these women were paid was managed by the outing matron. In most cases, Native girls and women needed the matron's approval to withdraw their personal earnings.[96] Even so, these earnings were more than they saw for any on-campus labor conducted at their respective boarding school. So, women and girls often acquiesced. Yet they were nonetheless put to work around the clock daily, laboring into their own dispossession under the surveillance of a matron or employer. On the question of agency, there was little, and yet some Native women were able to advocate for themselves.

Returning to Josephine Natchez, we find evidence of agency and also some semblance of hope for a life outside of domestic work. During her brief time in the program, both school and outing officials advocated for Natchez to stay working in the Bay Area instead of returning to school. Upon receiving a petition letter from her employer asking to keep Natchez through the winter, Stewart Indian School superintendent Frederic Snyder approved the arrangement. Not long after the agreement, Natchez was eager to return to Stewart so she could finish her education and become a nurse. Her bags were packed for some time, suggesting that she unwillingly stayed due to the school's and outing officials' recommendation.[97] Already in receipt of only meager compensation during her employment, Natchez was docked a further $4.50 of her pay for ruining a bedspread and was forced to wait nearly a year before receiving her full wages. Natchez's outing record reveals the lack of agency many school-age girls had within the program. It also demonstrates her strong will and determination to return home, continue her education, and follow her dream of becoming a nurse.

Considering the gendered constraints, daily monitoring, and low-wage servitude imposed upon her, Natchez's force of will is significant. Moreover, it is crucial to note that while contracts established disobedience clauses for girls, they made no mention of house visits or inspections to determine whether employers provided girls with good housing and meals. They did not establish crucial details such as work hours, the kind of responsibilities or tasks required in the home, or paydays. Ultimately, outing matrons trusted the private, unmonitored homes that girls were sent to labor in, and checks and balances in the program were inherently one-sided—aimed at young Native women. While this brief discussion of contracts demonstrates Natchez's agency, it also highlights the constraints to which she was subjected. One common issue amid these constraints was wages.

Wages

As demonstrated by the case of Stella Healey, some of the women and girls in the outing program were breadwinners for their whole families. Remittances were common and often the main reason for girls to out in the Bay Area. For instance, Rosalie Patterson made it her priority to send her mother five dollars a month from her wages. Outing allowed her to take care of her family and have enough to buy things for herself.[98] Previous data on the Bay Area Outing Program indicates that in the 1930s, Indian domestic servants averaged just twenty dollars a month, or as much as 47 percent below the national average of thirty-eight dollars a month.[99] New data on outing wages is illuminating. Bay Area Outing Program wages varied substantially, falling between ten dollars a month at the low end to one hundred dollars a month at the highest. Teenage girls were regularly paid fifteen dollars a month or less, especially if they were enrolled in public school. In rare cases, wages were so low that matrons indicated them as such. Elaine Johnson, a twenty-four-year-old Ho-Chunk woman, worked briefly at a home in Alameda, earning such a pittance that the matron simply denoted her wages there as "small." Johnson was primarily in the Bay Area to train her voice, so perhaps the minor sum was allowable.[100] In only one record, an outing girl received no wages for her labor. In 1931, sixteen-year-old Grace Boone, a young Pomo woman, received no earnings while "training" for a month at the Schmidt home in Berkeley. The next year, she received only room and board for working over nine months at the Rose home in Oakland. Simultaneously, Boone somehow managed five days at a Burlingame home, thirty-five miles away across the Bay, at the rate of twenty dollars a month.[101] Aside from these outlier examples, the average monthly recorded wage for all outing girls and women was roughly $22.50 a month. This includes all documented wages from 1926 to 1944.[102] For comparison, in 1939 full-time female domestic servants in California averaged about $545 annually. In contrast, Native outing women would have averaged under $300 annually—or about 55 percent less than the state average.[103]

However, it is important to remember that young women still enrolled in boarding school only saw one-third of their actual monthly pay. Two-thirds was paid "through" the superintendent of the young woman's boarding school.[104] On average, these women received only $7.50 per month—all of which was managed by the outing matron. Graduates of boarding schools and women of age would receive their full wages but were still subject to the matron's financial guardianship. For example, Lucy Egan, a Paiute woman from Owyhee, Nevada, began outing in 1926 at the young age of fourteen. The Stewart Indian School student outed on summer and winter breaks. During her outing tenure, she worked for eight homes in Berkeley, Piedmont, Oakland, and San Francisco, garnering twenty-five to fifty dollars a month in wages. In 1930, when she was eighteen years old, Egan gained access to her full wages. On her outing contract—which was especially common during 1930—Matron Royce crossed out the stipulation, "two-thirds of the [wage] to be paid through the superintendent of the school."[105] While Egan now received her full wages, she still had to petition the matron for access to them.

In August of 1930, Egan wrote Matron Royce from her outing placement at a Presidio home in San Francisco, "I wanted to ask you last Thursday if I could have all this month paid. . . . If you say 'yes' I'll be very much obliged. Will you phone and let [my employer] Mrs. Wright know?"[106] Not only did Egan have to request access to her funds, but she also had to inform her employer. Certainly, a young Indian woman with money was considered a dangerous thing. She might frivolously spend it on a cab fare or a night out in San Francisco. In return, Matron Royce responded, "You may have your month's pay if you need it for clothing. However, I expect you to start a bank account next month."[107] Royce's comment on clothing shows that matrons and employers both had assumptions about "good" and "bad" ways Native women spent money. Her final note about the bank account shows that Royce was willing to let Egan control her own funds. This kind of olive branch was extremely rare and is perhaps suggestive of Royce's annoyance at having to manage Egan's funds.

High Wages

A small percentage of women in the Bay Area Outing Program earned considerably higher monthly wages. These were usually women who were at least eighteen and typically more experienced. Haskins argues that higher wages were seen as an incentive for Indian girls and signified "the successful integration of Indian women into the domestic labor market economy."[108] In the Bay Area Outing Program, higher wages were especially prevalent in the late 1920s up until about 1932. Harriet Cleveland earned eighty dollars a month at a home in San Francisco—nearly the highest earnings recorded in the outing files. Her rate was only second to Persia McCarthy, who earned one hundred dollars a month while working at a San Rafael home in 1929. Records note that McCarthy was "very quick" and "is most capable—efficient—Wonderful cook."[109] High wages were typically rare, and subject to economic conditions. For example, in 1928, Theresa Williams, a Yurok and Tolowa woman from Klamath, began working for the program when she was twenty-one years old. For about seven months, Williams worked at a home in Berkeley, earning fifty dollars a month. In 1929, she transitioned to another Berkeley home, where she earned seventy dollars a month. In the fall of 1929, she earned a very high sum of seventy-five dollars a month at a home in Ross, California. Williams enjoyed these high wages into 1931. By 1933, however, her wages had fallen drastically. While working a few months at a home in Oakland, Williams earned twenty-five dollars a month. In December of that year, her wages increased slightly to thirty dollars a month at a Hillsborough home.[110]

Thana Thompson similarly enjoyed higher wages in the late 1920s. In 1929, just shy of her nineteenth birthday, Thompson began working for a Piedmont home earning fifty dollars a month. She continued in this same home until November of 1932. Thereafter, in January of 1933, Thompson began working in Oakland for thirty dollars a month, or 60 percent of her previous wages.[111] In March of 1933, Matron Royce wrote to Thompson's mother, commenting on the decrease of wages: "I am wondering how the depression is affecting you folks up there, it is rather bad here. Wages are much lower than they were several years ago, so Thana is not making as much as she used to."[112] Indeed, the Depression had a major effect on outing wages. Whereas in the 1920s, women could at times earn fairly large sums, that had all changed by 1933. In fact, overall, monthly outing wages failed to recover. Post-1933, wages remained around twenty-five dollars a month. In only a few cases did women achieve 1920s-level wages in the 1930s.[113] By the late 1930s, wage levels had begun to improve, but in 1939, wages again stagnated as a result of the Golden Gate International Exposition. A flood of laborers to the San Francisco Bay Area affected outing wages. Organizers of the program were aware of this downward wage pressure. On May 1, 1939, Mildred Van Every—in her capacity as Indian Service social worker—wrote to Mabel Whipple about a position. She regretted the pay, explaining, "We have been under great difficulty in getting more than $30 to $35 a month for household employees since the fair opened. So many women are here from the middle west looking for employment."[114]

Unpaid Wages

Where some women in the outing program enjoyed higher wages than their peers, others were pressed with lack of payment of wages. Employers commonly "forgot" to pay their servants and delayed or settled those payments. In the summer of 1929, Delphine Holbrook—the same young woman pictured in the 1927 *Oakland Tribune* article from the introduction—worked at an Oakland home earning thirty dollars a month. By August of that year, Holbrook and her friend Phyllis Washoe had not been paid their last month's wages. The two Washoe women worked together to secure their earnings. On August 27, 1929, Holbrook wrote, "We are writing and asking you for our money of the last month's payment. We are in need of some clothes and we could buy them much cheaper here than we could there. Please reply soon as possible and let us know if we are entitled to our last month's payment."[115] Interestingly, Holbrook not only conveyed her need but also defined that need as clothing—deemed an acceptable expense in the eyes of outing matrons and employers. By October, however, the debt remained. In a letter to Superintendent Snyder at Stewart, Royce explained that Holbrook's employer claimed that she assumed that her husband had paid the debt and would be mailing a check in the full amount shortly.[116]

Other women in the program similarly pleaded for their due wages. Velma Fred, a student from Chemawa, worked for the program in 1929 and returned home to Redwood Valley, California, in May of that year. Thereafter, she had yet to receive her wages. On May 21, 1929, Fred wrote Matron Royce for assistance: "Mrs. Royce please get that money from Mrs. Sirard and send it to me. As she don't know my address. And Mrs. Royce I did everything for her. I mean did all the cooking, made the beds, clean all the rooms. And I think I should get over $7.00 anyway. I may not worth it in my behaving. But Mrs. Royce please do help me to get it." A month passed, and Fred remained unpaid. On June 24, 1929, Fred wrote Royce again, pleading for her assistance: "Dear Mrs. Royce I am writing and asking why Mrs. Sirard hasn't sent me my pay for working for her. I certainly would appreciate it very much if you would kindly look into it for me as I am very much in need of it."[117] Weeks later, Royce sent a check to Fred with her remaining balance from Sirard. However, the matron took the liberty of garnishing $1.50 of those wages for Fred's subscription to the Community Chest of Oakland.[118]

In the summer of 1929, twenty-one-year-old Clara Shaw, a Paiute woman and Sherman graduate, had a similar issue. She was at home, in Nixon, Nevada, in between placements and still waiting on unpaid wages from her previous employer, Mrs. Armstrong. On August 29, 1929, Shaw wrote Royce, "And I also worked for one week. She did not pay me for that. I supposed to get that. I worked hard that week and I think I should get that. If she gives the money to you, please keep that for me."[119] Nearly two months later, Royce wrote Shaw informing her that Armstrong was mailing a check shortly.

Whereas Holbrook, Fred, and Shaw secured their due wages, some women were less fortunate. For example, Stewart Indian School student Bertha Daniels, a Blackfoot and Maidu woman, worked for the outing program at various Piedmont, Oakland, and Berkeley homes from 1931 to 1932. One of the employers was a Mrs. S. West in Piedmont, where Daniels worked for roughly seven months at fifteen dollars a month. Daniels's file reveals that she was not paid once during her time at the West home. Instead, the homeowner gave her occasional petty cash and paid for a pair of shoes, a perm, and her monthly carfare. A detailed document shows that Daniels's seven months of wages in the amount of $105.00 minus the abovementioned expenses of $47.38 came to $57.62 of wages owed to her. Though a clearly established debt remained, Daniels was forced to settle with the employer for $30—about 52 percent of what she was owed.[120]

Fighting for Commensurate Wages

Many young women negotiated with their employers to set a monthly pay rate. In some cases, this was arduous. For instance, Sue Andrews Morgan, a member of the Colville Confederated Tribes and graduate of Cushman Indian School—formerly Puyallup Indian School on the Puyallup Reservation in Tacoma, Washington—relocated from Los Angeles to work near her husband, who was stationed in Vallejo at Mare Island. At the time, Morgan was about thirty-two or thirty-three years old and was accustomed to a forty-dollar monthly wage working at a Los Angeles refuge center. In the summer of 1935, she wrote to Van Every, asking to meet local Indian girls and expressing some interest in working in the Bay Area. After a series of letters between the two and a possible picnic meeting with the Native women in the outing program, Morgan agreed to work for a Miss Ellis at a home in Berkeley.

At the start of her employment, Morgan wrote Van Every a "short note" to clarify her pay rate demands. In regard to her meeting with Miss Ellis, Morgan wrote, "I found her very pleasant. . . . One thing[,] I couldn't get her to promise to pay me $40.00. And in the future if she still doesn't see to pay me my price; I am only going to promise you that if she don't I don't want [to agree] to stay with her for only $35.00."[121] Morgan agreed to a weeklong trial in the Berkeley home but insisted that she would not stay past the trial if she was not paid her accustomed rate of forty dollars a month. Ellis's disregard for Morgan's pay would have meant a sixty-dollar reduction in her annual wages, or nearly two months of docked pay. That Morgan worked for the outing program during the Great Depression points to the likelihood that every dollar contributed to her survival and well-being. If Morgan was anything like other Native women working in the Bay Area during this period, she would have sent some of her wages back to her family in Colville, Washington, which underscores that the additional five dollars a month was more than just a wage; it was a means to support an entire family.

Morgan's letter to Van Every was a subtler form of resistance, but a resistance nonetheless. Morgan was well aware of the value of her skills and insisted that if she was not going to be paid her "price," then she would go elsewhere. In fact, that is what Morgan did. After her weeklong trial in the Ellis household, Morgan stayed only another three days, terminating her employment on August 1 of that year. Her outing record indicates she was paid only a thirty-five-dollar rate for the ten days of her service, which reveals that she did in fact leave for lack of commensurate wages. While it is not clear what employment Morgan held in the interim, nearly two months later, her husband was transferred to San Pedro, and the two returned to Los Angeles. Presumably she was able to return to her longtime position in the city. It is certainly understandable that Morgan would have greater agency and experience than her teenage outing counterparts, yet her case demonstrates that Native women refused to keep themselves in less than ideal situations and fought for the wages they deserved. The same could be said for Leona Godawa.

In 1932, Leona Godawa, a Modoc woman, worked for a Mrs. Marston in North Berkeley for twenty dollars a month. The twenty-two-year-old was responsible for a large family in a six-bedroom, three-bath home. The work proved difficult for Godawa, and she did not want to stay. On October 28, 1932, Godawa wrote Royce, "Dear Madam I have told my lady that I would leave on Sunday. I wish you would come for me, I shall be waiting. These people are swell but I think it is such a large family for me. I would be more pleased if you'd find me a place near my sister if you can. I don't really care to do cooking. I'll be waiting for a reply." Godawa received no word from Royce. A month later, she was pushed to the brink. She wrote Royce again, this time venting her frustration about the low pay. On November 21, 1932, she wrote the matron, "I've been very disappointed with the children here, and I really think the work is a little too much for me for so little amount of money. At first I understood that I was to get $30 a month but I am only working for $20. If Mrs. Marston really wants help I should think she should cut out giving parties and pay her helper at least $25.[122]

Child rearing, along with the house duties, was demanding and, for only twenty dollars a month, unacceptable. Godawa continued, "I'm sorry that I cannot stay here any longer than this month. If you could only try and get me a place where there's only three or four in a family, and all adults I'd probably be glad to assist the lady. But if you couldn't do that my sister and I would gladly return to San Francisco. Mrs. Royce do you place the girls in San Francisco?" Ever the concerned older sister, Godawa also inquired about her sister Lois's wages: "I'm very sorry for my sister at Mrs. S[. . .]'s for she has complained about many things that she didn't like. How much is she supposed to get at the end of the month? She's done most of the cooking and laundry, and housework. I'll be very glad to hear from you."[123] True to her word, Godawa left the Marston home and briefly transitioned to a temporary placement in San Anselmo. Shortly thereafter, both Godawa sisters left outing work altogether.

Four Winds Club

Throughout the early years of the Bay Area Outing Program, little community existed in which Native girls and women could participate. Live-in domestic work was already quite isolating, and girls were lucky if they and a friend were placed in nearby homes. Such an arrangement was rare, and usually only a result of girls advocating for close placements. Toward the end of Matron Bonnie V. Royce's career with the program, new organizational opportunities began to arise for Native girls and women in the program. This was especially true after Matron Mildred Van Every replaced Royce.

Van Every was closely affiliated with the YWCA in Oakland and realized the program's need to offer social activities for Native women working the Bay Area. Indeed, the "Y," as outing girls and women called it, had various clubs and organizations for working women in Oakland and the greater Bay Area. One of the first official clubs formed at Oakland's YWCA was the Four Winds Club.[124] It regularly met on Thursdays, when domestic workers had their day off, and became a central meeting place for Native women in the Bay Area. Within the organization, women held leadership roles and had the opportunity to delve into community organizing. Although always subject to the will of Matron Van Every, Native women in the club wielded a kind of power and authority—quite different from their daily lives as domestic workers. Moreover, the formation of such a social organization meant that assimilation was not working as planned. In addition to creating a community space for outing women and girls, this club grew to include Indians from other realms of the Bay Area, including college students and military personnel. Native men also became involved in the Four Winds Club.

In December of 1932, the *Oakland Tribune* published an article announcing the Four Winds Club's upcoming Christmas party. The spread includes a prominent photo of Marie Penrose, Paiute, and Allen Hunt, Pueblo, both in what appears to be traditional dress. The article announces, "Eastbay Indians representing 20 different tribes will come to Oakland next Thursday night to participate in their annual Christmas celebration at the Oakland Y.W.C.A., 1515 Webster Street. The program which will proceed games and dancing will feature an Indian interpretation of 'The Christmas Story,' in tableaux presented by members of the Four Winds Club under the direction of Mrs. Clarence Blackman." Certainly, the "Indian interpretation" would have fascinated local white socialites and women reformers of the time.[125]

The article further explains that the special program featured "the appearance of Allen Hunt in a dance, 'Chant Unto the Great Spirits.' Hunt, grandson of the famous war chief 'Red Fox' of the Pueblo tribe is known to members of his tribe as 'Spyawaka' or 'Whitefeather.' Also participating in the tableaux and dances will be Marie Penrose also known as 'Nashua' or 'Running Deer,' a member of the California Piute [*sic*] tribe." Others in the cast included women from the outing program: "Elaine Johnson, Singer,

Savina Scott, President of the Four Winds Club; Lucy Egan, Avis Hooper, Esther Babb, Mary Srk, Marie Penrose, Winifred Nelson, Lucy Nixon, Tony Rodriguez and Rose Primrose." While certainly captivating the interest of *Tribune* readers, the article demonstrates a very involved Four Winds organization that tapped into the community of Native women and girls outing in the Bay Area as well as Native men. Within the space of the Four Winds Club, Native cultural representations were not only acceptable but celebrated. By the mid-1930s, the Four Winds Club had gained further traction in Bay Area–based newspapers, demonstrating a lively social calendar. In November of 1934, the *Oakland Tribune* announced that the Committee on Indian Girls' Work would host a Thanksgiving dinner at the YWCA for the ladies of the Four Winds Club.[126] The dinner, held on Saturday, December 1, came two days after Thanksgiving, suggesting that outing girls worked the holiday and celebrated at a later time. Certainly, the dinner would have been a welcome respite and encouraged community participation. Such commitments would have been formally recognized by employers, who would have felt obliged to grant women time off. A few months later, in February of 1935, the *Oakland Tribune* reported that the Four Winds Club would host an event the following day to "welcome all Indian girls who have recently come to the Bay region." Over afternoon tea, the guests to be greeted were "Mrs. Agnes Malts, and Misses Mary Williams, Florence Elliott, Virgie Brittain, Pauline Mesket, Elfie Davis, Bernice Williams and Marjorie Peters." Evidently, some of the members of the Four Winds Club were affiliated with the Y's Industrial Clubs Council and planned to attend the upcoming Industrial Girls' Conference in Fresno.[127] In effect, the Four Winds Club acted as a reception center for outing women and girls and a conduit into larger organizational efforts across the state of California. It was a place where women could connect locally as well as regionally.

In addition to afternoon teas, dances, and dinners, the Four Winds Club hosted events for Native children. In 1938, the women of the Four Winds Club held a Halloween party at the YWCA for Native children in the East Bay.[128] Members assisted with games and refreshments and created space for Native children where there was none. Initially, the Four Winds Club was exclusive to single or newly married women in the outing program.

However, as more Indian people came to the Bay Area for educational pursuits and military jobs, the Bay Area Indian community grew; along with it grew the club. Frances Jack, a Pomo woman who worked in the Bay Area in the 1930s, fondly recollected the Four Winds Club. On Thursdays, when most domestic workers had their day off, "everyone"—all the Indians in the area—would go to the Y for the Four Winds Club. Once a month, the women in the club hosted a dinner and dance for the Native men attending UC Berkeley. Jack also recalled annual Christmas parties and dances. During the holiday season, the Y began a tradition of delivering Christmas baskets to the Indian community living in Oakland.[129]

By the Second World War, the club had grown even more, developing into an organization for both women and men. Genny Mitchell, Karuk, worked for a telephone company in Oakland in the late 1930s. She recalled the Four Winds Club's monthly gatherings for those in the "service," including social dances once or twice a month. Mitchell reflected that "[the club] was my only social life. I didn't know of any other way of going about it. I was never one to go to bars or dance halls or anything."[130] The club offered a safe, contained space to socialize and meet other Indian people. After Mitchell married, she and her husband became more active in organizing Four Winds Club programming. They were likely involved in the planning of the club's annual holiday events. In November of 1944, the Four Winds Club hosted their annual Thanksgiving dinner at the YWCA. The one-dollar dinner was free for all servicemen. A month later, the club hosted a Christmas party for servicemen, not unlike the one held twelve years prior. At this especially intertribal event, Native men and women dressed in regalia and exhibited dances from their communities.[131] When the war concluded, Mitchell noticed that more families came to the club instead of single people. There were also at least 150 members representing twenty-seven tribes.[132] The organization eventually outgrew itself, paving the way for the Bay Area Indian community in the form of the Intertribal Friendship House (IFH) in Oakland.

Reflecting on the ebb and flow of the club, Mitchell exposed the underlying intentions of the organization: "In the beginning, the Four Winds Club was supposed to be for working girls from reservations or from the schools. They brought them down here to work in homes, in rich people's homes."[133]

The club, she felt, was "one way they were trying to keep control of them, too, so they wouldn't be running off to the bars and places they shouldn't be going." Mitchell herself found the Four Winds Club gatherings to be a harmless way to socialize without venturing off to a more dubious establishment. Undoubtedly, Matron Van Every and the YWCA felt that Indian girls were better off socializing with one another in a controlled environment under the Matron's watchful eye. So although certainly a vital space for the Native community and a testament to the intertribal identity that grew in the Bay Area, the Four Winds Club was first established as a means to control the social lives of Native women. Nonetheless, in return, Native women organized and created new possibilities for their children and their families.

Native people "struggled" over domesticity.[134] Outing presented a predicament—the promise of wages and public schooling bound to the likelihood of undesirable conditions, surveillance, and lack of agency. For Native women during this time, domestic work was woven into their boarding school "education." When they were not laboring on school grounds daily, for example during summer breaks or after graduation, the "natural" occupation was live-in domestic work. This was a trade that was fraught with disciplinary issues. Participating in the Bay Area Outing Program system meant taking an automatic pay cut from already meager wages—in some years this was as much as 47 percent below the national average.[135] While adult women had more of a choice than their adolescent outing counterparts, there were few options besides domestic work. Regardless of their age, women in the program were subject to the matron's surveillance, approval, or consent. Participation in this system meant being subjected to the Victorian morals of the outing matron and one's employer. Live-in work was isolating and demanding of one's time. Ostensibly, the work seemed to afford Native women some independence. Instead, the program treated these Native women like wards—unnatural children—within a system of government "maternalism."[136] Despite the calculated assimilative mechanics of this settler project, Native women challenged these circumstances and resisted. They negotiated for better wages, left undesirable situations (when they could), and established the foundations for a Bay Area community that survives today. They navigated this contentious program and profession while asserting their individual needs. Faced with the pervasive force of the assimilation doctrine on Native bodies, Native women complied, contested, and actively unsettled domesticity.

THREE
"Indian Girls Prefer Park to Housework"
Criminalization, Surveillance, and Runaways

IN THE SUMMER OF 2017, I attended a Washoe basket-making workshop at the Intertribal Friendship House (IFH) in Oakland, California. "IFH," as it is affectionately known, is the backbone of the Urban Indian community in the East Bay. There, the Native community gathers for community feeds, Christmas parties, and cultural events like traditional cooking classes and clapper stick–making workshops. IFH dates back to the early twentieth century, when, on their afternoons off, Native women domestic workers organized the East Bay Native community through a group called the Four Winds Club. This club, affiliated with the Oakland YWCA, was created in the 1920s as a social organization composed of Native women domestic workers and later Native men enlisted in the military. Nearly a century later, we know this organization as IFH. The current building on International Boulevard has housed the community for over six decades.

On a warm June afternoon, amid colorful community murals, community language activists and friends of mine instructed youths and elders on how to create their own pine needle basket. At the tail end of the event, I sat with community elders who had all attended Indian boarding schools in their youth. These elders had come from various tribes, including Washoe and Shoshone. A few of the women had themselves worked in outing programs. The others were children of participants. These elders had attended Stewart in Carson City, Nevada; Sherman in Riverside, California; and Haskell in Lawrence, Kansas, among other boarding schools. As a I joined their group, they were reflecting on their time in boarding school. One woman cherished those years, saying, "If somebody came up to me today and said, 'I'll take you back anywhere you want to go,' I'd say, 'Take me back to high school, 'cause those were the best damn years of my life.'" Another joked, "You won!" A few others were less forthcoming. Talk of boarding schools turned quite naturally to stories of runaways. One woman who attended Stewart told a story about how she and some friends had run away from the school. They somehow managed to secure a car and drove fifteen miles into Washoe Valley before turning themselves in. Amid laughs and exclamations, she admitted that they just wanted to see what the "hoopla" was about running away.

A second woman who had attended Sherman but lived around Stewart in her youth recalled how a few boys from the Stewart School had decided to run away and stole her family's station wagon. They were trying to get back to Arizona. The boys made it over 220 miles from Stewart but were pulled over by highway patrol in Tonopah, Nevada. Her parents' car was eventually returned, a bit worse for the wear.

As the event wrapped up, their conversations returned to the present day—off-reservation tribal meetings, their grandchildren, and the next A's game. But what this moment proved to me is that runaways are still alive in the cultural memory of Native people. In a rather regular social setting at IFH, these elders reflected a communal memory of resistance. They celebrated the runaways and were eager to know what the "hoopla" was all about. They excitedly shared their stories and laughed about the few hours of freedom they and other Native students had enjoyed away from Indian boarding schools. Some were caught, while the others turned themselves in. But their conversation is embedded in a long history of colonial processes that bleed into the present and demonstrate a collective memory of resistance.

We will never know how most runaways may have reflected on their experience. Did they enjoy their fleeting moments of freedom? Was running away thrilling, frightening, or both? In what precarious situations did runaways find themselves? Did some just want to see what the "hoopla" was all about? The majority of these stories will remain untold. But the truth is that despite the oppressive force of federal indoctrination and assimilation, Native children and young adults resisted in the way they knew how.

While running away may have been a last-ditch effort or a little bit of fun, these runaways attempted to carve out a space for themselves. Their actions demonstrate Native resilience in the early twentieth century.

In the summer of 1922, the *Berkeley Daily Gazette* published an exposé revealing early twentieth-century traces of Indian women's labor in the San Francisco Bay Area. Notably, it covered the recent absence of said labor—four girls had run away from their places of employment. In large capital letters, the article declares, "Indian Girls Prefer Park to Housework." The article employs stereotypical tropes, claiming that "the call of the open was stronger than the city home for four Piute [*sic*] girls." Allegedly, these young Native women had camped out at Oakland's Lakeside Park before they were discovered by a police officer and "turned over." The last words of the article explain that the girls were "placed" in Berkeley and Piedmont homes for summer work, and they were under the care of Mrs. B. V. Royce, who served as matron for the Bay Area Outing Program.

Runaways, sometimes referred to as deserters by federal officials, have captured the mind of scholars, Native communities, and relatives of escapees.[1] Indian children who ran to the safe sanctuary of home and family personify a spark of resistance that gives light in the often-dark reality of Indian assimilation programs. This chapter examines the understudied facets of gendered Indian labor and carcerality in the context of western outing. I do so by exploring early twentieth-century outing runaways and Native women in California's juvenile justice system. I illuminate Native women's resistance to settler colonialism and argue that outing functioned as a carceral space that privileged criminalization and incarceration of Native women. In turn, Native women resisted the worst elements of outing, especially by running away. Historians have primarily focused on runaways in the context of Indian boarding schools.[2] Few have examined those who ran away from outing programs, nor have they detailed young Native women's carceral experiences while outing. To this end, I consider the powerful and painful stories of women and girls who expressed their dissatisfaction, ran away, stayed out past curfew, and found themselves in Bay Area "detention homes."[3]

My use of the term "runaway" considers a spectrum—women who had public departures and those who quietly absconded in the night, at times not garnering the outing matron's attention until days or weeks later. This term also considers those who left without permission. I use the term "incarceration" to mean both the literal confinement of outing girls in Bay Area jails and juvenile detention centers and confinement of girls within outing homes. Carcerality is not just caging, but also containment, confinement, and limiting movement. As Sarah Haley notes, carcerality can reinforce racialized constructions of gender and gendered divisions of labor. Therefore, confinement of girls within outing homes, limiting their movements, and subjecting them to the limitations of domestic work is an extension of carcerality. Settler societies control and contain and do so in various forms. Scholars agree that reservations and Indian boarding schools were designed to be carceral institutions.[4] Consequently, outing homes as extensions of schools were a form of confinement. The fact that runaways existed illuminates the carceral nature of these homes. Yet, the carcerality of outing programs remains largely unexplored.

This analytical shift changes our understanding of assimilation-oriented labor policies. Understanding outing as a form of carcerality highlights how outing programs are extensions of the carceral framework of boarding schools. They therefore require containment, surveillance, and punishment. And importantly, this subjects Native women and girls to carcerality. Ultimately, I find that outing women resisted containment, constant control, sexual surveillance, and labor exploitation.

Certainly, a key factor in incarceration is first criminalization. Carceral studies scholar Luana Ross argues that understanding Native criminality requires tracing the evolution of federal policies, the process of being made deviant, and the politics of confinement.[5] Indeed, while criminalization often occurs with crime, certain behaviors can be criminalized. In the case of Native women in the early twentieth century, simply being deemed deviant was sufficient. Further, at the turn of the century, the sexuality of working-class female youths in urban areas was read as a threat that concerned the public.[6] Sexual expression, whether confirmed or presumed, was immediately identified as delinquent or criminal behavior and frequently led to a young woman's incarceration. In short, young working women of the era were caught in an interconnected web of social fears that rendered them sexually deviant and criminal. This was especially true for Native women as racialized subjects. Where the average young working woman's sexuality would have been surveilled by the larger society and its criminal justice system, Native women's sexuality was specifically monitored by the outing program. Their sexuality was policed in order to create gendered labor exploitation. Thus, I argue that Native women and girls were disproportionately criminalized and incarcerated in the outing system.

In this chapter, first, I briefly review the existence of runaways in both Indian boarding schools and outing programs. I connect this to the literature on Native women, criminalization, and sexuality, demonstrating how Native people were marked as criminal and how the era intertwined notions of criminality and sexuality. Second, I turn to twentieth-century Bay Area newspaper articles, which reported on runaways in the program's infancy. While these articles are not the only coverage outing received, they articulate the lengths Native girls went to outwit their matrons and escape the program.[7] Here, I argue that localized rhetoric sought to convey the charity of the Bay Area Outing Program while justifying the control of Native women. Third, I examine federal records to demonstrate how the outing program and local detention centers policed and contained Native women, who were seen not as victims but rather as perpetrators— criminalized and subject to unreasonable policing. Woven throughout these cases is a fear of promiscuity and the need to control Native women's sexuality.[8] These records demonstrate the government's detailed management and exploitation of women in the outing program—but most importantly Native women's resistance to it.

Runaways and Criminalization

Scholars have largely focused on the central role that runaways played in resistance to Indian boarding schools. Boarding school runaways, or "deserters," were so common that each year, schools intentionally overenrolled to account for them. Desertion rates were especially high in the first months of school, when students were most homesick.[9] At Stewart Indian School, one year, ninety-one students ran away—or roughly 32 percent of the student body. Roughly 10 percent never returned. For those that did, local law enforcement played a role.[10] Schools regularly captured runaways and offered cash rewards for escapees. Students left for several reasons, including malnourishment, overwork, mistreatment, abuse, discrimination, and confinement. Nonetheless, running away was difficult and a last resort. Female runaways were subject to more dangerous threats than boys and were more obvious—and therefore not always successful.[11] Runaway stories vary, but in some cases, children were found in very dangerous situations. For instance, in December 1905, four girl runaways from Stewart were found unconscious from cold and exhaustion in negative-three-degree weather.[12] Boarding school "desertion" was a serious offense, and some runaways were corporally punished. Consequences for Bay Area Outing Program runaways were less severe. Matrons often gave girls another chance, revealing the context of exploited labor—the "second chance" to be exploited again. The goal was to discipline Native women into labor relations.

Though scholarship on outing runaways is incomplete, it is clear they were common. For instance, at Haskell, outing girls quit their jobs in response to stifling rules, overwork, and undesirable conditions.[13] Parents, too, had reservations about the program. While some encouraged their children to "out" so that they could earn spending money and gain new experiences, other parents criticized the program for subjecting their children to long, strenuous hours of labor. Many parents believed their children became ill because they were physically overworked. At Sherman, runaway girls had decidedly more urban exploits. One outing participant ran away repeatedly with another girl and frequented bars in a nearby city, enjoying forbidden freedoms.[14] Sherman outing girls had an unusual degree of agency in negotiating leave and family time. There, officials were inclined to grant Native women leave to prevent them from running away. Students also disliked outing. Some girls broke the rules of their outing contracts and tested their employers by staying out late, smoking, refusing abstinence, and befriending

Indian girls of "bad influence." Others left because of low wages.[15] Ultimately, runaways, whether from boarding schools or outing programs, would have faced the law.

Historically, Native people perceived as behaving outside the law have received harsher sentences for racialized infractions.[16] In fact, in the latter half of the nineteenth century, Native youths were often tried as adults and incarcerated in California prisons such as San Quentin.[17] This context sets the stage for outing women, who were additionally targeted for deviant behavior. Outing matrons enforced strict codes of conduct, including sexual restraint. They policed and surveilled their wards to ensure compliance. Native women who frustrated these standards—especially regarding sexual activity—were reprimanded and incarcerated.[18] Native women were under the guardianship of the outing matron, but legally, all minors in California were subject to parens patriae. This doctrine gave the state power over all children and youths identified as delinquents. Outing girls were often cited for "status," or noncriminal, offences, such as mingling with immoral companions or wandering the streets after curfew. These noncriminal offenses nevertheless led to their incarceration in detention homes. Moreover, because criminality was often linked to issues of the home, single parents—especially single outing mothers—were closely surveilled, subject to criminalization, and at risk of sterilization.

In early twentieth-century California, criminality and sexuality were deeply intertwined, and juvenile justice institutions routinely interrogated youths about their sexual activity. All reform school inmates were tested for sexually transmitted infections (STIs), but girls were forced to undergo invasive pelvic exams. In detention homes, girls were subject to a medical examination, a psychological evaluation, STI testing, and pelvic exams.[19] In Alameda County, incarcerated outing girls in the juvenile court endured such invasive exams.[20] Juvenile justice was gendered, and girls were incarcerated for sexual "crimes," whether confirmed or presumed, and regardless of their status as the victims or the perpetrators.[21] Incarceration usually marked girls as "sexually deviant." As I show in the testimonies of Native women laborers in the Bay Area Outing Program, Native women were subjected to these explicitly racialized and gendered social anxieties in addition to the experience of labor exploitation, further restricting their already regimented lives.

Tracing Outing Runaways

In 1922, over the course of several weeks, the *Berkeley Daily Gazette* published three articles on the subject of runaways in the Bay Area Outing Program's infancy. These articles provide early context for Native women's resistance and set the stage for their subsequent refusal into the 1930s. Evidently, these publications were prompted by the outing matron, Mrs. B. V. Royce, who sought assistance with apprehending runaways. In these years, the Bay Area Indian population was quite small, and girls were isolated from any sense of community and each other. Some Bay Area Outing Program runaways were characterized as the social type, looking for amusement in the city, yet their circumstances turn out to be closer to the experiences of "deserters" from boarding schools. Whether on account of homesickness, mistreatment, or overwork, these girls sought their only viable option—running away.

The article that introduced this chapter captures the early history of runaways in the Bay Area Outing Program. On August 17, 1922, the Thursday evening edition of the *Berkeley Daily Gazette* declared, "Indian Girls Prefer Park to Housework." Supposedly, these young outing girls camped out at Oakland's Lakeside Park before being discovered and "turned over" to the police. The article explains that the girls were "placed" in Bay Area homes for summer work, under the care of Matron Royce. In this article, Indian women are identified as unassimilated, "wild," and needing discipline. The title alone maintains that these four girls *preferred* the outdoors to domestic work—thus framing their deviancy. They are not only disobedient but also primitive and undomesticated. This language casts the outing program as necessary and benevolent, rather than exploitative.

The rhetoric employed here harks back to the kind of "Indian" that boarding schools were meant to transform and civilize. The "call of the open" suggests that these young women were uncontrollably driven outdoors—

marking them as wild and uncivilized. "Deserted" contends that they abandoned outing—a supposedly charitable endeavor. The girls were deemed ungrateful lawbreakers—criminal enough to warrant police intervention. Indeed, "turned over" is the passive terminology that the newspaper preferred to describe the reality of their capture: arrest and jail. Matron Royce is cast here as a *maternal* caretaker looking after the best interest of the Indian girls—and they are cast as her deviant foils. In twelve quick lines, the article declares outing as necessary to discipline and contain Indian women. Two months prior, the *Daily Gazette* published a similar article.

In boldface type, the paper declares, "Two Indian Girls Reported Missing." Two sixteen-year-old Indian girls had "disappeared" earlier in the week. The missing girls in question had gone to San Francisco with two other Indian "school girls." Both were employed as domestics and came from a cohort of sixty-five young women from Nevada to work during the summer. Of the four, only two returned to their live-in workplaces. The article reports that "it is believed the . . . girls were homesick and started on foot for the Indian reservation." This article uses much of the same rhetoric of deviance from the other article but also establishes a binary—Indian girls who obeyed and those who deserted. The article declares that these two runaways, Ella Bender and Lena Piper, had been "employed" as domestics. Such a term implies a contractual arrangement rather than an exploitative one. The operative word "disappeared," moreover, suggests they vanished without a trace. The article insinuates that, as runaways, they were disloyal and fickle, fleeing from respectable work.[22]

In the same way that the previous article is underpinned with "wild" rhetoric, this article accuses the girls of running "on foot" to their Indian reservation in Nevada. These words establish their "primitive" nature and declare the two as "untamed," unlike their more obedient counterparts. According to federal archives, all sixty-five girls would have traveled by train or bus to the Bay Area. Yet, this account inspires an image of Indian girls running hundreds of miles, barefoot. Once again, the paper affirms that Royce is "in charge" of the girls, underscoring her supposed interest in their well-being.

A third article in the *Daily Gazette* dated August 25, 1922, reported another disappearance. The article announces, "Indian Girls Are Reported Missing."[23] Allegedly, five Indian girls, "tired" of domestic work, had "disappeared" from their "good homes," where they "paid for their board by doing housework." Once again, the paper alleges that the girls "started on foot" to their reservation. As in the previous articles, Indian girls are presented as idle, even ungrateful for their "good" homes and pay. That the girls "tired" of their work evokes laziness and indifference, as if the girls were simply bored and left. The article does not mention that these children might have been physically exhausted from the difficult labor they performed, and it skirts around the fact that they were apparently unpaid—they were merely given room and board in exchange for their labor.[24] Indeed, the mere mention of pay marks them as "ungrateful" for work.

As with the previous article, the author supposes that the girls started "on foot" for their reservation. Similar to the "call of the open," the description of these girls is as wild and undomesticated. These "pupils"—boarding school students—were from the Blackfoot Indian Reservation in Montana, roughly twelve hundred miles away from Berkeley. The accusation that they would go "on foot" to Montana is laughable. In fact, if these runaways resembled those that escaped from boarding schools, they might have train-hopped home.

Like those published before it, this article states that the girls were under the "care" of Matron Royce. While asserting wardship over the girls, the wording highlights Royce's supposed compassion for the children. Yet, the article reveals otherwise. Three of the girls had been gone for at least two weeks—unaccounted for and alone. This begs the question of whether Royce adequately cared for the girls and their safety. If anything, this delayed report reveals the federal government's outright neglect and mistreatment of Indian girls. They may have been monitored and controlled, but not protected.

While we cannot know the specific reasons these eleven girls ran away, we can imagine some of the circumstances: homesickness, physically demanding work, the isolation of live-in positions, or the culture shock of city life when so many had come from rural communities. The articles do not reveal how Native women lived under constant surveillance from their employers as well as their outing matrons. The surveillance, however, was selective. There is no evidence that officials performed regular house calls or home visits to ensure employers treated girls properly. These private spaces were potentially dangerous.

Altogether, these runaway articles tell a one-sided story apparently crafted by Royce herself. Through racialized and gendered rhetoric, these three reports frame Native girls as criminal deviants. Constant police involvement highlights the fact that they were certainly treated like criminals. As these articles do not question the difficult conditions of forced domestic work, readers were led to believe these acts of resistance proved that Indian girls *must* be disciplined, contained, and assimilated. In these reports, the outing program and Royce's work are presented as necessary—a beneficial program to *civilize* Native women, exploit their labor, and establish a relationship of enforced servitude. While we cannot know precisely why these young women ran away in the summer of 1922, remnants of the archive tell a fuller story.

Native Women's Testimony

In the spring of 1929, seven years after the summer of runaways, Vivian Cooper, a sixteen-year-old Pomo girl from Guidiville Rancheria in California, entered the outing program. Her father arranged her placement through Mrs. Keenan, a Ukiah-based public health nurse. Cooper worked at homes in Richmond, Oakland, and Alameda, while earning fifteen to twenty-five dollars a month.[25] Shortly after Cooper's arrival, Royce informed Keenan that Cooper "seems to be a nice girl but has no training at all; she had three places in all of which she has failed. I am hoping she will improve with experience."[26] Indeed, Cooper did not stay long at the home she was assigned. Though employers colored Cooper as inexperienced and "untrained," Cooper attributed her displeasure to the demands of the work.

On July 9, 1929, Cooper left a position at Mrs. Muldown's house without consent. Royce reported her departure to Keenan in hopes of locating her, admitting, "I [believe] she has gone home as she appeared to be dissatisfied in each home in which she worked."[27] After a series of letters between Royce and Mendocino County officials, Cooper was located at her aunt's home in Santa Rosa. In an August 1929 letter to Royce, Cooper had the chance to tell her side of the story. She was forthcoming about the reason for her departure: "I left that place because I did not like her children and also that I have to work too much just for fifteen dollars a month. . . . When I left that place I did not tell or say any word to her. . . . I am awful sorry, leaving that place without letting you understand why I left. Please send my clothes to Hopland Calif."[28] Significantly, Cooper was not apologetic for leaving; rather, she was sorry that she had not explained *why* she left. As Royce had noted, Cooper was dissatisfied in each outing home where she had worked. For so little pay—two-thirds of which she would not even see before it was sent back to Sherman—the demanding work was simply not worth it. Her 1929 departure did not appear to hinder Cooper's brief return to the program in 1932. Ultimately, Cooper was not the only one to leave for wage issues.[29]

Bernice Hunter, a Stewart Indian School student, joined the outing program in the fall of 1930 at nineteen.[30] She arrived with a cohort of young women and girls from the boarding school and started off in a Piedmont home at fifteen dollars a month before working her way up to thirty dollars a month in homes in Berkeley and San Anselmo. Hunter's file is one of the few that indicates a "raise."[31] Moreover, Hunter's file is unusual in that while outing, she interacted with all three of the women who supervised the outing program: Matron Royce; her assistant, Jeannette Traxler; and finally Matron Van Every. Whereas Traxler and Van Every were cordial with Hunter, Royce washed her hands of the girl. During her roughly five-year stint in the outing program, Hunter contracted an STI and convalesced at the Stewart sanatorium. Once Hunter recuperated, Royce hesitated in taking her back. The matron despised sexually active girls and did not hesitate to express her anger. On February 10, 1932, in a heated letter to Superintendent Frederic Snyder of Stewart Indian School, Royce called Hunter a "moron" and a "moral degenerate." These words were not just denigrating but reflect a eugenicist orientation.[32] Royce identified Hunter as "feebleminded" and accused her of promiscuity and criminality. Nevertheless, as if through gritted teeth, Royce agreed to place her once again, adding, "I know that she will never be able to hold a place for any length of time and will probably become infected again."[33] Royce expected Hunter to contract another STI and "fail."

In fact, Hunter did hold a place. After a nine-month hiatus, she returned to work at the Huber home in San Anselmo. Records indicate that though she and a friend occasionally socialized late with Filipino men, the family was "well satisfied with her," and she was "treated like one of the family."[34] Though the family was apparently content with Hunter, the feeling was not mutual. After working nearly three years at the Huber home, Hunter left. In a July 5, 1935, letter, Hunter wrote Matron Van Every from San Rafael, explaining her decision:

> I know you are angry at me for leaving all the sudden. I guess you don't blame me if you had to work from 6:30 in the morning until [around] 9:30 at night. There is one thing I like to talk about. . . . See I mean Mrs. Huber never paid me for two months. I tried to ask her but she said she paid me. . . . This is how it happened; she'd pay in the middle of every other month. I wonder if you'd get it for me and I'd appreciate it very much if you do. The following are as it come. For December she paid me January 4th, never paid me for January. February 28th for February. April the 18th March. May 23 for April, never paid me May if you come I'll explain it to you.[35]

As a live-in maid, Hunter worked grueling fifteen-hour days. Though she received a raise from twenty-five to thirty dollars in the Huber home, a demanding schedule and the family's failure to pay proved the final straw. Ultimately, Van Every secured one month of wages due to Hunter. However, the matron's notes indicate that Hunter "did not give an intelligent reason to Mrs. Huber" for her departure.[36] Despite her awareness of the unpaid wages, Van Every gave little credence to Hunter's reasoning. Hunter's experience demonstrates two major points: sexually active outing women were especially targeted, and dissatisfaction was common throughout the outing program.

Ida Moore, a Mono woman from Auberry, California, was twenty-three when she came to the outing program. She started at two homes, located in Richmond and Oakland, at forty-five dollars and thirty-five dollars a month. In February of 1931, she returned for a brief stint at a Piedmont home, where she earned forty dollars a month.[37] After about a week, she worked for a

Mrs. Maurice in Pleasanton for thirty dollars a month. On February 22, 1931, Moore wrote to Matron Royce, appealing for better pay:

> My dear Mrs. Royce, just a few lines to let you know that I do not like it out here, and I am staying out here only a month. So I wish you to get me a job in Oakland. Also I want more than $30 a month as I need it very badly. I will be over about the 10th of next month. Have you seen my sister yet? How is she getting along? If you have a place now I would like to know. You know Mrs. Royce I need a better-paying job than this one. Mrs. Maurice is a dear woman to work for, but I do have to have something better. I hope to hear from you real soon.[38]

Much of Moore's urgency was because she was pregnant with a summer due date. But it is also clear that, however brief her previous positions, she had a history of higher pay—as much as fifteen dollars a month more than what Mrs. Maurice paid her in Pleasanton. Despite Moore's appeal, her wages were not raised nor was she placed closer to Oakland. In fact, Mrs. Maurice's home was her final place of employment in the outing program. In spring of 1932, Moore sent a few more letters to Royce on her own personalized stationery, reporting a healthy ten-month-old baby boy. She and baby were well taken care of the Fort Bidwell Indian Hospital.[39] Though Moore requested domestic work in Oakland in a separate letter, Royce explained that jobs were "scarce" and wages "much lower" than before. Moreover, the matron mentioned she would need at least twenty-five dollars for one month of board for her baby.[40]

In lieu of working in Oakland, Moore beaded a belt that she arranged for Matron Royce to sell.[41] In times when wage work was scarce, many women and families affiliated with the Bay Area Outing Program used their connections with the matrons to sell Indian crafts like beaded objects and baskets. Whereas Moore used her outing connections to secure supplementary income, not all women and girls were as fortunate, especially those whose outing was marked by late-night socializing and accusations of theft.

A year after Vivian Cooper fled Mrs. Muldown's home, seventeen-year-old Martha Graham was placed in the same Alameda home. The Chukchansi woman from Coarsegold, California, outed from 1930 to 1933 in Alameda,

Oakland, and Lafayette, earning fifteen to twenty dollars a month.[42] While at Mrs. Muldown's house, Graham wrote Royce, requesting winter leave: "Just a few lines . . . asking you if I could go home . . . next month for my Christmas Vacation. Oh yes did Mr. Snyder send the money to you . . . ?"[43] Intriguingly, Graham's letter includes an annotation, undoubtedly written by Royce. It states, "Do Not allow to go if it can be prevented." This rare annotation demonstrates the practice of keeping girls at work and away from their families as much as possible. Records do not reveal if Graham returned home for break but do show that she requested funds. Though she attended public school, Superintendent Snyder of Stewart Indian School managed her finances. It took requests like these for girls to secure their hard-earned money.

Though Graham had a spotless record, she experienced a rough patch during the next four placements. In January of 1932, she was hospitalized for a gallbladder operation. When she returned to the outing program that fall, she purportedly "went wild" and brought a man into her employer's home. Thereafter, Graham ran away and was found inebriated in a park. Her employer accused her of stealing, and local papers reported the incident.[44] Graham was undoubtedly arrested, detained, and subjected to invasive exams. After the incident, Traxler called Graham a "problem case in delinquency" and indicated that she had fraternized with an outing woman who was known for trouble. Despite these transgressions, Traxler gave her one last chance. Finally, the matron placed Graham at the Whitaker home in Lafayette.[45] Graham's experience indicates that accusations of theft and the desire to return home were often the impetus for running away or challenging the matrons. Undoubtedly, bringing a man into her employer's home had marked the young woman. That infraction alone would have made her subject her to closer surveillance and criminalization.

Della Smart, a Paiute girl from Winnemucca, Nevada, attended the Stewart Indian School when she arrived at the outing program in the summer of 1929. That summer, the fourteen-year-old worked at two separate homes in Oakland and Niles for about three days. On August 1, 1931, Smart returned to the outing program to work briefly at a Berkeley home.[46] By August 26, Royce reported that Smart, along with Lottie Cleveland and Catherine

Snapp, had been missing for two days and nights.[47] Once Cleveland and Smart were recovered, their employers refused to take them back. Both girls were promptly sent back to Stewart Indian School. According to Royce, Smart "staid [*sic*] out late whenever she had an afternoon off" and the last time did not return to her position. Royce further asserted, "I hold Della responsible too for the absence at the same time, of Catherine Snapp and Lottie Cleveland."[48] Matrons especially disciplined girls they assumed to be ringleaders.

Smart had a track record for staying out late at night. That, paired with the fact that she had gone missing and her employer was unwilling to take her back, left Royce with little choice but to return her to Stewart. Whereas some girls and women were given a second chance, Smart was not afforded another opportunity. These four months were Smart's final stint in the outing program. She was not the only Native woman to suffer consequences for her transgressions.

Loretta Crabtree, Pomo,[49] came to the outing program with her sister Evelyn Joaquin in 1935. She was eighteen years old when she joined the program and worked in Piedmont and Oakland homes for twenty-five dollars a month. In December, both sisters left their jobs without giving notice and returned to Covelo, California.[50] A year later, in December 1936, both sisters wrote to Matron Van Every in search of outing work. The two sent separate letters. Joaquin was especially adamant to return to the Bay Area so she could see her son, who was hospitalized at Stanford Hospital. Her letter from Santa Rosa reads,

> Dear Friend, Miss Van Every I must write to you dear. I want you to find me a job please. I have not seen my boy for a month now and it is worrying me to death. I will do everything you wish me to do, that is in obeying your orders . . . oh! my, I must be near my poor little son. He seems more happier when I see him often. I'd tell you lots of things on why I quit before but it is best to tell you in person. I am glad that I took my sister home when I did. My mother was sick and [there was] no one there so we went. She is with mother now taking care of her. Please Mrs. Van Every if you can get me work in San Francisco or Palo

> Alto any place near I'd be so glad. I never gave you any trouble did I? And my wages were so small for the work I did. . . . I am well and strong as ever before. You can depend on me so please do not turn me down . . . my little boy needs me.[51]

Joaquin's letter was apologetic and remorseful and sought to befriend Van Every. Although she offered some account of why the two sisters left, her son was clearly the driving force for her desire to return to work in the Bay Area. Significantly, Joaquin had to market herself to the matron, asserting that she was "dependable" and "strong as ever" and insinuating that her low pay would not be much of a burden. Her sister Crabtree had a similar but shorter appeal, conveying her regret and fond memories of the matron. Crabtree's letter reads, "Dear Miss Van Every, I'm sorry to bother you again. I just have to work. I'm very sorry that I came home the way I did. Now I have more sense. If you would please find me work the last of the month, please. How are you sis [?]. I often think how nice you were so kind. I'll try not to disappoint you."[52]

Crabtree appeased the matron in the same way as her sister but went a step farther, stating that she will "try not to disappoint." These letters reveal some of the performances Native women undertook to reconcile with the matron after having run away. Before responding to the sisters, Matron Van Every reached out to Edith A. Murphy with the California and Mendocino County–based Federation of Women's Clubs. Matron Van Every wondered if the girls were "stable enough to adjust themselves."[53] In response, Murphy fervently discouraged the matron from taking on Joaquin. Yet, although Crabtree was "not a boarding school girl"—referring to her lack of domestic training—Murphy endorsed her.[54] On January 6, 1937, Matron Van Every wrote to Crabtree, offering her the opportunity to out: "I feel sure that I can find a suitable place for you, however, since you are willing to try harder, after you[r] experience last year. Please bring a medical certificate with you, which will be of real help in securing a place."[55]

Despite Joaquin's remorseful letter and her plain desire to be near her son, Murphy's disapproval prohibited her from returning. And while Matron Van Every moved forward with Crabtree, records do not indicate that she returned. Perhaps Crabtree did not want to work without her sister, or maybe she found work elsewhere. Nonetheless, the case of these two sisters illustrates some of the strategies runaways enacted and how they were received by matrons.

In more extreme circumstances, women who challenged the outing program's rules dealt with police and were forced into juvenile detention homes. In 1934, Marjorie Peters, a seventeen-year-old Klamath girl and Chemawa student, joined the outing program. She had short stints at three homes, earning fifteen to twenty-five dollars a month. Her first placement, at the Brill home, proved difficult. She had to do heavy labor, like carrying wood and coal, and could not get her ten- and twelve-year-old charges to cooperate. After about a month, Peters left the home. Thereafter, in the Harney home, the employers accused her of stealing a fountain pen and an umbrella. They also claimed Peters received frequent calls from boys on the telephone. The matron placed her in a third home in Mill Valley.[56] In the summer of 1935, she became ill and returned to Humboldt County to recover.[57] Though Van Every discouraged it on account of her after-hours socializing, she returned in November of that year. As was common in the 1930s, Peters was permitted to return after providing a medical clearance confirming that she was "free from evidences of venereal or other infectious or contagious diseases."[58]

In late November, the matron placed Peters with Mrs. Seifert. On December 10, Peters stayed out all night and was taken to detention the next day. Though authorities recommended she be returned home to Humboldt County, Van Every chose to give Peters another chance. On December 15, she was placed with Mrs. Whitaker in Lafayette—the same home Martha Graham had worked in two years prior. Van Every saw the position as Peters's "last chance . . . to make good" with the threat of being sent back home should she fail.

In January 1936, Peters stayed out all night twice, after which the matron gave her yet another chance. In March, Peters returned home for a visit. Though she was scheduled to return on March 10, Peters instead stayed with her half brother in San Francisco. The next day, Van Every apprehended Peters and sent her to the detention home. Oakland probation officers insisted that she leave and alerted authorities in Del Norte County.[59] Peters was sent back home on a Greyhound bus.[60] Peters's file reveals that women who broke curfew and stayed out late socializing were criminalized. Outing contracts established rules and guidelines of the program, including curfew. For instance, women and girls were not allowed to leave their employers' homes at night without proper escort. Therefore, unless chaperoned by their employers, outing matron, or some other recognized authority, girls broke curfew. While these were largely the rules of the program, matrons relied on the police to apprehend girls; therefore, these programmatic infractions would turn into formal legal actions. Minor infractions such as receiving phone calls from boys would have marked Peters as deviant. Though she committed no crime, these status offenses led to her incarceration. She was not the only one to be detained.

Similarly, Sadie Sam, a Paiute girl, experienced police intervention and was incarcerated at a detention home. Sam entered the outing program around 1923 as a student at Stewart Indian School. On July 3, 1923, in a lengthy letter to Stewart superintendent Frederic Snyder, Matron Royce reported that Sam had been hanging around with "bad company." Reportedly, Lena Donnely, a Stewart student and former outing participant, had been "taking some of the other girls to San Francisco and keeping them out late at nights." Sam was one such girl and left her outing placement at the Thayer home for four days before returning. Royce wrote to Snyder, "Of course, I know that she is living an immoral life, but I have no proof of it"—meaning she believed Sam was sexually active.[61] Sam continued to work at the Thayers' home but left again a few days later. She was given another chance and stayed out all night a third time, upon which Sam began to pack her bags to leave. At this, Matron Royce asked Mrs. Thayer to call an officer to apprehend Sam and detain her in a detention home. Reportedly, Royce sent her home that evening, presumably to Yerington, Nevada.[62] Matron Royce was especially apt to send young Native women to the local detention home, especially when she felt the young woman in question was uncontrollable or reprehensible.

Winifred Nelson, a Klamath girl of fifteen years old, came to the outing program in the fall of 1932. She worked in homes in Oakland, Berkeley, and Piedmont. Nelson's wages averaged fifteen dollars a month—to be expected during the Depression. However, one brief home in Oakland paid Nelson a low ten dollars a month—one of the lowest monthly wages recorded in the program.[63] Nelson had a troubled time in the outing program, beginning with her first placement at the Benninghoven home in Oakland. There, Nelson walked half a mile to Oakland High School for her studies. She was overwhelmed by the large student population and disliked the home. After a few months, Nelson ran away and was apprehended in San Francisco and detained in a detention center.[64]

On January 4, 1933, Royce wrote Nelson's parents to inform them of their daughter's departure. "We made every effort to locate her and finally asked help of local authorities. They . . . found her in San Francisco. . . . She is now in detention there." Royce continued, "Considering Winifred's behavior . . . I think she would be better off with you at home."[65] That same day, she reported the escape to Superintendent Boggess of the Hoopa Valley Indian Agency, stating, "She is so young and a very attractive girl and she needs close supervision."[66] Indeed, Nelson had just turned sixteen and yet was responsible for a household.

Royce's letters demonstrate that the outing program required and desired "docile" servants and resolutely refused to employ Native women and girls with any "behavioral issues." This preference reveals the hypocrisy of the program's supposed interest in Native girls' health and well-being. Moreover, Royce's comment on Nelson's attractiveness exposes the matron's fear of promiscuity and the desire to police Native women's sexuality.

While Royce strongly disapproved of Nelson, the sixteen-year-old felt similarly toward the matron. In intimate letters to her sister, Nelson aired her grievances. These unmailed letters appear to have been confiscated by Royce to censor the young girl.[67] Nelson wrote,

> Greeting sis . . . what did you all do New Year's Eve? I celebrated in a big way. I'm attending the Oakland High School taking business, math, Spanish . . . instead of sitting at the school I come home and work like a slave. These people I work for are [unusual]. . . . What people. Royce said that she'd get me another place but I suppose that is after I graduate. . . . I don't get Thursdays off. Just Sunday afternoon till 6, and I

have to be home, sez Lillie, but if I get in earlier than 11:30 something is wrong. Spent a week in the Juvenile Detention Home, are those good girls there. Say, they sure are tough, they use to smoke tea . . . anything to [be] disobedient. I got sassy twice. It isn't a bad place, we have court everi friday and do they ask questions, & they sure examine a woman. Boys stay there too also babies. They sure believe in balling [bawling] a person out. How is Jeanette Beaver & her wagon [wagging] tongue and the rest of the [g]ossipers including Mrs. Nelson.[68]

Nelson began by proudly listing her course schedule at Oakland High—certainly a more thorough education than she received at Chemawa. But the promise of schooling was eclipsed by domestic work. Instead of studying, she came home and "work[ed] like a slave." And though she had expressed her misgivings to Royce, the matron did not secure her an alternative position. Unlike most girls in the program, Nelson did not get Thursdays off. Instead, she had Sundays off—less than twelve full hours of freedom. Whereas some girls might be able to catch a matinee or window shop, Nelson could not. Further, she was expected to stay away from the house all day, with no friends or acquaintances.

Nelson reflected on her time in detention and when she was "sassy," perhaps resulting from her recent celebration of New Year's Eve in a "big way." Though she asserted it "isn't a bad place," she revealed the gendered surveillance and scrutiny in detention. Her veiled statement "they sure examine a woman" reveals that she likely underwent an invasive pelvic exam and was interrogated about her sexual history. Girls like Nelson who authorities placed in detention were presumed to be promiscuous degenerates. Detainees were yelled at or "balled" (bawled) out. There is no way to know if a young Native woman like Nelson would have undergone more scrutiny than her non-Native peers. In her tongue-in-cheek farewell, Nelson reminds us that there was a world outside of the detention center and the outing program. Her family, friends, and loved ones were living their lives while Nelson was stuck. She was alone, desiring connections and trying to stay positive.

Midway through January of 1933, Royce gave Nelson another chance and arranged for a second outing home in Oakland adjacent to her high school. Nelson managed just one week at the Fiene home before the homeowner accused her of theft—a slip, some toothpaste, cigarettes, and aspirin. On January 15, while Royce and Fiene met with Nelson to confront her, Nelson ran to her room in the home and perhaps in protest—or to numb the pain—drank from a bottle of Lysol.[69] She was immediately rushed to the hospital and had her stomach pumped.

Nelson's cry for help clearly reflected her need to go home, yet Royce insisted on keeping her in the Bay Area. Under the matron's watchful eye, Nelson was sent to recover at the outing program headquarters—Royce's own home in Piedmont. This may reflect Royce's sense of guilt in the situation and her desire to set things right, yet it was not uncommon for the matron to bring in girls she felt needed close supervision. Indeed, Royce's "care" manifested as tighter surveillance and control. The specialized attention was entirely unwanted.

On January 18, 1933, Nelson wrote that she was "spending a week here with Royce, maybe longer. . . . Boy I almost died last Sunday. Don't tell anyone, had my stomach pumped up Highland Hospital. Was I sick—I took Lysol. Ole Royce made me so mad. Now she tries to be so damn nice to me."[70] A day later, Nelson wrote a fourth letter to her sister, airing her complaints: "You probably have heard all the mess I've been in, it sure was tough. I sure had a lousy place & ole Royce insisted I should stay there, but nothing doing, I'm here at her place at present, what a life, I sure hate it here. I'm going to school. . . . It's O.K. there is over 3,000 students . . . & it is crowded . . . it sure is raining down here. . . . I have to walk to sch[ool] that's what I hate."[71] In this final letter to her sister, Nelson is honest about her complete hatred for Royce, the outing program, and her overcrowded school. Nelson had had enough. That very evening, Nelson did not return home from school. Instead, she stayed out all night with a fellow outing girl. Reportedly, the girls had been drinking and hanging out with "Mexicans." In the early morning of January 20, police apprehended the girls and sent Nelson back to Royce's home at 5:00 a.m.[72] For a second time, Nelson was sent to a detention home and awaited the matron's decision.

About a week later, on January 28, Nelson was sent home. Though her first stint in the outing program was over, she would return in December of 1933. Considering all that she went through, Nelson's homecoming must have felt like a relief. Her decision to return later that year highlights the extent to which many girls and their families relied on outing wages.[73] Nelson's story reveals the dark side of this supposedly benevolent institution. For Nelson, outing work was akin to slavery. Her hard work eclipsed the promise of school life, and she had very little choice in her placement. She was lonely and desired independence from a meddlesome matron and accusatory employer. She also craved real connections. When she had had enough, Nelson found ways to blow off steam—ignoring her curfew and socializing into the night. The cost of those moments of freedom was incarceration. The outing program pushed Nelson to the brink—ingesting Lysol. It was an all too apt metaphor for how domestic work thrust Native women into a toxic, sometimes dangerous place.

Bernice Nelson, Winifred's older sister by two years, came to the outing program when she was eighteen. She worked in 1933, at the height of the Depression. Her low wages of fifteen dollars a month reflect the economic slump. At the first home in Richmond, Bernice was lonely; she reportedly "cried all the time." The second home, in Berkeley at Mrs. Scott's, was Bernice's longest steady employment; she lived in the home for five months. Bernice's file indicates she was "well liked" at the Scotts', but she apparently left for "no reason."[74] Thereafter, Bernice transitioned to the Harvey home in Oakland. Again, Bernice got on well with the Harvey family, but like other girls in the outing program, she had difficulty securing her wages. On February 13, 1934, Bernice's mother wrote Mrs. Traxler the following:

> . . . and about Bernice. I wish you would find her another place. I understand the people are very nice to her and like her very much but that just cannot be helped as Bernice needs her money the same as the other girls. I should think it wouldn't be any trouble to find her another place. Mrs. Harvey just gives her about a dollar or so on her days off and she can't buy anything with that. Is she placed just for her room and board? I understand thru Mr. Boggess that you are there to see that the girls one and all get a square deal.[75]

In response, Mrs. Traxler notified Bernice's mother that her daughter and Mrs. Harvey came to a "satisfactory arrangement." Traxler added that she was aware of the unpaid wages and advocated she take another placement.[76] It is not clear what the arrangement was, or if Bernice received her total pay, but she continued to work at the Harvey home.

That fall, amid the usual outing work, Bernice and her sister Winifred both learned what it was like to be vulnerable Native women in the city. On September 20, 1934, an assailant abducted Bernice and Winifred shortly after their dance lesson. He forced the sisters into an automobile with the threat of violence. Reportedly, the assailant promised to drive the girls home but instead took them further east, to Moraga Road in Oakland. The culprit pushed Bernice down a hillside while Winifred screamed for help, thankfully attracting attention. Though the two were victims, they were promptly arrested and taken to the Oakland city jail. Reportedly, they were intoxicated while the driver was sober. As no charges could be made against the girls, they were dismissed from jail the next day. Their employers willingly took them both back.[77] Perhaps Nelson and her sister were left relatively unscathed, but their run-in with a predator and the police demonstrates how dangerous the city could be for them. Although they were the victims of this abduction, it was the sisters who were treated as criminals. To echo Stormy Ogden, violence perpetrated against women and girls can put them into the criminal justice system, where they are seen not as victims, but rather as offenders in the eyes of the state.[78] Though girls and women who were met with police force, jailed, and detained were quite common, rarely was there a case where a woman would have not suffered much retribution at all for her actions. Such was the experience of a Klamath woman, Thana Thompson Mitchell, who came to the outing program to become a nurse.

Thana Thompson was from Hoopa, California, and was nineteen when she came to the outing program in the summer of 1929. She was a recent graduate of Sherman Institute and desired to enroll in nurses' training. That fall, Thompson and a cohort of girls from Sherman, including her friend Ivora Nelson,[79] enrolled at the Children's Hospital in San Francisco. At the start of the program, Thompson earned fifty dollars a month at a Piedmont home—an impressive sum compared with the average outing wage.[80] On top of domestic outing work, Thompson was engaged in practical training at the hospital across the bay. Her demanding schedule was filled with regular and sometimes daily exams, as well as in-depth instruction on respiration, anatomy, nutrition, and even nurses' cookery. Her days were so arduous that Thompson was once shocked to learn she and her fellow students had an hour or two to themselves.[81]

The toll was too much for Thompson's friend Ivora Nelson, also Klamath and Hoopa, from Eureka, California. Nelson was reportedly dissatisfied with her experience, and her mother advocated for her to return home. By early September of 1929, Nelson chose to leave nurses' training and the Bay Area. She returned a few months later to continue outing work. Meanwhile, Thompson continued her training. On April 14, 1930, Thompson wrote a letter to Matron Royce at 1:20 a.m., during her night shift. She described the difficulties of the demanding work:

> My dearest friend, I was told to tell you that there is to be a meeting. Dr. Glazer told me to tell you to be sure and come. I think he wants to talk to you (Wednesday). It rained so hard yesterday didn't it? How are you? I haven't seen you for a long time. Come over to dinner after the meeting or before if you possibly can. I am so sleepy I could gladly go to bed and enjoy it. I am through with my charting—I'm going to make supplies as soon as I finish this little note to you. Excuse my terrible writing please—but—you know how full of energy one is when they're drowsy. Being on night duty is like living in the land of upside down—you eat your largest meals at 12 at night and sleep in the daytime.[82]

Letters reveal that without the company of her good friend, Thompson felt lonely and regularly sought visits from Matron Royce, who had a strong relationship with her and her parents. Indeed, on some occasions, Thompson addressed letters to Royce as "Dear Godmother." Their relationship was a rare example of what appeared to be an amicable friendship with an outing matron. Throughout Thompson's outing years, Royce facilitated the sale of her family's baskets to help them make ends meet. On one occasion, Matron Royce advanced the Thompson family $17.50 for baskets she planned to sell for them—a very generous sum.[83] Though Thompson received much support and encouragement from the matron, nurses' training proved difficult. In May of 1930, Thompson wrote to her parents, informing them that she had left the hospital.[84]

This news was regrettable for both Thompson's parents and Matron Royce. Both parties hoped she would return to nurses' training in the fall. Records do not indicate that she did. However, Thompson returned to the outing program in September 1930, where she continued working at the same Piedmont home for fifty dollars a month.[85] Matron Royce called her a "girl to be proud of" and consistently advocated for the young woman.[86] This long-standing relationship seems to have colored the way in which Matron Royce responded to Thompson's eventual departure from the outing program.

On February 2, 1931, Matron Royce reported to Thompson's parents that she had left without her "permission."[87] Though the matron encouraged Thompson to contact her parents first, the young woman instead left for Los Angeles of her own accord. Reportedly, she asserted to the matron that she was of age and taking care of herself and desired no supervision from anyone. Whereas most girls and women who left without permission were met with some kind of reprimand from the matron, Thompson was not. Though the matron expressed confusion as to where such behavior had arisen from, she nonetheless told the Thompson family, "Don't worry too much about Thana for after all she is 21 years old and we cannot restrain her if she wants to be on her own."[88] Few women in the outing program earned such acknowledgment of their free will, much less escaped chastisement from the matron. Undoubtedly, the apparently genuine friendship between Royce and Thompson and Royce's pride in the woman influenced her independence. Thompson's file reveals that if women honored the aims of the program, to improve themselves and cultivate ambition—and most importantly if they sustained a friendly relationship with the matron—they could be afforded freedoms other girls and women were not.

Participating in the Bay Area Outing Program meant being subjected to carcerality on multiple levels. Native women suffered confinement in the outing home and literal incarceration in Bay Area detention centers, and they were figuratively incarcerated by a social system that allowed them no other path to self-determination and the means of survival than their submission to a society that regarded them as menial labor. Their rebellions, then, are more poignant because they may not have been able to imagine another reality for themselves and yet were still able to snatch moments of happiness and freedom in fleeting hours, out past curfew with friends or partners.

Considering the confines of outing, there are several reasons why Native women and girls would choose to exit the Bay Area Outing Program. The cases I examined here point to homesickness and loneliness, especially in the program's infancy. For some young women—particularly in the summer of 1922—running away was their only escape. Later, Native women ran away or left without permission on account of being overworked and underpaid. Some were not paid at all. These were less-than-ideal conditions, and criminalization and surveillance also contributed to their departure. One young woman had to carry wood and coal to the home and care for defiant children. Others were accused of theft or sternly punished for staying out late and socializing. Outing women and girls who hoped to let loose and experience the city made opportunities for themselves. But in these cases, they were criminalized, assumed to be promiscuous, met with police intervention, and detained.

While this chapter has explored the experiences of women who ran away, it is crucial to note that many Native women returned to the outing program. Outing work was difficult and low-paid, but wages were essential. So, women who left without permission or knowledge or fled in the middle of the night found themselves with no other option than to return to make a living. These runaway women and girls seized the only tool that seemed available to them, and when they needed wages, they returned. It is also noteworthy that their ability to appease the matron and secure a second chance facilitated this process. The complexities of this push-pull situation often brought runaways back to the outing program.

As my analysis of federal archives proves, those with confirmed or presumed sexually based infractions—getting phone calls from boys, for example—were marked as deviant and subjected to further surveillance. These women were incarcerated in Bay Area detention centers and subjected to invasive exams and interrogation. Here, Native women became confined on two counts—first through the outing program and second through detention. In the Bay Area Outing Program, labor, incarceration, and sexuality intertwined to create oppressive circumstances for Native women. They were disproportionately criminalized and incarcerated in this system. Furthermore, utility in domestic labor was paramount; if a girl was no longer "useful," she was discarded and sent home. Considering the mechanics of the Bay Area Outing Program, a young woman's escape is neither unreasonable nor surprising.

For Native women, outing functioned as a space of incarceration and criminalization. In response, they resisted the worst elements of outing—containment, constant control, sexual surveillance, and labor exploitation. Women were drawn to the Bay Area Outing Program to experience city life and provide for their families yet found that the program was invested in their dispossession. The women whose stories are examined here pushed back. They expressed their dissatisfaction, ran away, stayed out past curfew, and resisted in the ways they knew how. Native women's testimony tells us that despite the structure of this settler project, Native women challenged its oppressive system.

FOUR
Breaking the Family
Outing Mothers and Indian Child Removal

THIS CHAPTER EXAMINES how the Bay Area Outing Program affected the Indian family. Throughout the program's roughly two decades, Native women and girls sought a vibrant, better life through domestic wage work in the Bay Area. Many followed sisters, cousins, or other family members into the program. But what happened to young mothers or their children? Three main questions drive this chapter: How did the Bay Area Outing Program affect the Indian family? How did Native women fight against Indian child removal? And what circumstances did the children of outing mothers face in the early twentieth century? To this end, I closely examine stories of Native women involved with the outing program who had children, who were thought to be sexually active, or who became pregnant in the Bay Area. In the outing program, Native women's sexuality and reproductive capacity were central issues. Women with young children and soon-to-be mothers risked their positions, for employers and matrons viewed children as a barrier to live-in employment. Most women were forced to choose between outing work and their children. Further, outing records reveal that matrons heavily scrutinized Native mothers and those recently pregnant while in the Bay Area. Indeed, matrons' assumptions about Indian mothers and Indian families informed their regular interventions.

First, I briefly historicize federal notions of Indian families and Indian mothers in the early twentieth century. This sets the stage for the context of Indian child removal—that is, the removal of Native children from their homes and families.[1] From this broader analysis, I briefly examine the context of sexuality and pregnancy in the outing program. Finally, I closely examine ten files that demonstrate how outing matrons and federal officials threatened to separate and sometimes succeeded in separating Native women from their children. Ultimately, I find that outing matrons directed Native mothers along three paths. First, mothers were encouraged to board their young and infant children at a local nursery or similar form of childcare. Second, if the child was six years of age or older, outing matrons encouraged mothers to enroll the child into a federal Indian boarding school. Third, women faced the most heinous of possibilities—outing matrons advocated that Native mothers place their children in foster care or put them up for adoption. Though not always achieved, this final scenario was a regular and looming threat.

Whichever of the three scenarios took place, the consequences reverberated throughout Native families. As Margaret Jacobs has argued, outing matrons and BIA officials paired with Bay Area–based institutions sought to uphold what Sau-ling Wong has described as "diverted mothering."[2] Wong defines this term as a process wherein "time and energy available for mothering are diverted from those who, by kinship or communal ties, are their more rightful recipients."[3] Instead, mothers are separated from their children, often in order to care for others. While certainly a contemporary issue, especially in the field of caregiving, diverted mothering has historical roots that can be traced back at least as far as the era of US slavery, when white enslavers' children took precedence over the care of enslaved black women's own children. In the Bay Area Outing Program, diverted mothing was achieved through institutional parenting by way of infant boarding, enrollment in Indian boarding schools, and adoption and fostering.

Unfit Indian Mothers, Unhealthy Indian Families, and Assimilation

In 1916, Commissioner of Indian Affairs Cato Sells authorized Bonnie V. Royce to manage the newly established Bay Area Outing Program. In that same year, Sells authored the foreword to *Indian Babies: How to Keep Them Well*, a thirty-page guidebook aimed at combating infant mortality rates in

Native American communities. The guidebook was designed to instruct Indian women in best practices for childrearing. The manual was filled with illustrative photos of an Indian mother and baby and included instructions on prenatal care, proper nursing, clothing, bathing, sanitation, and treatment for illnesses. Indian Service widely distributed the pamphlet across Indian Country, especially at federally sponsored "better baby contests" held in various tribal communities.[4]

While ostensibly instructive, the pamphlet was ultimately an attack on Native mothers and their families. In the foreword, Sells did not mince words. He wrote,

> My Friends: Do you know that one Indian baby out of every three dies before it is 3 years old because it does not have the right kind of care? Do you know that a great many of these deaths can be prevented? It is not natural for a baby to be sick. Health is its normal condition. It is a pity, therefore, that so many Indian baby lives have been lost because *their mothers did not know* how to keep them well. . . .[5] It is because so many Indian mothers follow wrong ideas in caring for their children that so many of them die.

These vicious words positioned Native mothers as the enemy of their children, harboring "wrong ideas" in the form of culturally and tribally specific motherhood—traditions that had been passed down for generations. Instead, the *Indian Babies* pamphlet attempted to impart the benefits of "scientific motherhood" for Native mothers and their families. Ultimately, *Indian Babies* was just one part of the "Save the Babies" campaign.

In August 1915, Sells gave a "Save the Babies" speech at the Congress on Indian Progress in San Francisco. The conference comprised three hundred to four hundred officials and employees of the US Indian Service.[6] Sells's speech, reprinted in the guidebook argued for instructing "ignorant" Indian mothers on the proper way of caring for their infants, thus revealing how federal officials regarded Indian mothers and their families. At the conference, Sells argued, "It is our chief duty to protect the Indian's health and to save him from premature death. We can not solve the Indian problem without Indians." Though seemingly more concerned with the stability of his vocation, Sells continued,

> The new campaign for health in which I would enlist you is first of all to save the babies! Statistics startle me . . . approximately three-fifths of Indian infants die before the age of 5 years.[7] Of what use to this mournful mortality are our splendidly equipped schools? I earnestly call upon every Indian Bureau employee to help reduce this frightful percentage. Superintendents, teachers . . . everyone can do something by instruction or example, the physician with his science, the nurse with her trained skill, the matron with her motherly solicitude, all of us by personal hygiene, cleanliness and sobriety.[8]

In these last few words, Sells arrived at what he believed to be the real issue—dirty, unclean, "drunken Indians." Sells blamed Indian families yet neglected to acknowledge the settler colonial circumstances that shaped Native health and issues in the Indian home—poverty created by colonial policies, lack of access to health care and nutritious food, and inadequate sanitation, to name a few. Quite plainly, settler colonialism created these conditions. Yet, the commissioner continued. He argued that motherhood applied under "intelligent and friendly direction" would save Indian babies from their "untimely graves."[9]

In a final gendered plea, Sells argued that the proper education of Indian girls must emphasize home nursing, child welfare, motherhood, sanitation, and, unsurprisingly, "intelligent housekeeping" and "attractive home making."[10] As ever, the argument targeted Native women and girls and emphasized the need for domestic work. Sells believed that if Native women accepted and reproduced Euro-American domesticity, they became capable of properly raising their children. Only through assimilation could Native women earn the right to mother.

Outside of Sells's speech, the *Indian Babies* guidebook includes much of the same ideologies. While the pamphlet includes useful advice to new mothers, it seethes with racist assumptions about Indian mothers and their families. *Indian Babies* argues that Indian homes were unclean, overcrowded hotbeds for disease. In the eyes of Indian Service, Indian mothers had been taught and perpetuated bad practices that led to wild, naked babies. Traditional baby carriers were unhealthy. Infants were liable to be surrounded by alcoholic Indians poised to spread disease. Indian mothers—through negligence and ignorance—caused "dead babies." The fact that disease and malnourishment resulted from settler incursion was absent from Sells's guidebook. The fact many tribes could no longer rely on traditional subsistence and were forced to lean on inferior foreign foods was lost on the commissioner. He did not explain that the theft of Native land and resources left Native communities destitute.

Sells's speech paired with the larger Save the Babies campaign demonstrate that the Indian Service considered traditional Native family patterns and medical practices "antiquated and dangerous."[11] Federal officials hoped that through the Save the Babies campaign, Native women would discover the superiority of Western medicine, shun tribal practices, and embrace patriarchal gender roles. Instead of seeking assistance from their extended family networks, Native women would look to field matrons and physicians. Western medicine thus allowed the settler nation to assert its colonial power while undermining Native families and communities.[12]

The arguments put forward in the Save the Babies campaign, Sells's treatise by the same name, and *Indian Babies: How to Keep Them Well* undergirded the Indian Affairs operation. Unless a Native mother could properly assimilate and embrace "scientific motherhood"—and perhaps even if she did—Indian children were better off raised in an institution than by their own mothers and families. White individuals used this "rhetoric of rescue" to justify the taking of Native children, even in the case of living parents and extended family members. The fact that Native women were regularly regarded as unfit, amoral, and promiscuous drinkers only solidified this notion.[13] The overarching narrative affirmed, whether fostered, adopted, or sent to an Indian boarding school, Indian children would have a better life. Certainly, some Native women may have believed their child could have a better life without them. Therefore, Indian women with the capacity to conceive were rendered mere surrogates. In the absence of their "competence," the government would properly parent and raise their children.

Policing Sexuality, Pregnancy, and Unspeakable Violence

The notion of Native women as "unfit" mothers fueled fears about Native women's sexuality and reproductive capacity.[14] Outing matrons who operated the Bay Area Outing Program embraced Victorian ideals that lauded sexual restraint and maintained strict codes of conduct. The government's use of Victorian ideals to regulate Native women persisted well into the early twentieth century. Despite being outdated, these ideals were deemed practical in managing and influencing Native women's behavior. Federal programs designed to "fix" the Indian problem targeted Native children as the future of their race and, *especially*, young women as procreators of that race. Consequently, federal officials cultivated a series of fears grounded in Native women's reproductive rights, and outing matrons policed Native women's sexuality in various ways, monitoring who they socialized with and seeking health clearances intent on detecting venereal diseases.[15] Such health clearances attempted to locate promiscuity and gauge whether girls were sexually active. Because all Native women were required to submit health clearances, all women were routinely implicated. Native women who defied these standards—especially in regard to sexual activity—were reprimanded and incarcerated. Matrons in particular feared Native women's sexuality. While sexually active Native women were deemed "promiscuous," they were seen as especially dangerous because such acts could lead to pregnancy.

Program leaders saw pregnant women in the outing program as particularly risky for two reasons. First, their child would be considered a barrier to their live-in employment. Second, as previously mentioned, officials believed Indian mothers posed a threat to their own children. In the eyes of the government, Native women were negligent, unfit mothers. Indian homes were unclean and overcrowded. In turn, federal officials believed that Indian children needed to be saved by institutional intervention. The outing program ignored Native women's maternal and reproductive roles in favor of their roles as workers. Consequently, women who became pregnant in the outing program were often forced to make difficult choices.

In the event of pregnancy, outing matrons were very concerned with Native women's ability to "properly" mother, but they rarely troubled themselves with the idea of consent. They regarded sex itself as a transgression, therefore—as records substantiate—officials did not distinguish between consensual sex and assault. While not explicit in the archive, it is possible that some Native women in the outing program became pregnant as the result of sexual assault. The connections between settler colonialism and sexual assault on Indigenous women are well-documented.[16] Also, individual outing girls in the homes of their employers were isolated and vulnerable. Further, if the outing home emulated colonial space, sexual violence within the outing program was undoubtedly possible. This reality, compounded with the prevalence of sexual abuse in Indian boarding schools, renders abuse probable.

Indeed, scholars have found that sexual violence was and is widely experienced in live-in domestic service as well as day work in the private homes of employers.[17] Outing records are predictably less than forthcoming on the subject. There are discussions in the archive about women in love and in what are portrayed as consensual relationships with the fathers of their children, but matrons and federal officials were largely concerned with women marrying the men who were "responsible" for their "condition." Such neutral terms leave little room for interpretation of consent. Moreover, officials assumed that Native women were ultimately responsible for engaging in sexual intercourse. One example in this chapter reveals that federal officials often suspected Indian girls of falling for a "false" love affair. Whether intercourse was consensual or not, the blame was placed on them.[18]

Native Women's Testimony

As a system, the Bay Area Outing Program was a racialized, gendered labor construct intent on the control of Native women's bodies. Where the outing home may have been shaped by male domination, the program's everyday operations were managed by outing matrons. This decidedly feminized labor force was envisioned to instruct Native girls and women in "civilized," "Americanized" values. In practice, matrons wielded a great deal of power, including surveillance and management over Native women's lives and bodies—particularly with regard to their reproductive capacity. The following stories speak to this detailed management and describe how the Bay Area Outing Program affected the lives of Native women and their children. These stories extend the histories of abuse toward Native women and their families during the process of territorial expansion and the removal of children from Native homes. While seated in the twentieth century, these stories are part of a much longer history that illustrates the enduring effects of settler expansion.

These cases reveal how the outing program threatened to separate and at times succeeded in separating Native women with from their children to make them more available for domestic work. Gendered domestic labor was designed to break the Native family and allow mothers entrance into society through labor exploitation. Most outing mothers were forced to choose between outing wages and their children. These files also demonstrate how outing matrons feared that their charges might become pregnant or engage in interracial relationships, and how they regarded Native women as "promiscuous," on occasion doubting the paternity of their children. These cases also reveal how outing matrons would "force a marriage" if necessary. Additionally, these files show how single mothers struggled to survive in the Bay Area under the constraints of domestic work, as well as how fathers advocated for their daughters. My analysis of these stories thematically engages outing matrons' three central methods of removal: first, by boarding infant children; second, by enrolling Native children into a federal Indian boarding school; and finally, by attempting and at times succeeding in the fostering or adoption of Native children. While these methods are distinct, at times Native women and their children experienced overlapping and intersecting methods of removal. For example, a child may have been forced into an infant boarding home and later sent to boarding school or adopted. Regardless of the method, these ever-present risks existed in the Bay Area Outing Program.

Boarding Homes

Agnes Dyer's story speaks to the common pressures of infant boarding home placement, especially among young single mothers with multiple children.

Dyer, a Paiute woman, participated in the Bay Area Outing Program in the late 1920s and early 1930s.[19] The MacDonald family in San Francisco employed Dyer, and she left the position in the summer of 1931. She was roughly thirty-four years old. At the time, she had two young daughters. Helen was about ten years old, and Alice was about three. That year, the Children's Agency, a subsidiary of the Associated Charities of San Francisco, became involved with the Dyer family. On August 28, 1931, Elizabeth Peterson of the Children's Agency wrote to Matron Royce regarding Dyer, "There is a grave suspicion that [Agnes] is again pregnant. I think you had better be sure about this before placing her. . . . Will you please impress upon her the fact that there is no place in California where her children can be cared for. She insists they can be sent to Fresno."[20]

Peterson then began to question the paternity of one of Dyer's children, noting that "she dislikes me very much on account of the attitude I took in [regard to] the affair between her and [a younger man]. I felt that she, as an older woman, was the one to blame. Also, I find there is a grave suspicion that the father of that baby was not [him], but the brother who is married to the maid in Mrs. Graupner's home. What do you think?"[21] Matrons and officials of this and other "welfare" organizations of the time were highly concerned with questions of chastity and morality, holding Native women to an at-times impossible standard. They regularly questioned the parentage of Indian children and whether they were "illegitimate." Meanwhile, women like Agnes Dyer were simply trying to earn a living in the city.

A year later, Dyer's children were again the objects of BIA administrators' interest. On October 9, 1932, Esther Adamson, a social worker at Stewart Indian School, wrote to Dyer's again-employer Mrs. J. R. MacDonald. It seems MacDonald had inquired as to whether Dyer's children could be boarded. Adamson explained, "I have made several inquiries regarding a possible boarding home for Agnes Dyer's children, the youngest especially, but nothing has come up." She then turned her focus to the condition of local Indian homes: "The families are [so] unusually crowded by their own children and grandchildren's return to the parental roofs that the suggestion of an additional one is not even considered, much less found acceptable." Perhaps the "addition" to which she referred was the child Dyer was suspected of carrying the year prior. Adamson then admitted that even Dyer's eldest child, a four-year-old, could not be enrolled at Stewart until she was at least six.[22] She concluded, "The only suggestion that seems at all possible would be to try to get a more agreeable relationship between Agnes and the court officials who supervise the placement of the children."[23] County, city, and BIA officials targeted Dyer and many other Native women—especially those with more than one child. Ostensibly, these bureaucrats feared that Native children would be neglected or abandoned by their own mothers. But in practice, Native women were separated from their children so that they could more properly labor as live-in domestics.

Sadie Sam, a Yerington Paiute woman, is another example of what the outing program expected of mothers with young children. Sam entered the outing program around 1923 as a Stewart Indian School student. She was a former runaway and was incarcerated at a detention home in her early outing years. Later in her life, as a wife and mother, Sam continued outing work under the supervision of Matron Royce. In the summer of 1927, while Sam was in Yerington, Nevada, with her family, she wrote Matron Royce requesting funds from her account. She noted that her son Bobby "is [a] fine big boy now."[24] In return, Royce sent the funds. In an October 1927 letter, Sam thanked the matron and sent her regards to the fellow outing women, saying, "Give all the girls I know my love." Sam expressed her longing for the Bay Area but recognized the fact that she would be forced to leave her son if she returned. "I just get the longing to go back there sometime. But it's my boy. I don't like to be dragging him about all the time. If I go I have to leave him here and I don't like to. He likes my mother and father and talks good Indian now. I sometimes think he'll forget his English but I talk to him he understands. But always wants to answer in Indian."[25]

The promise of wage work came at a cost. The outing program forced Sam and other mothers like her to choose between their children or the program. Sam was unhappy "dragging" her son about but then longed for the friends she made in the Bay Area and wages that could support her family. In the fall of 1928, Sam planned to return to the Bay Area Outing program. Her husband was not well or working, so Sam hoped the work would allow her to provide for her family. She planned to keep her son at home with her parents in Yerington, Nevada. On November 10, 1928, she wrote Matron Royce, declaring, "I am not taking Bobby with me because my mother and father give him good care. I don't think he would like it if I take him away from them because he likes to be with them all the time."[26] While Sam had to work far away from her baby and family, she was fortunate to leave her son with his grandparents. By contrast, many young mothers outing in the Bay Area would have had to board their children in a home or institution until they were old enough for boarding school or worse—adoption or fosterage. With the outing program's strong ties to Catholic charities, the Children's Home Society of California, and similar adoption-driven institutions, the latter was certainly possible.

In 1931, Amy Bethel, a sixteen-year-old Mono woman from North Fork, began working in the outing program. For the next few years, Bethel worked at various homes in Oakland and Piedmont, earning ten to fifteen dollars a month while attending Oakland High School. After a brief hiatus, she returned to outing work in 1935, 1936, and 1937. After enrolling in courses at Merritt Business College, Bethel briefly worked as a typist in San Francisco at the Indian Warehouse. There, she garnered a whopping $120 a month.

In September of 1941, Bethel gave birth to a baby girl named Charlene. Because of postpartum complications, she and her daughter convalesced at the Salvation Army Home in Oakland for a few months before Bethel was strong enough to return to work. In the winter of 1942, Bethel worked as a domestic at a Piedmont Pines home in Oakland. The employers forced her to board her baby, and she was unhappy with her working conditions. On January 7, 1942, she wrote Matron Van Every to vent her frustrations: "Things get pretty lonesome way up here out of civilization, when you look out the window and all you see is a great big ugly water tank. Oh well, can't be surrounded with all the bright lights all the time." Bethel explained that she had not heard from her daughter's father since November of the previous year, when he sailed off to war. She managed the monthly boarding fee but lived on a tight budget. She explained to Van Every, "I have my baby paid up to February 1st. She's cost me $55 so far. I pay $20 plus her clothing a month. I make $45 so you can see what I have left."[27] Indeed, after paying nursery fees, the single mother earned less than twenty-five dollars a month.

Roughly half of her monthly wages went to boarding her daughter—simply because her job demanded it.

In the summer of 1942, Bethel transitioned to a new home in the Rockridge neighborhood of Oakland. There, she cared for a family with three children while managing a four-bedroom, three-bath house. The former typist found the work tiresome and especially difficult, for she longed for her baby. Worse, in the midst of the war, she failed to locate her daughter's father, Frank Murphy. On June 22, 1942, Bethel wrote Matron Van Every formally requesting her assistance in locating Murphy. The new mother told the matron the last time she saw him was at the Salvation Army Hospital after she had given birth. Bethel explained, "At that time we talked of my baby's support. I told him it would cost $30 a month plus her clothing, to have her taken care of. He told me then he would send me the money." Bethel lamented, "We had planned to marry, but my being in the hospital so long prevented our marriage. Also we did not know if his Squadron was being transferred to Foreign Service."[28]

In the postscript, Bethel expressed her desire to reconnect with her daughter and to transition out of domestic work:

> I've been sort of thinking of changing jobs where there is less work. You know I tire very easily. There are three children here and also a large house. So you can see there's plenty work. Now that school is out the children sort of get on my nerves—you see I get so lonesome for my baby—thinking of how she's getting along (I worry a lot over her father—not knowing where he is) putting it all together just any little thing upsets me. It sort of makes the lady here feel bad because she doesn't know what's wrong with me. My mother has told me so many times if I could get support for my little girl to come home and take care of her myself—that any child needs their own mother.[29]

Bethel felt guilty for not being in her daughter's life. While she cared for three children at the Rockridge home, her employers and the outing program prevented from caring for her own. Bethel suffered from diverted mothering, a social reality for many women in the outing program. The program ignored Native women's maternal and reproductive roles in favor of their roles as workers.[30] A single mother like Bethel was forced to make a difficult choice and regretted that her wage work kept her from her own child. Just like Sadie Sam "dragging" around her son Bobby, Bethel had little choice in the matter. Shortly after these letters to Van Every, records reveal that Charlene's father was sent overseas. He was reportedly captured, and there is no record of whether he survived. By November 1942, Bethel transitioned to clerical work at an office job, working long nights and weekends. She considered leaving to work in the shipyards, where "the rest of the gals" made all "that do-ra-me."[31] Yet even outside of domestic work, Bethel was still without her daughter. While Charlene now lived with her relatives in North Fork, she was even further away from her mother. And Bethel was, as ever, "lonesome" without her. At the time, the young mother was in the midst of applying for federal support for her daughter so that she might regain custody locally. Records do not reveal if Bethel secured these funds or if Charlene's father was ever found.

These three cases demonstrate the prevalence of Indian child boarding practices. Whether through outing matron intervention, county officials, or the young mothers themselves, Native women were encouraged and at times pressured to board their children in local homes or institutions. Separation from their children was largely a requirement of live-in outing work—forcing mothers to choose between their work and their children. In Dyer's case, boarding school officials attempted to remove her youngest child to a boarding home. Her older children were already being raised by Stewart Indian School. Native women like Dyer who had more than one child were often targeted by county, city, and BIA officials. Sam was unhappy "dragging" her son around but needed outing wages to support her family. Whereas some women had no family to turn to, Sam's parents gladly raised her young son. Surely if they had not, he would have been sent to a boarding home. Initially, Bethel boarded her infant child in a home so she might continue outing work. But she missed her baby, and almost half of her monthly wages went to boarding fees. Ultimately, Bethel felt guilty for not being able to care for her daughter while busy raising her employer's children. In practice, the outing program facilitated diverted mothering, prioritizing Native women's roles as workers. While these young mothers struggled to maintain relationships with their children, boarding Native children turned out to be the least invasive scenario imposed on them.

Boarding Schools

Maude Mitchell's story reveals the ever-present threat of child removal in the form of boarding schools. Ultimately, her daughter was threatened with both removal to a boarding home and removal to Stewart Indian School. Thirty-two-year-old Mitchell, a Pomo woman, arrived in the outing program in 1931.[32] She was a single mother raising two children, one of whom was enrolled at Sherman Indian School during her outing career. While Mitchell was employed for many years in the outing program, there were a few instances in which she reportedly "did'nt [*sic*] fit in" at client homes, leaving after a couple of days. However, she had regular employment with a Mrs. Baxter in Oakland.

In 1936, while working for Mrs. Baxter, Mitchell struggled to raise her daughter Vera while also working as a live-in domestic servant. In the fall of that year, Mitchell terminated her employment at the Baxter household. One month later, an angry Mrs. Baxter wrote to the superintendent of Stewart Indian School, pleading for them to enroll Mitchell's youngest daughter so her maid could return to work. Baxter believed this was for Mitchell's "betterment" and that of her daughter: "Maude Mitchell, Vera's mother worked for me for six years. . . . I needed her at night, but it was impossible to leave Vera alone. . . . She is having much difficulty in supporting both Vera and herself. . . . I believe it would be a solution to this problem if Vera were accepted into the Indian school and educated as other Indian girls are educated."[33] Despite the fact that Mitchell terminated employment of her own accord, both Mitchell's employer Mrs. Baxter and the outing matron continued to see Mitchell's daughter as a barrier to her employment and, ultimately, Mitchell's successful assimilation. In fact, Matron Van Every researched the feasibility of placing Mitchell's youngest daughter in a county home against Mitchell's will. Van Every's ill-considered assessment did not consider the financial needs of the Mitchell family or Mitchell's desire to raise her own child. Mitchell did not take kindly to Van Every's interference.

During an office visit to the outing program, Mitchell declared to the matron, "I do not want to send my child to the boarding school. . . . You are to leave me absolutely alone and keep me off your list."[34] According to the records, Mitchell's daughter was not sent to a home or an Indian boarding school. Instead, the family separated their ties with the program and never returned.[35] Nonetheless, Mitchell's case suggests the outing program's larger intentions. Gendered domestic assimilation was designed to break the Native family and allow parents' entrance into society through labor exploitation. These women's experiences demonstrate that outing matrons and BIA officials regularly disregarded Native women's wishes for their children.

Other women's stories demonstrate the power matrons held over Native women and their children, particularly in regard to boarding school placement. Gertrude "Gertie" Wasson, a Paiute woman from McDermitt, Nevada, was raised at Stewart Indian School before coming to the Bay Area Outing Program around 1925. She was twenty-two. Wasson's file starts in the early years of the program's recordkeeping and is less complete than others; still, it captures the outing program's effects on the Indian family. During her outing tenure, Wasson worked at a home in Oakland, and later two homes in San Francisco. From her arrival, Wasson regularly butted heads with Matron Royce and wanted nothing to do with her while working in the Bay Area. After Wasson, who was in a relationship, became pregnant, Matron Royce sought to insert herself in the matter. Gertie wrote letters to her father, John Wasson, in which she openly complained about the matron's interventions.[36]

On July 6, 1925, John Wasson wrote a two-page letter to Matron Royce in defense of his daughter. She was pregnant, he said, and intended on marrying. He fully supported the marriage and desired no further interference from the meddlesome matron. His letter is an impressive example of a father's love for his daughter. After formalities, Wasson opened his letter with "I wish you would leave Gertrude alone. She's all right when you leave her alone. She old enough to look after herself." He continued, "If that boy love her and she loves him, leave them alone. We can't pick out her husband and his wife for them, so just leave them alone. Let them get married if they love each other."[37]

Wasson then noted that he did not have any opinions on white people getting married, so why should Royce about Indian people: "You know that our [Indian] people don't say anything to your children. We can't pick out your son in law. Same with me. So just let her alone. . . . These people here [Indians] just leave the young paleface alone, they don't bud [*sic*] in. . . . They just let them get married." He argues, "I thought any people, I mean Indians could get married any time, just as long as they're old enough. If they have their folks consant [*sic*] but I'm mistaken I see." At the close of his letter, John Wasson warns the matron one last time: "I hope I don't hear anything like that again from you. I'll write again from some friends if you interfere again."[38] On November 5, 1925, Gertie Wasson gave birth to her first child, William. William was given his mother's maiden name, and it appears she did not marry. Perhaps Matron Royce's interference worked. After giving birth, Wasson continued outing.

Over the next year, Wasson's father and sister Norma wrote Matron Royce occasionally to check in on Gertie. On October 27, 1926, Royce assured Norma that Wasson was still working in Oakland and the matron had secured a place for her nephew in a nursery. Reportedly, "The baby is a fine one, healthy and fat."[39] Like other babies in the outing program, William was separated from his mother to ensure she could maintain her live-in domestic work. While continuing to work in the Bay Area, Wasson became pregnant again. She delivered her second son, Benson, on November 7, 1927. William and his baby brother were born exactly two days and two years apart.

The next few years of Wasson's life are absent from the archive, but by 1931, the family was involved with the Children's Agency, a subsidiary of the Associated Charities of San Francisco. The agency worked to improve conditions in orphan and foundling asylums and also had an extensive record of placing babies and children in foster homes. On January 24, 1931, Elizabeth Peterson of the Children's Agency reported to Matron Royce that Wasson's children were committed by the juvenile court to the care of the agency. They planned to place William and Benson in a foster home, thus "leaving Gertrude free to go to work and contribute to their support."[40] Many Native women like Wasson were separated from their children simply so that they could labor.

In this letter, Peterson further claims that Wasson had a "rather borderline" "mental rating" and stated that her colleagues intended to commit Wasson in due time.[41] As Margaret Jacobs has argued, Native women who fought the removal of their children were in some cases deemed "feebleminded" and committed to institutions.[42] Such claims of low intelligence and incompetence discredited Wasson and prohibited her from advocating for her children. By the summer of 1931, the boys were transferred to the Infant Shelter in San Francisco. Though Wasson objected to sending her boys to Stewart Indian school, the shelter planned to care for the boys until they were old enough to enroll, at six years old.[43]

A year later, on June 10, 1932, a Miss F. Baringer wrote on behalf of the City and County of San Francisco's chief probation officer to BIA officials regarding the Wasson family. Reportedly, Wasson had four "illegitimate" children, among which, one—William—was now six and eligible to be enrolled at Stewart. However, Baringer noted, "Gertrude is most unwilling for this placement, stating that she had been very unhappy there and that she could not possibly consider placing her child there."[44] Baringer wondered if there was some other recourse. Nearly a month later, Frederic Snyder, Stewart's superintendent, learned of Wasson's dissatisfaction. On July 2, Snyder wrote Matron Royce, stating, "I am surprised to learn that Gertrude states that she was very unhappy while she was a pupil at our school, and, therefore, could not possibly consider placing her children here. I was not aware that she was unhappy, but on the other hand I felt that she was old enough to appreciate the protective advantages that were given to her while here."[45]

Whether or not Wasson would agree on the "protective advantages," it was not the first time she had expressed her reservations. Nevertheless, if she had no other options, she preferred the boys be sent together—even if they were two years apart.[46] In spite of Wasson's wishes, Royce mailed Baringer an application for William's enrollment.[47] Within a month, the Children's Agency confirmed that William would be transferred to Stewart at the beginning of the school year.[48] Outing records do not reveal how William fared at Stewart or whether his brother Benson joined him. However, Gertie Wasson's brief but difficult time in the Bay Area Outing Program demonstrates the profound forces that Native girls, women, and their families experienced.

Outing matron intervention was but one element that could be joined with city and county officials as well as BIA administrators.

These two cases demonstrate the pervasive practice of Indian child removal in the form of Indian boarding school enrollment. If the children of outing women were of age, they could easily be taken away. To the dismay of her employer, Mitchell freely chose to terminate her outing position. Working with her daughter in the home while attempting to manage the demands of her work was too much. In turn, Baxter meddled just enough, influencing Van Every's efforts to send Vera to a county home. Even after Mitchell was no longer officially tied to the outing program, she was still threatened with Indian child removal. Whereas Mitchell was successful in thwarting the matron's efforts, Wasson was not. Not only was Wasson at odds with Royce but also the matron may have succeeded in breaking her engagement, despite her father's intervention. Thereafter, Wasson's children were targeted by early social welfare efforts simply so she could work. Together with the matron, these organizations worked to discredit Wasson and attempted to institutionalize her. Meanwhile, they sought to enroll her eldest into boarding school, against Wasson's wishes. Yet again, the outing program prioritized Native women's roles as workers and did so by attempting—and in one case succeeding—to remove Indian children to boarding school. Outside forces judged Native women and their families, made efforts to separate Native children from their mothers, continued the cycle of boarding school trauma, and undermined Native communities. Amid these difficult times for Native women and their children, some women—especially young, first-time mothers—felt the pinch of trying to survive and work in the city with a newborn.

Fostering and Adoption

Whereas boarding school placement was certainly undesirable, especially for those who had experienced being raised by the institution, it was largely preferred over the fostering or adoption of outing women's children. The latter severed all ties between mother and child and sent a young Native child into a non-Native home.[49] However, while most women rejected the fostering or adoption of their children, some accepted it. Certainly, they were encouraged and likely coerced by matrons and other officials. Perhaps they believed that their children would have better lives without them. While their motives will never be known, adoption and fostering were a common tactic of removal. One woman whose story is presented here vehemently fought it. In spring of 1928, eighteen-year-old Daisy Plummer, a Paiute student from Stewart Indian School, came to the outing program.[50] Plummer had a brief first stint in the program before apparently being sent back to Stewart for an undefined transgression. On May 20, 1929, Plummer wrote from Stewart Indian School, professing apologies to Royce. Plummer admitted "what a mistake" she had made while in the Bay Area; "I am awfully sorry and sad today and I really to goodness don't know what I'll do if I stick around here. I'd rather work that's all. I miss the girls there now. Seems to me I am in a serious trouble or put in prison."[51] For Plummer, the outing program represented freedom, compared to the "prison" of boarding school life. She pleaded, "I just can't stand it here any longer. It's awfully lonesome for me no matter if the girls are nice to me. Every time I think of Oakland I had to cry and cry I was not even sick when I was at Mrs. Linden's. Only thing [that] bothered me was the cold. But now I feel over it." Apparently, her employer's home lacked heat. But the conditions were worse at Stewart.

Plummer begged the matron for another chance: "I have disobeyed you Mrs. Royce. . . . Please could you let me go back there and work. I will promise you I will listen to you. . . . I am real sorry for not doing what is right. It's because I stick around with bad girls and I do what they wanted to do. But if I can go back with you it would sure make me happy again." Plummer was calculated in her appeal and must have hit the right notes, for Royce gave her another chance.

Later in the year, when Plummer returned, she became pregnant with her first child. In January 1930, she delivered a healthy baby girl named Verna Jean. Plummer and her baby recovered at the Salvation Army Home in Oakland. In a letter to Royce, Plummer was apologetic again, but this time, she was inspired to advocate for better wages. "Mrs. Royce I really do hope that I will get better money this time so that I may bring my baby up in a right way. And I often get so discouraged sometimes but I am trying to forget the past and I know that I am going to be a better girl, I realize my mistakes and I know better now."[52]

Plummer had a tense relationship with Matron Royce, who was particularly hostile toward sexually active girls. Her run-ins with Royce likely colored the matron's decision to intervene with Plummer's newborn child. Within two months of Verna Jean's birth, Plummer got word that Royce intended to take her child away. Records reveal that Royce found Plummer to be irresponsible and foolish. The matron believed that Verna Jean would be better off in someone else's care. In a March 25, 1930, letter, Plummer scolded the matron:

> I was told about two weeks ago that you said you was going to take my baby away to some institution. Now Mrs. Royce, I really don't like that. But I'm going to stand by my baby no matter what happens. You have to write soon to Mr. Parrett [superintendent of the Walker River Paiute Agency] or my father right away. Because I can't stand it any longer. I am just worried. I cry myself to sleep every night for that. I guess you don't know how I love my baby. I am old enough and know better and can work and get more money by now. You may think it's best but not with me. I can't do that by giving up my baby. If [you] try that misses Royce, I'm going to write soon to father and he will probably come down and help me out. Because my father doesn't want me to do that at all. Well Mrs. Royce I hope you and I will have a talk whenever you like. When I am trying so hard to start all over. But seems as if though no one won't let me have a chance.[53]

Despite Plummer's warnings, Royce continued to intervene. By May 1930, she had arranged for Verna Jean to board at the Ladies' Relief Society nursery. But like most Native women in the outing program, Plummer appears to have not taken up the offer—much to Matron Royce's disapproval. By summer, Royce was again targeting Plummer. On June 21, 1930, in a letter to Superintendent Parrett of the Walker River Agency, Royce accused Plummer of being "irresponsible" and "slovenly in her work." Apparently, the new mother was socializing out late among "bad company." Royce added, "a negro is the latest."[54] Outing matrons frowned upon interracial relationships, especially with African American men. Because Native women were assumed to be promiscuous, these fears were rooted in miscegenation. Eventually, when the new mother was unable to keep her outing position, Royce forced her to labor at a neighbor's home. Plummer refused to work in that home and apparently "sulked and refused to come out of her room." Royce felt compelled to act. The matron declared, "I was therefore forced to place her in the Detention Home where she is at the present time."[55]

As if she had no choice, Royce washed her hands of the young mother and had her incarcerated in a detention home. Records do not reveal if baby Verna Jean was sent with her mother to be detained or separated from her during this time. However, the incident appeared to be the last straw for Royce. In a rather positive turn of events, Plummer and her daughter were sent home shortly thereafter, never to return to the outing program. Plummer's experience reveals that an infraction early on in the program could mean a rocky tenure in the outing program. A young unwed mother would be closely scrutinized, judged, and likely threatened with losing her child. Plummer's case also demonstrates that in their defense, Native women made use of patriarchal standards by petitioning the assistance of men in their lives. Apparently, matrons may have responded to male authority where they did not honor the authority of Native mothers themselves. Ultimately, Plummer was neither the first nor the last woman to be threatened with the removal of her child.

Josephine Green's story speaks to the common pressures of adoption, as well as the complexities of single motherhood. Green, a Wintu woman, was nineteen years old when she began working for the Bay Area Outing Program in 1930. A public school student from Redding, California, Green worked in homes in Piedmont, Oakland, and Berkeley for roughly forty dollars a month. In early April 1930, Green and her sister Thelma contacted Matron Royce in search of work. The Shasta County laundry where the pair had worked had recently burned down, and the sisters, who were financially responsible for their younger siblings and ailing father, were unemployed. On account of their familial obligations, Green requested wages of fifty dollars a month and expressed a desire for a "public" job: "I would like to have a job in a small store, or in an ice cream parlor or even washing dishes for a hotel. I would rather work in a public place than for a family."[56] Of course, only housekeeping positions were available in the outing program.

In response, Matron Royce advised, "Times as you know are hard and work [is] next to impossible to find. . . . Housework is always available, so if you and your sister are willing to go into homes and work we will be glad to help you. We will get the highest possible wages for you."[57] Interestingly, Royce rarely made such wage promises to prospective outing employees. Perhaps she took pity on the high school siblings who were thrust into such responsibility. Rather coolly, the two replied, "We are both perfectly willing to do housework until we can find something we like better."[58]

Toward the end of the month, on April 22, 1930, Green started work in a Piedmont home. Shortly afterward, she transitioned to the Leydecker home in Oakland, where she was employed for some time. In early January of 1931, Green became pregnant. According to records, the father of her unborn child was a married man with his own children. Whether this child was the product of an affair or assault the records do not reveal. As previously discussed, outing matrons and federal officials did little in the way of discussing consent and were more concerned with holding Native women responsible for sexual intercourse. Green continued working nearly up to her due date, and on October 8, 1931, she gave birth to a baby boy named Daniel, or "Danny."[59] Like other outing girls and women, Green recuperated at the Oakland Salvation Army Home.[60] While still outing and earning roughly forty dollars a month, Green somehow managed to pay off a twenty-five-dollar "maternity fee" as well as a twenty-dollar monthly fee for the care of her son while at the home. In an undated letter to Matron Royce, Green discussed the debt and ended her letter with a curious final statement: "I am trusting you to do your best and say nothing to no one for my sake. But more for the sake of my baby."[61] Perhaps she desired to keep secret the debt or the nature of it. After giving birth, Green continued outing.

Records do not indicate precisely when, but sometime after Danny was born, Green married and became Josephine Ford. In the summer or fall of 1932, she delivered her second child. Sometime after the birth of her second baby boy, Ford decided to board Danny with a sixty-year-old woman by the name of Bernice Upson. Upson raised Danny with the help of her daughter

Beryl under the understanding that she was to be paid for her services. However, the recently married Ford, busy with her new family, became indebted to the Upsons in the amount of three hundred dollars. Rather than press Ford for back wages, the elderly caretaker continued caring for Danny without pay for over a year. Perhaps because Danny was considered an "illegitimate" child, or her new husband did not want to raise him, Danny remained outside of the Ford family circle.

In March 1934, Matron Van Every sought to address the issue. In a visit with Van Every, Ford expressed that she desired to keep Danny but had financial issues. Her husband had little steady work, and though he apparently did not object to raising the child, they could not afford it. At the visit, Ford maintained that she did not want her son placed in an institution. Roughly a week later, on March 26, 1934, Matron Van Every and her assistant, Jeannette Traxler, returned to the home. There they met Ford's two-year-old son and noted that while the Relief Commission paid the family's rent, they were "comfortable." When Van Every questioned Ford about her son Danny, Ford said she would have to adopt him out, stating, "I've decided this is what I have to do. I want to get it settled." Van Every believed that Ford was aware of the steps involved and informed her of the Children's Home Society of California.[62]

Three days later, Matron Van Every spoke with a Mrs. Marie White of the California Children's Home Society. White argued that unless Ford assumed the responsibility of her son Danny, "the child must be adopted out."[63] She further directed Van Every to ask for Ford's "full cooperation in the case." Over the next month, Van Every and Mrs. White worked together to ensure Danny's adoption. By April 12, 1934, Ford, who was pregnant with another child, signed the relinquishment papers. The aging Mrs. Upson, who had clearly cared for Danny, agreed that adoption would be best and was charged with delivering the boy to the Children's Home Society.[64] We cannot guess what Danny's future held, whether he knew he was Native, or if he one day contacted his biological mother. What is clear is that the outing program was invested in adopting out Indian children and that it destabilized Indigenous families and their communities. Sadly, Danny was not the only child to endure this fate. Native women and their families often fought federal efforts to foster or adopt out their children. At times, however, Native women acquiesced to these wishes. Whether they lacked the stability to raise their children or believed their children could have a better life without them, we will never know.

Other women's stories demonstrate adoption practices in the outing program as well as an example of mothers who were accused of refusing to raise their children. Avis Hooper, a Shoshone woman from Owyhee, Nevada, was twenty-one years old when she began working for the Bay Area Outing Program.[65] The former Stewart student was employed at eight different Bay Area homes from 1927 to 1934, working in Oakland, Richmond, San Francisco, and Berkeley. She earned an average wage of forty dollars a month at each position. Within a year of Hooper and her sister Hattie's arrival, their father, Sam Hooper, wrote to Matron Royce to inquire about his daughters. On March 7, 1928, their father wrote, "I would like to have a long letter from you telling me all about my daughters. . . . How are they getting along? What are they doing? And why do not they write to me?"[66] In response, Royce reported that both were well, but that Avis had been hanging around with "bad company."[67]

Nearly a month later, on April 11, 1928, Royce wrote Sam Hooper again, informing him that his daughters had given her "considerabl[e] trouble lately." Reportedly both had been going out with soldiers, and Royce warned, "I think Avis will be a mother this fall sometime." In an attempt to evaluate the match, Royce found the soldier to be a "mean, unprincipled young man" who "refuses to do anything for Avis." She continued, "He says he is not responsible for her condition." Royce, who often advocated marriage in the case of pregnancy, admitted to Sam Hooper that "I might be able to force a marriage but do not think it advisable under the circumstances. He has no funds and would surely not live with her or support her." The matron trusted Avis Hooper's father with the decision: "I would like to have your opinion of the case and we will do whatever you think best. We will be able to take care of Avis and her child here if you want her to remain here. She has had her lesson and I think it has made an impression on her."[68] As ever, Royce relished a teaching moment.

On September 21, 1928, Avis Hooper gave birth to her daughter Jacqueline at the Salvation Army Home in Oakland. In a letter to Royce, Hooper related, "I am very happy with her she is the dearest little darling, wish you could see her." Hooper reported that fellow outing employee Amy Tuohy also had delivered a girl, and both were well taken care of at the home. And as if with a newfound purpose, Hooper declared, "I sure am very anxious to get out and work for her as soon as I can get back my strength again."[69] Rather than wait for Royce, the two mothers found assistance in a San Rafael–based woman named Genevieve Martinelli. In October, Martinelli pulled Hooper, Tuohy, and their babies from the home.[70]

Royce found Martinelli "splendid" and appreciated her generosity with Hooper and Tuohy. However, she feared for the babies' health in San Rafael and was concerned that the mothers paid Martinelli "so little" for food and care for their daughters. While Hooper and Tuohy were not officially engaged in the outing program, Matron Royce still involved herself in their affairs and most importantly maintained control over their wages and bank accounts. When Hooper requested her wages from Royce, the matron elected to forward all $51.53 to her home Indian Agency in Owyhee, Nevada, even though Royce knew that Hooper was located in the Bay Area and that her decision would make things difficult for the new mother.

In a letter to the Indian agency at Western Shoshone, Royce admitted that Hooper was furious when she learned her wages were beyond her reach. Undoubtedly, Hooper needed income to care for her child. In this same letter, Matron Royce, apparently wounded and fed up, complained, "Avis is the first girl to positively refuse my supervision."[71]

Ever the concerned father, Sam Hooper got word of his daughter's disagreement with the matron and wrote Royce to hear her side of the story.[72] In response, Royce explained that Hooper refused to go home, that she was still in San Rafael, and that she had treated the matron with "great disrespect."[73] Royce had essentially washed her hands of Hooper; she found her to be one of the greatest challenges she had experienced to that point in her career. Hooper purportedly hung out with the "bad company," was unchaste, became pregnant, and navigated the Bay Area in her own way without heed to the matron's offers of help. In many ways, Hooper's time in the Bay Area was an outright affront to Royce's authority. Within the year, Hooper was back home in Owyhee, Nevada. But she was not yet done with the Bay Area.

On October 2, 1930, Hooper wrote to Matron Royce, declaring her desire to return to the Bay Area. As ever, with the few economic opportunities available, Native women were driven to outing labor. Hooper, aware of the animosity she once shared with the matron, strategically apologized for her previous behavior. Hooper declared she wanted to work "under" the matron's "guardian[ship]" and said, "I apologize to you Mrs. Royce [for] the way I did with Amy [Tuohy]. She was [the] cause of everything." Hooper assured Royce, "I sure will be [a] good girl and mind you cuz I love to work hard and earn money and support my little girl."[74] Royce was quick to accept Hooper back, agreeing to another trial.[75] Hooper continued working in the Bay Area for the next few years, eventually becoming pregnant again.

Hooper gave birth to a baby boy, whom she named after his father, James Haas. While she continued outing work, she boarded him with a Mrs. Louisa Dalen, who cared for the baby from the time he was ten days old.[76] In the spring of 1934, Hooper's sister fell very ill, and Hooper returned to Nevada to be with her family. On March 16, Hooper wrote from Owyhee, Nevada, to Royce's assistant, Jeannette Traxler. Hooper was wondering what to do with her son, Jimmie, who was still with his caretaker, Mrs. Dalen. She felt awful for "neglect[ing]" him and knew that Dalen could not always care for the boy. She suggested that his paternal aunt and uncle care for him—for they "wanted him long ago." Hooper gave Traxler Jimmie's father, James Haas's, address and left Traxler to make the arrangements.[77]

Following an institutional shift in the outing program, Matron Van Every took over for Royce and Traxler. In the fall of 1934, Van Every searched for James Haas but was unable to locate him.[78] On further investigation, the matron found that Hooper was in debt to Mrs. Dalen for well over a year of unpaid caregiving. In a letter to Superintendent McNeilly, Van Every urged, "We shall need to make some plan for this little boy, not 3 years old."[79]

On October 25, 1934, Mrs. Dalen became ill and could not take care of Jimmie. With no other recourse, she asked Van Every if arrangements could be made for his temporary removal.[80] At this, Van Every wrote to Acting Superintendent L. B. Patterson, urging him to make a plan for the boy. At three years old, he was too young for boarding school. Moreover, the monthly child support from his father had stopped the previous month, and he was nowhere to be found. While Mrs. Dalen gave Jimmie excellent care, she could no longer afford to do so. Van Every explained, "The first plan any of the social agencies will suggest is to send a little boy home to his mother."[81]

With little institutional memory on the case, Matron Van Every sought to research the prospects of placing Jimmie in a home: "In the past 10 days, I have gone to the various agencies . . . concerned with children's social welfare. The child placement Bureau has [made] Indian placements . . . in the past and . . . found them very difficult, in fact impossible, especially when the child is of such a[n] Indian cast of features as is this little boy." Jimmie, and apparently other phenotypically Indian children like him, were impossible to place. Moreover, Van Every admitted that no agencies were "willing to have him assigned to an orphans home" as McNeilly had suggested. According to Van Every, "the man [Jimmie's father] in the case has carried the financial responsibility well for over two and a half years, especially considering his doubtful parentage"; therefore, Hooper should take responsibility and Jimmie should be sent home.[82] As ever, the newly installed matron reduced Hooper's situation to a soap opera drama of "doubtful parentage."

During the winter months that followed, Van Every and BIA officials worked to get Jimmie reunited with his family. On January 5, 1935, Jimmie was sent to his grandmother's house in Owyhee, Nevada. By springtime, however, Van Every learned that Jimmie was being cared for at the local hospital in Owyhee. In a March 4, 1935, letter to Mrs. Dalen, Jimmie's former caregiver, Patterson informed her he "has won the hearts of all the Hospital personnel" but "his mother has no desire to care for him, and since we have been unable to place him with a private family our medical personnel is taking care of him."[83] Patterson's mean-spirited words suggested that Hooper refused to mother. Without Hooper's side of the story, we might agree. But a mother with young children during the Depression undoubtedly had challenges. And the local hospital provided relief. Outing records end shortly after this exchange, but other records show a story of family reunification. In 1940, six years after Van Every joined the case, Jacqueline and Jimmie were living with Hooper and her husband in Elko, Nevada.[84]

In the face of attacks on Native families during the time, this story of reunification feels like a victory. And while Jimmie's early years were precarious, the fact that his placement or adoption was impossible meant that he would not be separated from his family. Not all Native children would experience this. This case reveals the complexities of life for Indian families in the outing program. Particularly in the ways that federal officials attempted to discredit Native women. Indeed, a case such as Hooper's might be used to justify the undermining of other outing women's parental rights. Ultimately, this brief file shows how, in such circumstances, BIA officials like McNeilly and Van Every preferred that Native children be sent to an orphanage or "placed" with a family—that is, adopted out or fostered.

While much of the outing program's concerns focused on Native women and girls employed by the program, they also at times dealt with nonaffiliated Native women—especially in relationship to their reproductive rights as mothers. In the winter of 1943, for example, Lillian Penrose, a seventeen-year-old Yerington Paiute student at Stewart Indian School, became pregnant. On January 20, 1944, Ernest C. Mueller, principal of Stewart Indian School, wrote to Mildred Van Every, reporting that "one of our girls is found to be pregnant and it is necessary to find some place more suitable for her than the Carson Boarding School." Penrose's mother had apparently passed away, and Penrose had no home to go to. In the past, the school had sent at least one other student to San Francisco with a similar pregnancy case. The principal continued, "She is three months pregnant with a negative Wassermann one month ago. The boy responsible is located at the Reno Army Air base she thinks and is willing to marry him."[85] As ever, federal officials sought to marry off Native women, especially once they became pregnant. Marriage itself was a method of containment for Native women and idealized among outing matrons and various federal authorities. Mueller's mention of a Wassermann test, moreover, indicates that authorities were concerned that Penrose may have contracted syphilis or another venereal disease.

On February 5, 1944, Mueller wrote again with new information. While Penrose was one of Stewart's "nicest girls," he surmised that "girls of her age often get into difficulty through some false love affair which this happens to be."[86] Reportedly, there would be no financial remuneration from the "boy" involved. He was a first-class private in the Army and was already married, with a family to support. Therefore, Mueller petitioned the matron to assist with transferring Penrose to the Booth Memorial Hospital in Oakland.[87] There, Penrose could offset the hospital fees by doing domestic work for a few hours a day.[88] Finally, Mueller stated that provisions would have to made for the child, as according to his contacts, "Indian babies are not adoptable in the State of California." In response, Van Every noted that she had a great deal of experience with Indian girls at the hospital, and thus Penrose's expenses could be paid once she was employable. Further, she noted, Mueller was misinformed, "because Indian children have been legally adopted whenever there is one available for adoption." She added, "It is quite possible that a foster home can be found for this baby."[89]

By April of 1944, Penrose was getting along nicely at Booth Memorial Hospital. Penrose informed Van Every that she wished to keep her pregnancy a secret from her father and planned to place her baby for adoption.[90] Near the end of the month, the hospital secured authorization from her father, Archie Penrose, to treat his daughter for "diagnostic tests."[91] While Penrose appeared to have a normal pregnancy, she did suffer from a swollen gland that led doctors to believe that she might have tuberculosis. If so, she posed a danger to other patients at Booth Memorial Hospital, which was unequipped to handle such a case.[92] Moreover, because she was not an Alameda County resident, Highland Hospital was unable to provide a full diagnostic test. Penrose was running out of options. On May 5, 1944, Muriel Smith informed Van Every of the situation: "You will remember that there is a social problem also involved, that if possible, Lillian's community remain ignorant of her pregnant condition."[93] Another letter two days later indicated, "Lillian is very hesitant to return to a hospital where she may run into people who she has known formerly."[94] Whereas normally Penrose would have been sent to the Stewart or Schurz sanatoriums, these were not an option if she were to keep her secret safe. And keeping her secret safe also meant keeping on track with plans for having the child adopted.

Shortly afterward, doctors confirmed that the mother to be was in fact tubercular. They arranged for her hospitalization at the Hoopa Hospital in Northern California—far from her community in Nevada. Reporting to Van Every, District Medical Director Hunt added, "Lillian seemed to be an intelligent girl, and it might be possible to keep her around the hospital and train her as a hospital employee."[95] As ever, it was Penrose's capacity to labor that seemed to most interest the "guardian" figures surrounding her. Not long after the exchange, on August 12, 1944, Penrose delivered her baby in the Hoopa Valley Hospital. Rather than give her baby up for adoption as she had initially planned, Penrose chose to return to her community and raise her child at her aunt's home.[96]

In late September of 1944, a disgruntled Superintendent Ralph Gelvin wrote to Van Every, "It almost floored us to have this information as we have been trying so hard to protect this child and keep in secrecy all her troubles, then she left the hospital and came right in the area where we had been so careful to keep the news from. We thought we were helping her to meet the situation of life easily, but she has taken the old Indian way and shows no shame or disgrace, but feels quite proud of the fact that she has a baby. She will keep her baby."[97] Clearly for Gelvin, Penrose's life and that of her baby would have been easier had she adopted out her child. The fact that Penrose was proud of her baby seemed to serve as a personal affront to the superintendent, who believed she should be ashamed of herself. Instead, she took the "old Indian way," as if rejecting the civilities dictated by Euro-American values. These "old Indian ways" were the same as those that the Save the Babies campaign sought to dismantle.

Gelvin continued in his letter to Van Every, "After the baby is old enough, she plans to go to work in Fallon. We do not like this idea, but perhaps we can assist her into some other line of work. As you know, Fallon is in the defense area, and we have found too much immorality, especially from Indian girls. We shall try to protect her." Again, Gelvin was concerned for Penrose and her potential to fraternize with degenerate Indian girls. His concern remained with Fallon's Naval Air Station and undoubtedly the many servicemen situated there—so close to local Native women. In so few words, the superintendent feared promiscuous, sexually active Native women.

While records do not include Penrose's personal testimony, her actions speak loudly. Initially she may have believed that it was best to keep the pregnancy a secret and adopt out her child, as she was likely encouraged to. Federal officials must have agreed that adoption was best, as they worked carefully to manage the mother to be and keep her secret safe. Yet Penrose chose to keep her baby after delivering, asserting her right to motherhood. This choice incensed Superintendent Gelvin. It is revealing that he was furious not merely over the apparently painstaking details and resources it had taken to manage Penrose's secret but also that she had affirmed her ability to mother and taken pride in it. Certainly, Gelvin would have preferred Penrose to have accepted that her child was better off adopted. For an Indian child born of a young single mother, BIA officials preferred "placement" in the form of adoption or fostering. In the case of women who chose not to raise their children, this was commonplace.

In another example of how the outing program at times interested itself in circumstances beyond those of the Native women under its employ, in 1930, Matron Royce got involved in a case regarding a Cherokee woman who lived in Marin County.[98] While the woman was not an employee of the outing program, she and her son became the subject of much correspondence between BIA and county administrators. On July 26, 1924, twenty-one-year-old Frances Pensotti gave birth to her son Joseph at St. Elizabeth's Hospital in San Francisco. Pensotti relinquished her son for adoption on December 10, 1924. A Mr. Ryan, acting as "agent" for Joseph's father, made visits to the hospital to pay for Joseph's care. On February 15, 1927, Joseph outgrew the hospital nursery and was sent to the Little Children's Aid Society of San Francisco. Mr. Ryan's payments for the child stopped, and reportedly a "mysterious man"—perhaps his father—began to cover Joseph's board. Records reveal that no family visited him at the society.[99]

As he grew older, the Little Children's Aid Society secured a foster home for Joseph. He was cared for by a Mrs. Margaret Michael in San Francisco. According to BIA officials, "efforts were made to have him adopted," but they were never able to secure a permanent home. As was also the case with Jimmie, phenotypically Indian children were difficult to place. BIA records report that "no one wanted a child as dark as he."[100] Apparently with little recourse, and in line with other cases of Indian children in the Bay Area, officials waited for Joseph to reach the proper age so he would be sent off to an Indian boarding school.

In the fall of 1930, Matron Royce researched the feasibility of placing

Joseph at Stewart Indian School in Carson City, Nevada. Though "overcrowded," the school opened its doors to seven-year-old Joseph and another Indian child by the name of Rosita Elliott—a twelve-year-old Pomo girl who would grow up to work in the outing program.[101] On November 19, 1930, Royce wrote to Stewart School's Superintendent Snyder, arranging for their transportation.[102] Within a year's time, BIA administrators sent reports to Joseph's foster mother. Records reveal that his foster mother was "exceptionally fond of him" and "greatly upset" when he was taken from her and sent to Stewart. However, officials felt it was convenient and cost effective. According to an internal letter, "the Indian School plan was made because it was so difficult to secure the board money for the child and there was no other way to support him."[103]

Joseph remained at Stewart for about four years, until once again he became the subject of correspondence between BIA and county administrators. On November 25, 1934, Superintendent of Indian Affairs Alida C. Bowler wrote to Matron Van Every in search of more information on young Joseph. Apparently, Bowler and various administrators were unable to verify Joseph's life story. They doubted his parentage and uncovered disparaging gossip, reporting, "The mother's reputation is such that probably no one will ever know who was the father." Worse, after a federal inquiry, they realized that Joseph's mother was three-eighths Indian, meaning her son's degree of Indian blood was now insufficient for him to remain enrolled at Stewart. Bowler, determined to further investigate the truth of the case, concluded, "He is quite a fine little fellow and we would like to give him the best chance possible. He should be in a home rather than an institution."[104] Bowler's use of "institution" in this letter is curious. "Institution" may have referred to Stewart or possibly an orphanage. Nonetheless, once it was confirmed that he was less than one-quarter Indian, Bowler found the young boy now worthy of a home. Joseph Pensotti's blood would free him from the confines of Indian boarding school life. Did that also mean that his Indian blood was so inconsequential that he was worthier than his Native peers at Stewart?

On October 1, 1934, Matron Van Every responded to Bowler with little further information. Her predecessor Royce had recommended the child based on a letter from Carl M. Moore, then supervisor of Indian education.

But no further documents improved his case. In the first ten years of his life, Joseph Pensotti was abandoned and cared for by hospitals and institutions and, after a brief stint in a foster home, was sent to an Indian boarding school. There he perhaps finally experienced some kind of stability. But his life would yet again be disrupted. Joseph was sent to Stewart because no one wanted to adopt a child as "dark" as he was, yet he was pulled from Stewart because he was not Indian enough. Joseph's file ends after this final letter, suggesting that he was in fact removed from Stewart. We may never know what happened to this young man or if he or his descendants connected with his birth family. Nevertheless, the first ten years of Joseph's life demonstrate the precarious state of Indian children in the early twentieth century. Children could be passed around from institution to institution while county and BIA officials waited for them to reach an age where they could be sent off to boarding school. Children like Joseph who were "dark" or Jimmie whose features were too "Indian" often proved impossible to place. These children had especially difficult lives.

These five cases demonstrate the ever-present threat of Indian child removal in the form of fostering or adoption. In the case of eighteen-year-old Daisy Plummer, Royce threatened to take away her daughter almost immediately after her birth. The new mother was livid and threatened her father's intervention. Whereas Plummer was able to evade the matron's interventions, Josephine Green was less lucky. Records do not reveal whether Green's son Danny was the product of an affair or assault, but it is clear that she distanced herself from her newborn, first through infant boarding and later—after much encouragement—through adoption. Van Every and the Children's Home Society worked diligently on the issue. Mostly, Native women fought efforts to foster or adopt out their children. But at times they yielded. Hooper's case may have been used to justify the undermining of other outing women's parental rights, but it thankfully ended in reunification. As with Hooper, federal officials initially sought to marry off the recently pregnant Lillian Penrose. In lieu of marriage, officials sought to hide the student's pregnancy with the intention of adopting out the child. To their disgust, Penrose did not yield to their wishes. She took the "old Indian way" and, rather than hiding in shame, proudly chose to mother her newborn. Whereas Penrose rejected adoption, Frances Pensotti embraced the possibility of relinquishing her infant son Joseph. After a nursery, brief fostering, and a failed adoption, Joseph was passed around until he was old enough for boarding school—only to be ousted for not being Indian "enough." For Indian children, the intervention of outing matrons and the BIA was at times positive. In some cases, these officials worked hard to help abandoned or neglected children. Yet this assistance came at a cost, subject to the standards of the BIA. In this best-case scenario, outing program intervention equaled government-based childrearing. However, in the case of many mothers and Indian families, BIA intervention amounted to threats of children's removal and separation from their Native family.

This chapter has examined how the Bay Area Outing Program affected the Indian family and particularly Indian mothers and their children. My analysis of these stories demonstrates how outing matrons facilitated three central methods of removal: first, boarding infant children; second, enrolling Native children into a federal Indian boarding school; and third, attempting and at times succeeding in the fostering or adoption of Native children. Aside from low wages and poor conditions, Native women in the outing program faced unique issues directly related to live-in work. Women who labored in the program were in a predicament. While cooking, cleaning, and living in the home of their employers, Native women struggled to raise their own children within the home. They were chastised by both employers and outing matrons for having the audacity to raise their own. Women with especially young children and some first-time single mothers had it worse.

Outing records reveal that women with children—especially young children—were encouraged to board out their children in local nurseries or similar institutions. If the child was at least six years old, matrons, employers, and BIA officials advocated for enrolling children of outing mothers in an Indian boarding school. Finally, in the most precarious of situations, matrons attempted and sometimes succeeded in adopting or fostering Native children. While the latter was not always achieved, this final scenario was a regularly looming threat.

Whereas Indian children were seen as an obstacle to employment, officials assumed Indian women to be unfit mothers and Indian homes to be unhealthy and backward. Commissioner Sells, who authorized the outing program, claimed that Indian mothers simply did not know how to keep their children well. They were ignorant of best practices and raised their children in dirty, overcrowded, unkempt homes. The government decided that Indian women were meant to be not mothers but surrogates. The Bay Area Outing Program therefore presented an illogical contradiction. Native women were seen as incapable of raising their own children yet simultaneously deemed ideal caretakers of their employers' children. While Sells and his contemporaries chastised Native women's childrearing practices, these same abilities were considered appropriate in white homes when directed toward white children. Rarely did outing matrons or other officials comment on this ironic arrangement. Little was done to justify it. But policy and practice speak volumes. Further, these practices were in the interest of the matron's job security and kept the outing program running. Institutionalizing children allowed their mothers to be employed as domestics. Therefore, this illogical contradiction illuminates the intentions of outing. Labor was paramount, and motherhood was not. Thus, Indian children were better managed and raised by the state. Adoptive and foster homes, Indian boarding schools, and other institutions would better parent Indian children. In particular, women who had not yet assimilated to Euro-American norms needed to relinquish their children so that they would have better lives. In the face of overwhelming messages of inferiority and incompetency, it would not be surprising if Native women, especially young, single women with their entire lives seemingly ahead of them, internalized these ideas.

Some women, like Ford and Pensotti, felt their children were better off in the hands of the government. Perhaps because of economic hardship, lack of stability, or an unplanned pregnancy, these women felt their babies had needs they could not meet. Some women in similar circumstances still imagined better lives for their children. Gertie Wasson, for example, did not want her son William to be sent to Stewart, where she had been raised. As a product of the boarding school, she knew too well the suffering he would endure. And where some women consented to board their children out or relinquished them, others fought against it. Maude Mitchell and Daisy Plummer were vocal about their wishes in conversations with Matrons Royce and Van Every, refusing to have their children taken away. Plummer and Mitchell threatened to get their fathers involved in the matter, and when Mitchell had had enough, she left the outing program. Whereas some women could afford to board their children in local nurseries or were fortunate enough to leave their children with relatives, others could not.

As this chapter has examined, the early twentieth century was a precarious period for Native families involved with outing in the Bay Area. Outing matrons stringently monitored Native women and made it their business to manage many aspects of their lives, especially when it came to their children. At times, outing program officials worked hard to help abandoned or neglected children, but elsewhere they consigned children to Indian boarding schools to be raised by the state. Overwhelmingly, outing intervention amounted to threats of child removal and separation of Native children from their mothers. For many Native women outing in the Bay Area, there was a promise of city life and wage work. But this came at a cost.

Native women, especially as young single mothers, were often forced to choose between their children or the outing program. While some mothers were able to navigate these conflicting demands, others were not. Their experiences demonstrate that BIA officials regularly disregarded Native women's wishes, intervening with the help of city and county agencies in the effort to separate Native children from their mothers. In the face of these profound forces, Native women both complied and contested.

FIVE
Containment, Sexual Surveillance, and Bodily Regulation

Scholars have noted the simple yet poignant fact that Indian policy had profound effects on Indian bodies. Myriam Vučković argues that in the assimilation campaign of the late nineteenth and early twentieth centuries, "the body became a contested territory."[1] The creation and implementation of reservations, rancherias, and Indian boarding schools worked to transform and discipline Indian bodies, controlling them through productive labor, social relations, and sexuality. This control was gendered, often centering on Native girls and women. The Bay Area Outing Program was part and parcel of this project. Monitoring and exploiting Native women's bodies served the interests of the nation-state. Girls entering the outing program did so through various "scales of containment."[2] This term refers to the many levels at which Native women were contained in the early twentieth century. Their lives often started on regulated reservations, then passed into Indian boarding schools, and later into outing homes. In the Bay Area, they were subjected to further institutions of containment. This framework demonstrates the ways the settler state attempted and at times succeeded in managing and controlling Native bodies, and how it did so specifically through the Bay Area Outing Program. Throughout their lives, these girls and women experienced various forms of bodily control.

This chapter demonstrates how bodily regulation unfolded on Native women domestic workers in the twentieth-century Bay Area. Scholars have examined sexual health and sexual surveillance in the context of boarding schools and on reservations, for instance monitoring schoolgirls' menarche or Crow women's access to reproductive health.[3] While a recent study briefly examines mid-twentieth-century Urban Indian reproductive health, none have considered Urban Indian women's surveillance and health in the early part of the century, particularly as it connects to carcerality. This chapter addresses the overarching question, How did sexual surveillance in the Bay Area Outing Program affect Native women? To this end, I connect a brief history of early twentieth-century Indian health with the nationwide prevalence of sexually transmitted infections. While gonorrhea and other diseases were common, in the early twentieth-century United States, syphilis was by far the most deadly and difficult to treat. In my analysis of this highly stigmatized disease, I highlight how efforts to fight venereal disease targeted the "immoral" woman. These ideologies fused the notion of female delinquency and sexually transmitted diseases, leading to widespread policing of young women's bodies. I connect this history to sexual surveillance within the Bay Area Outing Program and the criminalization of Native women.

While some Native women may have appreciated the outing program, I focus on four illustrative cases to demonstrate prevalent themes throughout its history: bodily control, surveillance, scales of containment, and "care." In doing so, I examine the structural forces of outing—including a close look into local detention homes, asylums, and related institutions. Through these intimate stories and my analysis of "care"—particularly the violence of its application on Native women—I interrogate how Native women's bodies were surveilled and controlled by the settler state.

Indian Health and Sexually Transmitted Infections

In the context of this chapter, it is important to understand the basic foundations of Indian health and sexual health. In the early nineteenth century, Native peoples' access to government-based Indian health services was haphazard. The establishment of reservations—and with them, confinement—led to exacerbated health issues. Disease swept across Indian Country, resulting in large casualty rates. Minor improvements in the late nineteenth century still resulted in inadequate care and delivery of services. The Indian Service medical staff faced several challenges, including a lack of qualifications, inadequate staffing, limited resources, an excessive workload, and insufficient compensation. Given these circumstances, quality federal health care for Native peoples was impossible. Unhealthy conditions on reservations and in boarding schools negatively impacted the overall health of Native communities. Allotment policy mandated poorly constructed permanent homes that led to further spread of disease.[4] Moreover, officials filled Indian boarding schools at all costs, even if admitting potentially contagious children who had not received proper health care. As schools exceeded capacity, children were forced to share beds, towels, and other items that further spread infections. Amid disease and outbreaks, some administrators prioritized Indian boarding school administration over Native children's lives.[5] While some Indian officials attempted to improve sanitation and segregate contagious patients in Indian sanatoriums and hospitals, it was not enough. Throughout Indian Country, diseases such as tuberculosis spread like wildfire. By 1935, the incidence rate of tuberculosis among Indians was five times greater than among non-Native people.[6] This will be further addressed in chapter 6, where I focus on the tuberculosis epidemic and its effect in the outing program.

While tuberculosis devastated Indian Country, a silent epidemic of sexually transmitted infections (STIs) was widespread across the United States. In the early twentieth century, syphilis and other venereal diseases were regarded as a moral issue. Those who suffered from STIs were not considered victims but degenerates. Even so, serious diseases like syphilis were quite prevalent.[7] In 1918, syphilis affected anywhere from 5 to 20 percent of the US population.[8] By the 1930s, one in ten Americans had syphilis.[9] Syphilis is a bacterial disease—a blood-borne pathogen transmitted via sexual activity. The disease largely has three stages; first, simple skin lesions on the genitals; second, a rash on the body; and third, dilatation and/or rupture of heart vessels, as well as dementia or insanity. The medical narration of syphilis indicated an unhealthy body, one which in turn suggested eugenic notions of abnormality and criminality. Those afflicted with the illness were often slated for sterilization. Syphilis was a covert disease that could be transmitted without the knowledge of the sick or of the infected. Syphilis, unlike some diseases, is not immediately apparent despite its deadly nature.[10] While no reliable cures existed, a method of testing to identify the disease was discovered at the turn of the century.

In 1906, August von Wassermann discovered the serologic testing of syphilis, which revealed the disease at an asymptomatic stage.[11] In the early twentieth century, the "Wassermann test" became the most common means of identifying syphilis. However, treatment was difficult. Arsphenamine therapy could be effective but was toxic and difficult to administer, and it required years of treatment. Only 25 percent of patients ever completed the therapy.[12] For the most part, the United States prioritized venereal disease treatment (particularly syphilis) only during World War I and World War II. In fact, syphilis was the major cause of rejection among World War I recruits, which inspired anti–venereal disease programming. Such efforts were gender-biased, often blaming "loose women" with "khaki fever," or "khaki-mad girls," as purveyors of disease.[13] Later, the Great Depression eroded venereal disease control programs even as economic desperation increased the rate of prostitution and, with it, the spread of venereal diseases. Treatment could be expensive, and stigma hindered conversations about syphilis, contributing to its continued silent spread.[14] In 1939, California joined other states requiring syphilis testing for marriage license applicants as a means to prevent the disease from being transmitted to a spouse or future children.[15] The idea was that syphilitic individuals should not be allowed to reproduce.

Such ideologies colored the tone of efforts against venereal disease, especially with regard to young women. Fear of young women's sexuality and the spread of venereal disease went hand in hand with the eugenics movement. Sexually active "immoral" women were a threat to the purity of the nation.[16] Eugenicists feared that newly arrived immigrants would pollute the American gene pool, not just with their un-American blood, but by spreading venereal disease. The same was assumed of people of color. Accordingly, efforts to eliminate venereal disease fixated on and led to further policing of women, particularly younger working-class women. In 1918, during World War I, the Commission on Training Camp Activities—charged with making military training camps free from vice and venereal disease—adopted a new gendered policy: compulsory physical examination, detention, and quarantine of women suspected of harboring a venereal disease. Local governments enacted similar laws. Any woman suspected of having a sexually transmitted infection could be arrested and detained—without bail—until examined and confirmed negative. By March 1918, thirty-two states had enacted such measures.[17] Given the focus on STIs and female delinquency, the two became inseparable. Consequently, juvenile detention centers conducted compulsory pelvic exams aimed at determining whether girls were still virgins. Detainees were thoroughly interrogated about their sexual encounters, tested for STIs, and treated if ill. In early twentieth-century Los Angeles, all youths detained at Juvenile Hall were tested for syphilis and gonorrhea.[18] Bay Area–based outing girls were subject to these same policies in Alameda County juvenile detention centers, but as racialized subjects, they were especially targeted for fear that they would contaminate their employers. This was a common occurrence in the Bay Area.

Pathologizing People of Color

In late nineteenth-century San Francisco, Chinese servants, mostly men often referred to as "houseboys," were commonplace. They largely predated Native domestic workers. These men were already pathologized on the basis of their immigrant status. Because of the intimate nature of these men's work in white homes, health officials were quick to assert the threat the men posed to their employers' health. Rather than questioning the role of white heads of households in contracting disease from extramarital encounters, officials blamed Chinese men for bringing venereal disease into white homes.[19] Therefore, the Chinese domestic servant was paradoxically responsible for household cleanliness and also the transmission of STIs.[20] These racialized fears of contamination were present in California-based outing programs as well.

Throughout the late nineteenth and early twentieth centuries, the government pathologized Native people. The assumption that Indian girls were vectors for disease was prevalent among outing employers. For instance, in Southern California, before Quechan women from Fort Yuma could work in Los Angeles, they underwent detailed physical examinations. Physicians searched for chicken pox, diphtheria, measles, tuberculosis, typhoid, scarlet fever, smallpox, and whooping cough. These exams appeared to be less venereal in nature, but they still ran the gamut.[21] Even a clean bill of health was not always sufficient for employers, however. In 1934, after clearing a health exam, a fourteen-year-old Mojave girl arrived in Los Angeles only to be rejected by her outing employers. She had scratched herself on a bush and had visible lesions on her legs. The family was so frightened that she might spread disease in their household that they sent her away. News in the community traveled fast, and the young girl was never able to secure work in the area again. As Kevin Whalen argues, "Regardless of the quality of their work, young women in the outing system would always be viewed as possible vectors of disease."[22] These same fears subsisted in the Southwest in Tucson's outing program and inspired federal efforts to contain Native women's sexuality.

Morality, Controlling Sexuality, and Health Clearances

Tucson's outing program closely reflected the structure of the Bay Area Outing Program in that it was largely independent from Indian boarding schools and solely placed Indian girls and women. Likewise, its administration cultivated similar anxieties over sex and sexuality. Given the proximity of Tohono O'odham villages and the culture of Indian indenture in the Southwest, Native women domestic workers were common in Tucson at the turn of the century. As federal officials considered appointing an outing matron to manage these women, they did so with the knowledge of the recently scandalized Phoenix outing program.

The Phoenix Indian School had started its outing program in the 1890s and, in line with other western outing programs, largely operated as an employment agency privileging labor over education. The school placed two hundred students annually, the majority of whom were domestic servants.[23] In the fall of 1902, a scandal erupted in Phoenix: unsupervised reservation Indians were found gambling, drinking, swearing, and engaging in "immorality"—that is, sexual relations. The scandal resulted in what amounted to the closure of the Phoenix outing program. The program eventually reopened with the appointment of an outing matron named Amanda Chingren, who embodied a new systematic approach to outing. In addition to placing girls and inspecting their workplaces, she policed their activities at work and after hours to ensure no further scandals. Prior to placement, she required girls to submit health certificates to rule out pregnancy or STIS.[24] The Phoenix Indian School superintendent also granted Chingren the power to punish or jail local Native women, outing or not. Robert Trennert reports that Chingren could deprive girls of employment, force marriages, banish them to the reservation, and even have them jailed if their personal lives did not conform to her standards.[25] For the Office of Indian Affairs, policing and managing Native women was paramount.

Victoria Haskins argues that domestic employment in Tucson was centered on controlling Native women's sexuality. While there was consideration for ensuring girls' proper treatment, outing matrons who managed placements were expected to monitor their charges' sexuality—especially in the context of common-law and "plural" marriages and the fear of prostitution.[26] The "red slave problem," that is, the prostitution or concubinage of Indian women and interracial sex, was especially troublesome. The fear of Indian women being seduced by white men, becoming pregnant, and having mixed-raced babies was the primary impetus for hiring a Tucson outing matron.[27] Tucsonan housewives were similarly troubled over their housemaids and the "great dangers" present in the city. In the interest of the girls' "moral integrity," they signed petitions demanding a space for the girls' social interaction and recreation.[28] Local clerics supported the appeal under the pretense that it would save the young women from becoming "girls of the street."[29] While ostensibly for "recreation," the space was intended for containment and control of Native women and their bodies.

The program's first outing matron, Minnie Estabrook, worked to prevent "immoral" sexual relations among the young domestics and to provide both space and "amusements"—safe middle-class activities—that would keep girls from scandal. However, the threat of scandal was less about the girls than the program's reputation and that of the matron. The matron took her role in policing Native women's sexual lives very seriously. Once, she accompanied a police officer to an outing home, where they found an outing girl in bed with a white man. The two were swiftly arrested and charged for "illicit cohabitation." After the incident, the matron was deputized, granting her the power to independently raid and arrest her charges.[30] Estabrook was similarly invested in arranging marriages among outing girls and preventing "illegitimate" children.[31]

A later Tucson outing matron deployed an Indian policeman to ensure that girls returned to their outing homes on the weekends. Local Indian dances held on Sunday were especially concerning for fear that they might "debauch" young Native women.[32] This same matron was known for hosting "courting bees," where she engaged in matchmaking among outing girls and boys—extending her control over their sexuality and relationships. In Tucson, forcing or arranging marriages was a common practice—ostensibly to protect and uplift Indian women while espousing assimilation. For outing matrons, legal marriage seemed to equate to financial security and making women less vulnerable to abandonment. However, Haskins argues that marriage represented an intense distrust of Indian women's sexual and social independence.[33] Seen from this perspective, legal marriage was simply another form of containing and managing Native women and their sexuality. This further prevented the prospect of "illegitimate" children.

Brianna Theobald has found that field nurses on reservations—similar to their outing matron counterparts—dedicated particular attention to the "problem" of "illegitimate" pregnancies. Although these issues were considered inconsequential within Native communities, they often became justification for a Native woman's continued surveillance, or even coerced sterilization, by authorities from outside the community.[34] Some physicians were particularly proactive about sterilizing women who had been infected with a venereal disease. According to Theobald, in the 1930s and 1940s, Indian Service social workers became actively involved in arranging for the eugenics-based institutionalization and/or sterilization of Native women.[35] Indeed, these same tactics were employed in the Bay Area Outing Program. One of the first steps in that direction was outing health clearances.

In the 1930s, at the peak of the Bay Area Outing Program, matrons required all Native women and girls to submit a health clearance prior to placement. Whether fifteen years old or twenty-six, women could not secure a position without it. Superficially, these clearances were meant to protect homeowners from contracting illness from Native women—which frames Indian women as pathologically unhealthy. However, as with the aforementioned Tucson outing program and a similar program at the Sherman school, these health clearances were interested in a more detailed knowledge of the young women's sexual activity, if they had contracted sexually transmitted infections, or if they were pregnant.

For instance, in 1933, eighteen-year-old Hazel Emm, a Washoe and Paiute girl from Schurz, Nevada, was required to submit a health clearance prior to laboring in the Bay Area.[36] Similarly, fifteen-year-old Alice Marshall Nix, a Hualapai and Hoopa girl, received a doctor's note of clearance just days before her start of employment in San Anselmo, California. She was reportedly "free from all and any communicable diseases."[37] Marcie Martin, a twenty-three-year-old Mono woman from North Fork, California, participated in outing in 1931. Her record includes a note from a Madera, California, physician certifying a negative Wassermann test for syphilis.[38] The test results, dated a year prior, suggest that Indian girls might be expected to have these results on record and that some other agency or institution may have requested them. No other form of "health record" exists in Martin's file—indicating that outing matrons were indeed primarily interested Native women and girls' sexual behavior rather than their health more generally.

Records indicate that women and girls were required to have current health clearances throughout their time in the program. In 1934, about two years after her first stint in the outing program, Martin wrote to Matron Royce in search of another domestic job, promising to be "good."[39] She was also interested in returning to her old employer in Berkeley, Mrs. Gurnett. Martin wrote to Royce: "Find out whether if Mrs. Gurnett wants me back or not. . . . I do really want to find a job if you do want to place me. I'll be good if I [go] to Oakland. I['ll] be willing to get on [a] bus back soon."[40] In return, Royce's assistant, Jeannette Traxler, wrote Marcie reminding her that "before we can go further in regard to a position for you, you will have to send us a Doctor's certificate stating that you are in good physical condition."[41]

In other exchanges, matrons were more explicit about the fear of contamination among white outing homeowners. In 1935, Matron Mildred Van Every made notes on Patricia Ince, a young Native woman who was not outing, but one whom the matron had considered for outing work. Ince had contracted and supposedly recovered from syphilis. Van Every indicated, "I told her to get the medical certificate from the Yolo County Hospital, where she had last been treated, and if she was non-contagious she could be recommended for work."[42] Records reveal a few confirmed cases of syphilis and other venereal disease among the outing women. Overwhelmingly, however, the agency was interested in tracking and passing judgment on what it perceived as "promiscuous" behavior among girls and women in the program. Because all women post-1930 were required to submit health clearances, all women were implicated.[43]

In her analysis of midcentury Indian Relocation, Brianna Theobald found that relocation officers also required health clearances—perhaps based on their knowledge of the difficulties outing mothers had experienced decades prior. Relocation officers were skeptical that single mothers could achieve self-sufficiency in the city, for they would be burdened by the demands of both wage earning and childcare. This was an issue that was certainly present in the Bay Area Outing Program. Further, relocated individuals and families had only limited access to health insurance that did not cover childbirth. Labor and delivery in a local hospital could easily result in impossible medical debt. To preempt these issues, the BIA eventually mandated that all pregnant women be disqualified from relocation. To this end, individuals interested in relocation were required to submit Form 5-422, known as the Indian Family Health Certificate. This certificate required a doctor's examination at the BIA's expense.[44] Because Indian children were seen as a barrier to labor, one of the core goals was to rule out pregnancy.

Nonetheless, many relocated women sought medical care, particularly for delivery of their children at their reservation hospitals, simply because this medical care was free of cost. While this temporary return to the reservation was discouraged by relocation officers, they had no choice but to accept the conditions.[45] By contrast, in the Bay Area Outing Program, outing matrons and federal officials embraced reservation-based hospital care particularly for long-term illness and convalescence. This was rationalized by the fact that only county residents had access to long-term medical care in the Bay

Area. Because many outing women were Bay Area residents for only short and noncontiguous stints, this made many ineligible for such care. Outing women, however, were able to access a more limited range of local medical services, in particular support during childbirth and emergency (including dental) care. They sometimes paid out of pocket from their meager wages for these services. Outing matrons often tapped into local services to subsidize or completely cover outing women's medical costs. For instance, the Salvation Army Home was a common destination for single pregnant women. I encountered several cases in the archives of outing women who birthed their children at their Oakland location.

In the early twentieth-century United States, widespread disease afflicted Indian Country, and venereal diseases like gonorrhea and syphilis were prevalent. These infections were also present in boarding schools, though less is known about from whom students contracted the disease or if the act in question was consensual. This silent epidemic largely went unimpeded because of respectability politics and stigma. Antivenereal efforts particularly targeted the "immoral" woman. While the fear of contamination was gendered, it was also racialized. In Southern California and the Bay Area, outing women were required to submit detailed health clearances, including the results of testing for sexually transmitted infections. Even with a clean bill of health, however, employers feared that Native women would spread disease in their homes. In Tucson, these fears of contamination and delinquency inspired federal efforts to contain Native women's sexuality. Whether through orchestrated "courting bees," arrests, or arranged marriages, matrons policed Native women's sexual lives. This policing, in partnership with eugenicist ideas, could result in the institutionalization and or sterilization of Native women.

These were the conditions outing women experienced in the early twentieth-century Bay Area. Native women born on reservations and raised in Indian boarding schools experienced "scales of containment." In these institutions, they were surrounded by death and disease. Adding the unchecked epidemic of venereal disease in the United States only amplified these circumstances. Once in the Bay Area, they became objects of multilayered societal fears—of disease and contagion, and of STIs and immorality. Outing matrons, federal officials, and homeowners who employed outing girls and women maintained the mythology of Native women as prone to disease, naturally unhealthy, and sexually active. These young women were perceived as laboring yet potentially contaminated bodies that required control and containment. In short, the experiences of Bay Area outing women and girls was colored by pathologization, "immorality," and sexual surveillance.

Rosita Elliott

In 1935, sixteen-year-old Rosita Elliott outed for a brief stint at a Berkeley home. The young Pomo woman had attended Stewart Indian School until fifth grade. As with other girls her age, she worked for fifteen dollars a month. Within a week of her arrival, however, she was detained at the Alameda County Detention Home. Elliott's file is incomplete and does not indicate the transgression that sent her to detention. However, while incarcerated, Elliott underwent an invasive medical exam. The exam was likely paired with an interrogation about her sexual history. While the majority of detained women—and men for that matter—would have been subjected to such an exam, Elliott's file is unique, for it contains the Alameda County Detention Home exam record.[46] This rare document indicated that Elliott's hymen had been ruptured, though not recently. It also indicated that her last menstruation was three to four months ago. It is possible that Elliott was pregnant. Such an exam result would have marked Elliott as a "sexual delinquent." In detention, she was likely segregated from her peers to prevent "moral corruption,"[47] contributing to her experience of isolation.

We cannot know for sure if Elliott was pregnant, nor, as the matrons would have put it, who was "responsible for her condition." We cannot guess if the act was consensual. But the matron's actions indicate that she was expecting. This information would have been crucial for the matron to convey to authorities, particularly since Elliott was an orphan. Consequently, Matron Van Every, acting as a social worker, quickly notified the Mendocino County Welfare Department. While the county social agent was "surprised" to learn of the news, she promptly sent a check to Van Every to cover Elliott's return fare. She was sent home shortly thereafter. Although today we know a broken hymen is not necessarily indicative of sexual intercourse, authorities at the time considered it as proof. While Elliott's file ends after this letter, her experience is telling of the interconnected realities of labor, incarceration, and sexuality for Native women in California's juvenile justice system. It also briefly demonstrates the scales at which Native women were contained—in her case, both in her employer's outing home and in the Alameda County Detention Home.

Carrie Spencer

The following case further illuminates the scales of containment that encompassed Native women's lives. As a student at Sherman Institute in Riverside, Carrie Spencer and her peers were contained. When outing in Southern California, they were contained in their respective outing homes. Her containment continued while outing in the Bay Area. Spencer's file is incomplete and does not list her places of employment or pay. We do know, however, that while in the Bay Area she became pregnant, and Matron Royce forced her into the Salvation Army Home in Oakland. The home was a common destination for pregnant women, especially single outing mothers. Spencer's file indicates she was taken to the home against her will. On October 9, 1925, a fellow outing girl, named Avery, wrote Spencer from a seven-bedroom, five-bath Queen Anne Victorian in Oakland. She wrote, "Received your loving letter this morning and believe me I was sure glad to hear from you. Lola called me up the other day and told me that Mrs. Royce put you down there at the Salvation Army Home. Gee kid. But I am only glad that you are there so you don't have to worry. There is plenty of time for you to go to work again, and I know you will make good for your future."[48]

Over a month later, on November 19, Spencer wrote to Royce from the Salvation Army Home, "Pardon me I would like to know how long am I going to stay here, or do I stay here until I pay for the board? I guess it will be mighty hard for me to get out, if I don't hear from home."[49] Spencer was waiting to hear from her parents and clearly hoped for their intervention, to no avail. Months later, Spencer was still in the Salvation Army Home and had delivered her son. As a single mother, she was in the process of applying for aid. However, conversations regarding child support quickly led to discussions of committing Spencer to the Sonoma State Home—a notorious institution for the "feebleminded."

Superintendent Parrett of the Walker River Agency agreed that the young mother should be committed. He felt that Spencer's elderly parents could not care for her or her child: "They could not pay anything for Carrie's care in the past and are unable at present to provide anything for her present or future support, or for the support of the child." Parrett believed that Spencer and her child's only hope was institutionalization:

> If Carrie is committed to Sonoma, the matter of care of the baby still remains unprovided for. Our Indian schools will not take infants . . . but the case of Carrie Spencer is similar to some others which we have had where no thought or provision has been for the future. Carrie has no property, money, or otherwise, here, and is without means of support and her parents are barely able to get along and there seems to be no other alternative, except that Carrie and her child be cared for by the state or by some charitable institution.[50]

Shortly after Parrett's approval, Spencer was committed. In October of 1926, the Sonoma State Home granted her a leave of absence for six weeks.[51] In December, the Bishop Sub-agency wrote Royce to check in on Spencer's status. Some months prior, her father had apparently consented to an operation for his daughter, and the agent desired to know Spencer's whereabouts and "what was done with the baby."[52] For months, her parents had gone without information on their daughter or grandson. Even more heinous, the leave of absence paired with a vague reference to an operation suggests that Spencer may have been sterilized. The Sonoma State Home was infamous for compulsory sterilization, and a young woman like Spencer, with no money or resources and a child "out of wedlock," would have been a prime target. F. O. Butler, the medical superintendent at Sonoma—the same man who signed Spencer's release form—sold eugenic sterilization as not only a panacea for social ills but also a restorative procedure beneficial to the defective or diseased body. Contrary to popular belief, California state law allowed sterilization with or without familial consent,[53] but Butler was intent on getting said consent. Although Spencer's records are incomplete, it is very likely that she was sterilized while incarcerated at Sonoma.[54]

Years later, Spencer was still detained at the Sonoma State Home. On July 14, 1928, L. L. Goen, a Bishop Sub-agency official, wrote Royce on behalf of Spencer's parents, "Carrie's parents are anxious about her, in fact, worrying. They do not know why she is detained in the home." According to Goen, Carrie was recommitted to the Sonoma State Home and had been detained there for the last six months. Spencer's parents were worried for their grandson and desired to gain custody of him. Goen hoped Royce might intervene to "relieve the mental strain of the parents."[55]

In response, Royce was unforgiving, stating that Spencer had always been a "problem." She declared, "After her baby came, I thought she might settle down and care for it, but she was worse than ever." Spencer apparently contracted an STI, and Royce called her a "moral degenerate." Employing eugenic terms, Royce accused her of promiscuity and criminality. Local authorities—perhaps a detention home—mentally and physically examined Spencer, as a result of which she was recommitted to the Sonoma State Home. While separated from his mother, Roland Spencer was boarded with the Ladies' Relief nursery in Oakland. Reportedly, he received the "best of care." While Royce washed her hands of Spencer, she admitted to Goen, "I will recommend that Carrie go home if it is your desire and you think her influence at home will not be too bad."[56]

On August 2, 1928, Goen petitioned for Spencer's parole from the Sonoma State Home. Spencer's parents were "pleading" for their daughter and grandson to come home. In the petition, Goen had to confirm his own role in Spencer's continued surveillance: "If you are willing to parole her and send her and the child here [I] will supervise them and do the best possible to have her live a pure life. Should she become obstinate or unmanageable while here we may return her to your institution."[57] In order to be considered for parole, Spencer had to be surveilled and contained in another space—her home reservation in southeastern California.

Months later, Spencer was finally reunited with her son and her parents. In December of 1928, Goen reported to Royce, "It sure was a happy reunion. Carrie says she does not want to go back to Sonoma State Home, and has promised me she will be good, if we will not send her back."[58] Promises to be "good" were a tactic that Native women had to employ to break incarceration, gain some autonomy, and be reunited with their families. Fortunately, in Spencer's case, it worked. Nonetheless, her parole and freedom were dependent on continued supervision and surveillance, so she might live a "pure life." Shortly after the reunion, Royce withdrew the entirety of Spencer's outing wages—minus nearly five dollars—and sent the funds for Goen to manage.[59] Her file with the outing program ends shortly thereafter. Hopefully, Spencer never returned to the Sonoma State Home.

Spencer's case indicates the scales of containment Native women experienced. As an adult outing in the Bay Area, she was confined in outing homes and, after she became pregnant, was kept in the Salvation Army Home. Thereafter, she was detained by local authorities—likely in a detention home. Per their recommendation, she was thereafter committed to the Sonoma State Home against her will and that of her parents. Only after federal authorities assured her continued surveillance on the reservation was she able to return home and be reunited with her parents and son.

Patricia Ince

A similar case describes how sexual surveillance and containment went hand in hand, even for women not participating in outing programs. In the spring of 1934, a young Klamath woman named Patricia Ince came to the Bay Area from Woodland, California. The nineteen-year-old had been living in Woodland with her father after her mother had passed away. Ince had gone to school in Happy Camp, California, and had spent a couple of years at the Sherman Institute. She was not in the Bay Area for outing and had managed on her own, living with friends and then in an Oakland boarding house, enjoying life in the city. When Ince contracted an STI, however, the outing program intervened. As was fairly common, outing matrons or officials from the "Indian Placement Office" made it their duty to address issues among all Native women in the area. Jeannette Traxler, Royce's former assistant, took over for the matron and begrudgingly handled the case.

According to records, Ince came to Traxler for advice in seeking medical treatment. The University Hospital San Francisco had recently diagnosed the young woman with syphilis and she needed further treatment. Well aware of the stigma associated with STIs, Ince initially sought medical care under a pseudonym, "Peggy Phillips." However, when the hospital discovered the fact, she "became frightened" and, likely in fear of legal ramifications, fled. Traxler's notes on the case indicate that Ince was not one of "our working, supervised girls." According to Traxler, she "just drifted here and lived a promiscuous life."[60] Clearly Traxler had already washed her hands of the girl, well before she started on the case.

Still unaware of the pseudonym on March 9, 1934, Traxler wrote Superintendent Boggess of the Hoopa Valley Indian Agency in search of a "Peggy Phillips." The young woman needed at least a year of treatment for syphilis, and Traxler was investigating if the Indian agency could provide. Traxler added, "She is not one of our working girls and we have not had any supervision over her, but like all Indians they come to this office whenever in trouble."[61] Unsurprisingly, Boggess founds no record for the alias. After realizing that Ince had "disappeared," Traxler reached out to a social welfare worker in Woodland, California. On March 21, 1934, Agent Porter informed Traxler that Ince had returned to Woodland and was under the "care" of their probation officer, who took the young woman to a physician.[62] Days later, O. H. Lipps of the Sacramento Indian Agency explained to Traxler that in order for Ince to receive the necessary treatment, she needed to be committed to the Ventura School for Girls. Reportedly this was agreeable to Ince, and the probation officer would handle her transfer to the institution.[63]

The next year, Mildred Van Every replaced Traxler as the social worker for the US Indian Service. On January 24, 1935, physician George Uhl wrote to Van Every, indicating that Ince had been treated for syphilis by Yolo County for the last six months and that her last Wassermann (syphilis) test was negative. Uhl wrote, "I feel that she is now non-contagious at the present time, but that a continuous course of Anti-Luetic therapy is indicated to completely cure her condition."[64] According to Uhl, the issue was handled, yet records show that despite efforts to surveil and contain her, Ince's care fell through the cracks.

Only two days later, on January 26, 1935, Van Every wrote to the social welfare worker in Woodland. Ince had returned to the Bay Area, but contrary to Dr. Uhl's assertion, she had *not* received the necessary medical treatment. In fact, the Alameda Health Clinic indicated that Ince needed further treatment for syphilis and also gonorrhea.[65] It seems that while Ince had been in the Ventura home for three months, she received no treatment for her STIS. She was simply contained in one of California's notorious juvenile institutions. Ventura School for Girls was not a school but California's only female state reformatory. Though it opened with the goal of being a "progressive" correctional facility, within years of its opening, the institution faced charges for inhumane punishment, including restricted diets, solitary confinement, deprivation of medical care, and hosings.[66] Between 1910 and 1940, many youths from this "school" were sterilized with or without their families' consent, as allowed by California state law.[67] Though records are absent on this issue, it is entirely possible that Ince was sterilized while incarcerated in Ventura. Ince, ill, alone, and with nowhere to turn, stayed at the Alameda County Probation Home waiting for some recourse. It never arrived.

Van Every continued to research feasible treatment options for Ince, petitioning Roy Nash, field representative of the US Indian Service, on the case. She wrote that the Alameda County Clinic was "willing to take her for temporary treatments and I've gotten permission to keep her at the Alameda County Probation Home, though only temporarily. The Ventura Home for Girls does not house or treat venereal diseases." Van Every's research revealed that the Ventura home in fact did not treat venereal diseases. Whether or not her predecessors knew this, they had justified her incarceration at Ventura because she needed treatment. Ultimately that justification was a lie, suggesting the likelihood that the goal of sending Ince to Ventura was merely to incarcerate her and perhaps facilitate her sterilization.

Van Every's letter to Nash noted one other avenue of treatment. She wrote, "The Pacific Protective Society charges $20 a month which needless to say I cannot guarantee."[68] The society, based in Oakland, provided institutional care for "venereally" infected infants and girls under twenty-one years of age. The majority of girls were referred from juvenile court, and most were between fifteen and twenty-one years old.[69] In addition to medical treatment, the society focused on "social rehabilitation." Admitted girls were committed for at least a year or fifteen months on average. The "home, hospital and school" largely amounted to house arrest within the home.[70] While perhaps better than Ventura, particularly for its ability to treat venereal diseases, it was also another form of containment. Nonetheless, the fact remained that said treatment would incur a cost—monies the OIA was not prepared to cover. Matron Van Every explained that both the Sacramento Indian Agency and the Hoopa Valley Agency believed that Ince was a "county charge"—meaning they felt her county of residence should handle and pay for her medical treatment—a common practice at the time. Therefore, whereas the outing program in its guise as an extension of the OIA attempted to address Ince's care, Van Every's research indicated that no Indian agency was willing to actually provide or facilitate that care. Interestingly, Van Every cited Circular 3051, an internal OIA document regarding the order of "quarantining Indians with contagious or infectious diseases."[71] In the same breath, she called Ince a "public menace" who was nonetheless willing to be treated. Clearly, Van Every was aware of the seriousness of Ince's case but renounced the young woman and was ultimately beholden to Roy Nash's decision.

Nash's response was unsympathetic. He simply stated, "If she is not a federal charge, I see no way of hospitalizing her in Indian service hospitals. She will have to be taken care of just like any white girl under the same circumstances."[72] But Ince was not treated like any "white girl." She was treated like an Indian girl. She was shifted from carceral space to carceral space. First she was sent to a detention home, then she stayed with a Woodland probation officer, followed by three months at the Ventura School for Girls. Once in the Bay Area, Ince was in the Alameda County Probation Home. For nearly a year she had been shifted from one institution to the next. A young woman with an illness that can be terminal if not treated properly did not get the care she needed. Officials were more concerned with containing her than the disease.

On January 28, Ince was taken to the Alameda Health Clinic, where she was briefly treated. She left shortly thereafter. On February 5, Ince and, as Van Every put it, her "alleged husband" came into the outing office and asked Van Every to "call off the Police." Ince and her partner were well aware of the legal intervention her health issues had brought forth. Had she in fact been like any "white girl," she would have likely gotten the care she needed and evaded the authorities. Unfortunately, we may never know if Ince received the care she so desperately needed. Her file ends just after her visit to the outing office. Ince's case demonstrates that Native women—even ones not involved in the program—were subjected to scales of containment through the outing program. Though Traxler and Van Every attempted to get Ince the medical care she needed, their "help" or "care" equated to further surveillance and control of her body. Their assessment that she was a "promiscuous drifter" and a "menace" only made matters worse. Despite the energy spent on locating Ince and containing her in several institutions, the young woman was left without proper treatment. Even while outside of the scope of the outing program, Ince was nonetheless subjected to its control and surveillance.

Lila Keisner

Lila Keisner was nineteen years old when she joined the outing program in 1929.[73] Records suggest that before her placement, she had already been living in the Bay Area. Keisner worked at various East Bay homes between 1929 and 1933, garnering fairly impressive wages of forty to sixty dollars a month. She earned her lowest wage of twenty-five dollars a month at the end of her outing career. Keisner came from Beatrice, California, where she had attended public school. Prior to outing, she had her first child, Lesley, in January 1928. While she outed, her son was boarded at the Ladies' Relief nursery. This might explain her higher wages, as infant boarding typically cost twenty-five dollars a month. In February 1931, after working briefly at a Piedmont home, Keisner left and apparently married.

A few months later, in mid-April of 1931, Lesley's father gained custody of his two-year-old son and moved him to Ukiah.[74] On April 14, 1931, Keisner's sister Hazel wrote to Royce to inquire about her sister and the baby. Hazel wrote, "I wonder what is the matter with sis Lila. Seems to be something the matter with her and we can't figure her out. . . . I heard Lila gave her baby up. I wonder if it is true. . . . Do you know why sis Lila quit or not?" Apparently, Hazel had also outed in the past and sent her regards to Royce and all the girls "down there."[75] Royce never responded. Meanwhile, perhaps unbeknownst to her family, Keisner was pregnant again.

In July 1931, Keisner entered the Salvation Army Home in Oakland. On September 25, 1931, she gave birth to her second child, a boy named Clarence Ray. The young mother wrote Royce a month later. Her boy was "getting along just wonderfully." On the heels of losing her first son, Keisner seemed determined to keep Clarence. She wrote to Royce,

> I was planning on adopting my baby out but now I feel different and I'd like to get a place to board him until I can get a place to work and get a good start, and try and get one of my sisters to come down and have her take care of him during the day while I work. I'd like to get a place to work where I could go home at night, then by doing like that I'd feel more settled and feel more like I have a child of my own to struggle for, rather than keeping it in a boarding place all its life, cause this sure means a lesson to mean, by me and keeping him and having him near me all the time. And I'll be more happier and it will be a pleasure for me to work and to think I have something worthwhile living for.[76]

Keisner's desire to have her sister help watch her son and to be able to return to him in the evening was impossible within the constraints of outing. Live-in domestic workers were not allowed to raise their children in the home. There appear to have been rare temporary exceptions for some, but the majority of the time, young single mothers of infants were required to board their children—typically with the Ladies' Relief nursery in Oakland—the same home where Keisner's first child was boarded. Being an outing mother was challenging. Nonetheless, she clearly wanted to raise her son in the best way possible as a single mother. Later in the month, Keisner wrote with a detailed plan, sprinkled with ingratiating language to placate Traxler:

> We are getting along just fine and the baby weighs 10 pounds now, he's sure a big boy now. . . . Sure too bad I have to depend on you folks. I'm sure sorry how I acted in the past, but it sure taught me a lesson. I learned a lot since I've been here and I'm sure going to do my best after I leave, I know I can if I can have my baby with me, I feel more settled

then. If I can find a place to board him for three or four months until I get a start and after that I'm going to keep him myself.[77]

Traxler found Keisner a boarding home for Clarence for twenty-five dollars a month but warned that places were not plentiful and wages lower than when she last outed. No doubt the Great Depression was showing its effect. The best Traxler found was a temporary placement including the care of a child for forty or forty-five dollars a month. In order to pay for the care for her own child, Keisner would have to care for someone else's.[78] Keisner eagerly agreed to the arrangement as she didn't have "a cent."[79] After about a month and a half in a Berkeley home, Keisner returned to Beatrice, California, with baby Clarence. In January 1932, she told Royce that Clarence's grandparents "sure think the world of him" and that she was happily surrounded by her sisters.[80] Later she wrote Traxler, "My folks were sure glad to have me home, they are just crazy about the baby. He sure is spoiled."[81]

Later that fall, the Keisner family fell on hard times. In October 1932, Keisner wrote Royce in search of work for her and her sister: "Try your best and get us a job, we don't care how cheap they are. I am leaving my baby home with the folks." She concluded, "Any job, any place will do us so please help us."[82] For many Native families living in remote places, work was already scarce. During the height of the Depression, it was more so. The ability to send multiple daughters to the Bay Area to work meant the prospect of more wages and family security. Keisner did not get a response from Royce and wrote again a week later. She was desperate:

> Well I sure wish that you can find us some kind of a job because we are very very anxious to leave. As we need work very bad. Because we are sure having a hard time. It's sure a bad year. . . . Work is sure scarce up here, get us a job any place. Out of town, we don't care as long as we have some kind of cheap job either $15 or $20, just anything . . . as soon as possible. Before winter sets in. Please write and let us know we've been waiting every day for a letter. You certainly did a lot for me I know and sure appreciate every bit.[83]

Most girls who outed preferred to be placed in town—Oakland or adjacent cities—rather than Walnut Creek or other surrounding rural communities. Keisner had last worked for fifty dollars a month and was now seriously considering a 70 percent pay cut. Royce replied that work was so scarce and wages so low, "it would hardly pay you to come down, however if you are still so anxious to come, and will bring a clean health certificate you may come, if you are willing to accept what we may be able to get for you."[84] Within days, Keisner began working at a home in Alameda for twenty-five dollars a month.

A year later, Keisner stopped working in the Alameda home. Meanwhile, Royce was investigating Clarence's paternity in hopes of securing child support. "They," whether referring to Keisner and her partner at the time or some agency, were also considering adoption. Should the former plan not work out, Keisner's partner would "do his part" and bring the baby into the family. Royce kept Keisner's father, Henry, informed, adding that his daughter promised to send money as soon as she could and was looking into working in a fruit cannery.[85] A few months later, Keisner wrote to her father, pleading for him to keep Clarence. She was recently pregnant with her common-law husband, Ramon Chavarin, and he refused to raise Clarence:

> Dear Dad, Well . . . I'm left in the cold again. I told my husband about Clarence, and he said if that baby comes in this house, he said he'll leave and then I'll have two babies so what can I do? I'm worried to death. So here I am, he said he won't have anything to do with either of the babies. He said if Clarence stays away, he'll keep me and his baby but otherwise he'll have nothing to do with either of us. I'd give anything if you keep him up there, as I'll be bad off as I ever was. So please do it dad. . . . I'll never cause you any more trouble as long as I live dad. I'd be happy dad. Ans. Soon.[86]

Months passed, and by January 1934, Clarence was in the custody of the Children's Home Society in Oakland. Meanwhile, Henry Keisner was eager to get his grandson back.[87] Despite his interest, after some administrative correspondence Traxler declared to the Hoopa Valley Indian Agency that "I believe the old people [the Keisners] should not have the responsibility for this child."[88] Internal notes apparently written by Van Every reveal further opinions: "[Lila Keisner's] parents are old and poor, and her mother is almost an invalid and unable to take care of this child any longer."[89] At no point, however, did the Keisner family suggest they were incapable of caring for their grandson. The problem was that such intergenerational households were considered unacceptable by federal standards. A nonnuclear family was contrary to the aims of the outing program, even to the extent that fostering or adoption would have been considered a preferred solution. Henry Keisner would have to fight for his grandson.

On February 7, 1934, Henry Keisner wrote to Traxler with his intent to adopt: "I wrote to Lila sometime ago and told her if she would let me adopt Clarence I would keep him. But she never answered my letter. So I don't know what she wants. She said if I sent him down her husband would leave her with one more (baby). What do you think of it? Well I will wait till I hear from you again then I will see what you say as I am willing to do all I can to make it agreeable with all concerned."[90] A month later, the case had been taken over by the newly appointed matron Mildred Van Every, who conducted a visit at the Chavarin home. Lila Keisner and Ramon lived there with his parents and extended family. Given Chavarin's ultimatum, Keisner was resigned to the idea that "she could do nothing for Clarence." The two were not married, but Ramon said he would marry Keisner if he had the money for the license.[91] Given that Keisner was seven months pregnant with her third child "out of wedlock," Van Every was determined to effect a marriage. In addition to establishing a legible nuclear family, Van Every made a plan that would ultimately threaten Keisner with sterilization.

Days after the home visit, Van Every called on Berkeley policewoman Mrs. Lossing and made arrangements for Keisner to undergo mental tests.[92] Such tests, including an IQ assessment, would score and classify individuals on a scale ranging from "superior" at the highest to "idiot" at the lowest. Despite these tests' inherently racist biases and flaws, at the time they were regarded as scientific fact. Individuals who scored low, "borderline" or "feebleminded," for instance, were considered defective and beyond help. Most heinously, women who scored poorly on these tests could be slated for sterilization with the understanding that society would be spared from further defectives.[93] Shortly after Van Every reached out to Mrs. Lossing, a Mrs. Boynton, one of Lossing's volunteers, was on the case.[94]

Later in the month, Van Every conferenced with the Probation Department about a "procedure" for Keisner. The detailed notes walk through the steps of sterilization. The operation would need to be done at the Sonoma State Home—the same "home" where Carrie Spencer was institutionalized. It would cost twenty dollars a month for a total of two months of recovery. Alameda County would pay for sterilization of its residents. Though legally, the state of California was able to sterilize without consent, the notes indicated it was "necessary for the client to give her consent to sterilization." The final determination would be reviewed by the probation court judge for its "legitimacy," but only after "mental tests" were administered. Casually, the notes mention a Dr. Butler, the same the medical superintendent at Sonoma who implemented the most far-reaching eugenic sterilization program in the country. The notes then delve into carefully crafted deception, reading, "The client should understand the reason for [taking] a mental test. . . . The explanation shall be made so that the client will understand that she is to be helped rather than that sterilization is the end and aim of the mental test." In fact, sterilization *was* the end goal of these tests. Accordingly, "if the mental tests show her sufficiently below par, the recommendation [for sterilization] is made immediately." There was also a caveat: "If the IQ should not prove sufficiently low for sterilization, the client, giving consent for sterilization and if in the case otherwise seems right, sterilization may be done." Therefore, even if Keisner proved to be mentally fit, if she had already consented to the procedure and it "seemed right," she would be sterilized. These procedures were not limited to Keisner—other outing women were similarly targeted.[95]

Days later, Traxler confirmed her plans with Boggess at the Hoopa Valley Indian Agency. First, she inquired about the status of Henry's adoption of his grandson. Second, Traxler reported that Keisner "has lived, and is still living with a Mexican. He is unemployed, and they live with his people in a downtown Mexican district." She then confirmed the plans for sterilization:

"We are working on Lila's case, (as her health permits) to the end that something might be done to prevent more illegitimate children in the future."[96] Traxler's tone about Chavarin—"a Mexican"—reveals racist undertones that would have also influenced the premise for Keisner's sterilization. In addition to the disproportionate sterilization of Native American women, in early twentieth-century California, youths of Mexican origin were disproportionately identified as defective delinquents in need of sterilization.[97] Keisner's sterilization would therefore solve two problems. Internal notes indicate that Mrs. Boynton, the Berkeley Police Department volunteer, had visited Keisner. The notes conceded, "Since nothing can be done with Lila, anyway in the matter of sterilization for several months, the next two months may well be spent in understanding Lila and Lila gaining confidence in Mrs. Boynton. The mental test may be much more fairly gotten that way."[98] Therefore, Boynton's wellness checks on Keisner would begin the process of testing the young mother and bring her that much closer to sterilization.

The notes further commented on her unstable relationship, "Chavarin might put her out of the house any time. She seemed worried as to what would come of her, with a new baby on her hands. She said she would like to marry Chavarin." Keisner's partner was ready to throw her out on the street, but as a young pregnant woman, she relied on him for stability. The matrons accepted that fact and encouraged a marriage between the two. After continued house calls from Mrs. Boynton, Chavarin agreed to apply to the Civilian Conservation Corps, where he would work for twenty-five dollars a month.[99] Then Boynton contacted a priest who might "consummate" the marriage.[100] Days later, Traxler confirmed that Chavarin's earnings could be sent directly to Keisner. Boynton maintained that if "they could be married before he went away, it would be better for all concerned." Accordingly, Boynton would work to "[effect] . . . [a] marriage" between the two so "there shall be no chance for an error in Lila not receiving . . . Ramon's wages . . . for her support and that of the coming baby."[101] Again, though it was clear that Chavarin might put her "out of the house" at any time, Keisner was encouraged to marry him for stability and access to his wages. These forms of relation were easier to control and legible to the outing program and federal Indian policy.

Meanwhile, the issue of Clarence's adoption by his grandparents remained.[102] Traxler's notes on the issue reveal Henry Keisner's agony: "The grandfather said that he couldn't stand seeing the baby among strangers who might mistreat him or . . . not be kind to him. He said that although he was a poor man he would rather take care of his grandson than see him mistreated. He would be willing to adopt a baby legally if it would cost him no money." Thankfully, with the help of the Hoopa Valley Indian Agency, Henry Keisner could petition for adoption at the county courthouse in Eureka at no cost.[103] At the end of April 1934, just as the paperwork for Clarence was in process, Lila Keisner gave birth to a baby girl.[104] Midway through May, she married Chavarin and was "in good health and good spirits."[105] While we do not know for certain if Clarence's grandparents were able to obtain legal custody, the final letter in Keisner's file indicated that Clarence's case was "going along satisfactorily in every way."[106]

Keisner's experience in the outing program reveals a complex web of white legal relationship parameters, modes of surveilling and managing Native bodies, and tactics akin to Indian child removal. While in the Bay Area, Keisner found herself squeezed by individuals and institutions who sought to control her reproductive capacity and insert themselves into her family's relationships. Due to her family's financial deprivation, she was obliged to return to the outing program a second time; on this second occasion, she lost custody of her young son, was encouraged by the outing matron to marry her live-in partner, a man who had objected to her retaining custody of her son, and was eventually pressured into a series of tests with the goal of justifying a sterilization procedure on the grounds of her mental incompetence. Sterilization is often thought of as a quick procedure, when in fact Keisner's experience reveals a gradual bureaucratic process of state-exerted power—power that I argue is akin to Indian child removal. A goal of Indian child removal is to end or curtail an Indigenous future—whether culturally or biologically. Officials tried to do just that. Keisner's life choices were constrained by mechanisms of state repression. At the same time, in order to raise his own grandson, her father had to contend with a matron who believed the entire family to be "unfit." It is unclear if Henry Keisner was able to formally adopt his grandson or if his daughter was in fact sterilized, yet the Keisner family's experience demonstrates the steps to achieve such a heinous act. Her case demonstrates the modes of coercion and control that attempted to craft settler family structures and maintain subordinated labor.

Because Keisner was a Native woman, the outing program regarded her reproductive capacity as dangerous and worked with various organizations to contain that problem. Outing matrons partnered with the Ladies' Relief Society, the Salvation Army Home, the Children's Home Society, the Berkeley Police Department, and Indian agencies to accomplish Indian child removal. Being a single mother in the outing program was challenging. Keisner was forced to board her child, leave him at home with her parents, and twice to consider adoption. These were acceptable forms of motherhood that privileged her role as a laborer. The outing program desired forms of relation that were legible and useful to the settler state—marriage and a nuclear, laboring family. In many ways, the program saw itself as a temporary custodial institution that that became unnecessary after marriage. Therefore, Keisner's proposed marriage to Chavarin was in many ways another form of custodianship—with a little effort, the matrons hoped to be able to secure a financially stable arrangement. At the same time, Keisner's sterilization would prevent further children. Even as the matrons claimed sterilization was to prevent further "illegitimate children," they did so with the intention of marrying her off, revealing that the operative word was not "illegitimate" but "children." The matrons regarded her reproductive capacity as a threat. Intergenerational households and single Native mothers in unmarried relationships were contrary to the outing program. In turn, outing matrons made it their duty to manage these bodies and relationships into more acceptable forms of relation that were legible to and controllable by the settler state.

These four cases have contextualized a truth of the Bay Area Outing Program about the surveillance and hyperregulation of Native women's lives and bodies. Regulation went hand in hand with containment. Boarding schools and outing programs are often thought of as institutions of education or labor. However, considering "scales of containment" reframes our thinking to consider outing as a carceral institution. Indeed, it was an institution that many Native women ran away from and, when caught, were apprehended and confined. This frame allows us to see the structural forces at work in the Bay Area Outing Program. It was a program that worked with local social services agencies, detention centers, and other institutions to contain Native women. The scales of containment these Native women experienced started in their youth from regulated reservations to boarding schools and then continued into outing homes and subsequent carceral institutions. It is true that outing afforded some women a kind of freedom—especially from the hypercontrolled life of boarding schools. Yet many found their freedoms curtailed, especially in relation to sexual surveillance.

Rosita Elliott's case, with its rare account of a detention home medical examination, demonstrates the interconnected realities of labor, incarceration, and sexuality for Native women in California's juvenile justice system. As a young woman outing in the Bay Area, she was vulnerable to incarceration at the Alameda County Detention Home, as her rapid arrival at the center shows, only a few days after she began outing work. She was promptly sent to her "home" in Mendocino County when it was suspected that she might be pregnant—a home that may have been with the grandparents listed in her file, or perhaps some form of institution. Her case illustrates not only that sexual surveillance and incarceration went hand in hand but also that a young woman's ability to labor in this program was paramount. Carrie Spencer's case further indicates the scales of containment that Native women experienced. Throughout her life, she and other Native women like her were subject to various forms of institutionalized control—ultimately she was committed to the Sonoma State Home, where she was almost certainly sterilized. She was only released when federal authorities assured her continued surveillance and control on the reservation. Therefore, in order to live her life and reunite with her children and family, she had to be subject to these scales of containment.

Patricia Ince's experience clearly maps out the carceral and legal ramifications of sexually transmitted infections of the era. Ince was so aware of these issues that she sought medical care under a pseudonym. Even as a nonparticipant in the outing program, she was still subjected to intense surveillance and containment. Further "care," whether from outing matrons or probation officers, meant further surveillance and control of her body. Ince was passed around institutions yet never received the medical care she desperately needed. The outing program, Woodland Social Services, the Ventura School for Girls, and the Alameda County Probation Home and Health Clinic all failed her. In fact, they only succeeded in containing her. Women like Ince were subjected to these scales of containment despite the fact that they were not outing girls. Finally, Lila Keisner's case further demonstrates how Native women in the Bay Area Outing Program were socialized as workers, not mothers. Her experience reveals both marriage and sterilization as scales of containment. Together these tools of the settler state attempted to restrain and contain Keisner. Amid her own battles against federal and local officials, Keisner was slated for sterilization—a gradual bureaucratic process involving eugenic ideologies and mental tests. Meanwhile, her father had to fight to raise his own grandchild, and authorities worked to quickly marry Keisner off and be done with her. Keisner's experience reveals detailed modes of manipulation and control that sought to craft settler family structures and maintain subordinated labor.

There is no question that the state exerted power over Native women's bodies through the Bay Area Outing Program. This power was primarily expressed as a form of custodianship, wardship, and perhaps even "care." It was a care that fiercely controlled and contained Native women and ultimately led to atrocious consequences: a young girl possibly pregnant at fifteen and thrown into detention, another young woman institutionalized and separated from her child and family for years, another left untreated with a life-threatening disease, and yet another expecting her third child while being coerced into a marriage and involuntary sterilization. These intimate stories have revealed that whether through local detention homes, asylums, or related institutions, Native women's bodies were fiercely surveilled and controlled. Ultimately, for Native women, the Bay Area Outing Program presented a dilemma—the promise of wages bound to the likelihood of undesirable conditions, sexual surveillance, lack of agency, and federal management and control.

SIX
The Failure of Indian Health Care
A Negligent Privilege

THE BAY AREA OUTING PROGRAM was intent on managing Native women's bodies. While the previous chapter took up the concept of "scales of containment" and bodily surveillance, noting the forms through which Native women were controlled in the Bay Area Outing Program, this chapter focuses on the question of Indian health—or lack thereof. In particular, I examine tuberculosis cases in the Bay Area Outing Program and demonstrate the difficulties Native women experienced in accessing health care and especially tubercular care. Through this shift in frame, I show how the inconsistent compassion of the outing program's leadership intersected with federal negligence around Indian affairs, and more specifically the dangerous inadequacies of Indian health care services, to cost Native women's lives. Scholars have examined Indian health in the context of boarding schools and in specific tribal communities, but none have considered Urban Indians' health in the early twentieth century, much less that of Native women. This chapter addresses two overarching questions: First, how did the Bay Area Outing Program affect Native women's access to health care? Second, and in turn, how did the Bay Area Outing Program affect Native women's bodies?

To this end, I examine the state of Indian health throughout the nineteenth and early twentieth centuries, providing a context of federal negligence and rampant disease. I contextualize the fact that many of the women and girls who participated in the Bay Area Outing Program endured the ills of federal containment—atrocious health conditions and disease. I pay close attention to the tuberculosis epidemic in Indian Country and unpack popular eugenic theories of the time. Because Native people fell ill with tuberculosis (TB) in disproportionate numbers, many assumed that they were simply more susceptible to the disease than their non-Native counterparts. In fact, many believed that full-blooded Native people were more susceptible to TB than those of mixed heritage, thus reinforcing the eugenic notion that the epidemic was inevitable. Yet there was no connection between race and TB. The disease that ravaged Indian Country well into the mid-twentieth century was caused by extreme poverty and negligence. As I trace the federal response or lack thereof to Indian health care and wellness, I focus in particular on three case files. I closely analyze three cases of outing women who became critically ill with active tuberculosis while in the Bay Area. This chapter uncovers state violence shrouded in federal neglect, demonstrating how officials chose who they considered deserving of health care. Productive laboring bodies were crucial to outing. If Native women's labor could not be extracted, the program was not interested.

Indian Health Broadly

In the early nineteenth century, Indian health was not a priority for the Indian Service. With the exception of the occasional policy, government approaches to Indian health were largely haphazard. Although some treaties stipulated the creation of hospitals staffed by physicians, the government often failed to deliver. Further, the establishment of reservations exacerbated health problems. Diseases swept across Indian Country, resulting in major casualties. For instance, in 1833 a malaria epidemic swept in into California's Central Valley, killing more than twenty thousand Indian people, or roughly 75 percent of the valley's population.[1] In the late nineteenth century, a physician among the Ho-Chunk surmised that tuberculosis was "slowly, but surely solving the Indian problem."[2]

The 1887 Allotment Act encouraged the construction of permanent homes that, by contrast with traditional homes, were small and poorly ventilated and led to the further spread of disease.[3] Meager improvements in the late nineteenth century still resulted in inadequate care and delivery of services. Staffing led to further issues. Indian Service physicians were not required to have medical degrees; they—along with nurses—had been rejected by other federal agencies and were paid significantly less than their peers for treating well over a thousand patients a year.[4] These same physicians made do without the necessary tools, materials, and hospitals.

In the twentieth century, these issues persisted; various reports revealed "deplorable" Indian health conditions, most notably *The Problem of Indian Administration*, commonly known as the Meriam Report, which dedicated a thorough section to the inadequacies of Indian Health Services.[5] The federal report, published in 1928 and administered by the Brookings Institution, surveyed conditions on Indian reservations in twenty-six states. The document reads as an indictment that quantifies the Health Services' inadequacies. First, it delivers a critique of the Indian Services sanatoriums. Somewhat distinct from hospitals, these institutions, whether Indian-school based or not, were lacking. The report argues that sanatoriums were "underequipped for the primary service of curing or arresting the disease which necessitated bringing the Indian to the institution."[6]

Second, the report exposes persistently untrained medical staff and an inadequate number of staff more generally. According to Indian Service statistics collected in 1926, there was an alarming ratio of permanent graduate nurses per bed. For the 510 total beds available at school-based sanatoriums, only six graduate nurses were present, a ratio of one nurse per eighty-five patients. For the 261 total beds available at regular sanatoriums, only four graduate nurses were present, a ratio of one nurse per sixty-five patients. These statistics reveal that the presence of graduate nurses in Indian Service sanatoriums was deficient. What is more, some of these nurses had not received training. The report further reveals that some nurses had an "unsympathetic attitude towards patients," and one hears "complaints" of neglect from Indians.[7]

As a comparison, in 1930, San Francisco's tuberculosis hospital had 350 beds for tubercular patients, 60 of which were reserved for children.[8] This singular institution's capacity exceeded all of the total beds at regular Indian Service sanatoriums and accounted for nearly 70 percent of the capacity of school-based sanatoriums. Further, in the same year, in the East Bay, Fairmont Hospital—which was reserved for patients discharged from Highland

Hospital—had a total of 760 beds, 125 of which were reserved for tuberculosis patients. The Arroyo Sanatorium had a total of 180 beds, 40 of which were reserved for children. The Del Valle Farm, reserved for children who were "predisposed" to tuberculosis, had 84 beds.[9] These Bay Area institutions had a larger capacity to handle tubercular patients and significantly more resources than the entirety of the Indian Medical Service.

While these Bay Area institutions were open to all residents, predictably, those with life-threatening illnesses like tuberculosis were impoverished.[10] For instance, at San Francisco's tuberculosis hospital, a disproportionate number of poor patients could not pay for services. Therefore, the city provided free days of bed care for tuberculosis patients. In 1929, the hospital, along with the adjacent Health Farm in Redwood City, California, funded 142,134 days—or roughly 390 patients for every day of the year.[11] Because of state funding and health mandates established in 1916, these facilities raised standards of care from previous years, including the separation of TB wards from other hospital wards, separation of advanced patients from less advanced, and provisions on isolation and space between beds.[12]

Susan Craddock finds that the improved standards brought about class biases among some hospital administrators, to whom migrants and other indigent patients were considered "undesirable." Because of extreme poverty and an itinerant lifestyle, migrant laborers had a high incidence of illness, including tuberculosis. In the case of migrants, many county hospitals would not take them.[13] It is possible these same sentiments inspired Bay Area hospitals to withhold long-term care from Native women in the outing program. Instead, they were sent to Indian Health facilities.

Whereas these facilities had a shortage of beds and permanent graduate nurses, the Indian Medical Service also had a shortage of physicians and general employees at sanatoriums. One survey conducted in April 1927 found that the total number of employees at sanatoriums included a total of ten doctors, one contract doctor, and twenty-one nurses. The ratio of these employees per bed equaled 81.4 patients per doctor, 81.4 per contract physician, and 38.8 patients per nurse.[14] Not surprisingly, the Meriam Report indicated that the Indian Service needed to increase the number of staff, particularly physicians—who were largely only part-time. The report recommended that every hospital of fifty or more beds should have a full-time physician. To sufficiently address Indian health, the Indian Medical Service needed to replace contract physicians as soon as possible and employ at least twice the amount of currently employed physicians.[15] In short, the Indian Service medical staff were underqualified, understaffed, underresourced, overworked, and underpaid. Conditions in boarding schools made matters worse.

Overcrowded and unsanitary Indian schools were prime conveyors of illness—children contracted disease at school and spread it into their communities when they returned home. The boarding school environment was neither healthy nor safe. The failures of Indian boarding schools and their atrocious conditions created a student population with weakened immune systems who were highly susceptible to disease. The combination of malnutrition, hard labor, and unhealthy living conditions increased children's risk of developing active tuberculosis.[16] Outing girls who attended boarding school were raised under these same conditions. They would have had weakened immune systems when arriving to the Bay Area that would have worsened under the physical demands of domestic labor. Moreover, officials filled Indian boarding schools at all costs, even if admitting potentially contagious children who did not receive proper health care. Amid disease and outbreaks, some administrators prioritized their institutions over Native children's lives.[17]

Within boarding schools, trachoma (an infectious eye disease) and tuberculosis (an airborne bacterial disease) were widespread. They overflowed into Indian communities across the country. At its worst, trachoma could cause blindness, but, of the two, tuberculosis was deadly. TB, also known as "consumption," is easily spread through a cough or sneeze. Symptoms include chest pain, coughing up blood, weakness, weight loss, loss of appetite, and fever. TB remains a serious concern in many parts of the world and is still seen in some populations in the United States today, where drug-resistant strains are the most challenging to treat. Those infected with TB might not have an "active" case. Those with dormant tuberculosis have no symptoms, but in the face of a weakened immune system, the bacteria can become active and multiply in the body. Therefore, some can become sick immediately, while others might get sick years later, when their immune system is compromised. Age can activate a dormant case of TB. Also, housing, workplace conditions, and length of workday are known to play a role.[18] The most common form of active TB is lung disease, but the bacteria could invade other organs and spread to lymph nodes, bones, or the bloodstream. When in the lungs, TB causes the chest to fill with blood. Many of these patients will also experience a pulmonary hemorrhage at least once, and often repeatedly. In the early twentieth century and for patients today who lack access to treatment, once a hemorrhage has occurred, there is not much that can be done. In its worst form, patients cannot breathe, and they succumb to respiratory failure.[19] It is incredibly painful and, in the early twentieth century, was the main cause of deaths among Native American people.

In 1908 and 1909, TB caused 30 percent and 40 percent of all Indian deaths respectively. In Nevada among Pyramid Lake Paiutes, the incidence rate of TB was 33 percent and likely higher.[20] Compared to non-Indians, Native people were disproportionality ill with TB. Nearly a decade later, the Meriam Report estimated that the number of Indian people with either active or "arrested"—that is, dormant—tuberculosis was one in ten. Those afflicted with the highly contagious disease were often sent to sanatoriums, school-based or otherwise. The report critiqued these institutions, stating that both "as developed in the Indian Service, are, as has been said, generally below a minimum standard of efficiency, plant, equipment and personnel."[21] The report added that it was generally difficult to send patients to these institutions and that reservation-based physicians and nurses were wholly inadequate for the job. Furthermore, little was done either on reservations or in boarding schools to detect the disease in its infancy.

The Meriam Report further enumerated tuberculosis-caused deaths. According to the study, Native American people suffered seven times as many tuberculosis-caused deaths per thousand as in the general population. In some areas, particularly the Southwest, the numbers were, alarmingly, even higher. In Arizona, the tuberculosis-based death rate of 15.1 per thousand was seventeen times higher than the national rate. Diagnostic facilities and x-ray, laboratory, and tuberculin tests were not available in the Indian Service, and only on "rare" occasions were such aids sought from the outside.[22] In most cases, a diagnosis was not made until the case was well advanced.

Given the poor standards at Indian Service hospitals and sanatoriums, tuberculosis spread. As tuberculosis ravaged Indian Country, three main theories claimed to explain the epidemic. First, some people argued Indian people were simply more susceptible to the disease than their non-Native counterparts. An excerpt from a popular periodical speaks to this point. In the September 1901 edition of the *Indian's Friend*, a publication of the Women's National Indian Association, Reverend D. A. Sanford took up this conversation with his editorial "What Is Killing Our Indians?" Sanford presented various statistics on tuberculosis mortality rates among Native communities across the United States. In 1883, only four of fifteen Cheyenne youth had survived an outbreak of "consumption." In 1896, of a small a cohort of Cheyenne and Arapaho students sent to Carlisle Institute, nearly half had either contracted or died from some form of tuberculosis. In 1901, a small Oklahoma Indian community suffered eight tuberculosis deaths. Sanford reported that young people, especially those in school, were contracting and dying from the illness.

Sanford blamed Native people for high mortality rates. He stated, "The facts seem to be these: Tuberculosis has been inherited from past generations. It is in their blood. Nearly all have it in some form." And while reformers of the time—particularly Women's National Indian Association members—insisted that Indian people assimilate, Sanford ironically blamed civilization on further spread of the disease. He contended, "In their wild state, in an active out-of-door life, the disease in a measure was warded off, but under present conditions it develops rapidly. . . . The vices of civilization tempt [the Indian], and then idleness and vice help to develop the tubercular disease which he has inherited."[23] So while Native people were being swiftly ushered into assimilationist policy—not of their own accord—the disease they suffered was seen as their own fault. Sanford's eugenic beliefs unapologetically framed Indian people as responsible for their own deaths.

Another group of people argued that Indians were so overcome by the disease because they had never been exposed to it. This notion regarded Indian people as "virgin soil." These virgin soil theorists believed that Indians could become "tubercularized" and would eventually be able to resist the disease. Or perhaps more specifically, the survivors of TB could acquire resistance overtime.

The third prevailing theory was that full-blooded Indians were more susceptible to tuberculosis than those of mixed heritage.[24] Officials pathologized Indian people and their behavior, blaming them for the epidemic. They reinforced the eugenic notion that the epidemic was inevitable, nothing could be done to fix it, and that federal officials and the structures thereof were not responsible. Indeed, these notions relate to the biologizing of race through the emergent field of public health, as well as the pathologizing of culture through the emergent fields of sociology and anthropology.

It was not until the period between the 1930s and the 1950s that new research finally discredited such theories. There was no connection between race and tuberculosis. The disease that ravaged Indian Country well into the mid-twentieth century was caused by extreme poverty.[25] Although the BCG, or bacille Calmette-Guérin, vaccine began to be administered in 1921 in Paris and then globally, it was not implemented by the Indian Service until 1935. While today many countries with a high prevalence of TB use BCG to prevent childhood tuberculous, it was not widely available in the early twentieth century. In 1930, when BCG was introduced in Germany in a trial to inoculate babies, dozens died. The fatalities resulted from tubercular bacteria stored in the same incubator—not the BCG itself. However, the tragedy made many adverse to the vaccine. While BCG was not 100 percent effective against TB, it certainly led to a decline of cases.[26]

In 1935, while tuberculosis was widespread among the entire Native population in the United States, it was estimated that 51,635 Native people—or about 17 percent—were treated for TB in a hospital, sanatorium, or school infirmary.[27] The incidence rate among Indians was five times greater than among non-Native people.[28] Whereas Indian children typically had access to tuberculosis treatment at boarding schools, Native adults with the disease were left to fend for themselves. In the years after World War II, the Indian Medical Division had access to only three x-ray machines that could detect the disease.

The Native women who participated in outing programs had been subjected to these conditions for their entire lives. Born on reservations and raised in Indian boarding schools, they were surrounded by death and disease. Although Native women may have survived such deplorable conditions, they suffered from compromised immune systems. Women who may have contracted latent forms of TB in their communities or while at Indian boarding schools may have begun to show symptoms only when the right conditions arose, and by then, it was often much too late. Preventative health was nonexistent in the Indian Medical Service. In the worst-case scenario, those with underlying diseases remained undetected, thanks to the failures of Indian Health Service. In short, the experiences of Bay Area outing women and girls was colored by poor health. Overall, federal Indian health could be characterized by financial neglect and by inadequate resources and staff. The federal government was failing Native people and literally killing them.

Ivy Sam

Ivy Sam, a twenty-one-year-old Washoe and Paiute woman, applied to the outing program in October of 1930.[29] She attended public school in Coleville, California, where records indicate that she was "well liked." Sam worked in two Oakland homes from November 1930 to January 1931. Upon arriving to the Bay Area, Sam was four months pregnant and likely intent on securing wages before giving birth. On January 31, 1931, seven months pregnant, she entered the Salvation Army Home. The home was specifically designed for single mothers, and many outing girls convalesced there before and after delivering their children. However, complications required that she be transferred the same evening to Highland Hospital in Oakland—the county facility that provided both emergent care for the acutely sick and obstetric care.[30] On February 2, Matron Royce wrote to Superintendent Parrett of the Walker River Agency requesting assistance with Sam and another outing girl, Minnie Dock. Sam was hemorrhaging from her lungs—a common sign of TB, though apparently undiagnosed—and Dock had tuberculosis in her bones.[31] Both were gravely ill, hospitalized in emergency care in the Bay Area, and needed to be placed in a long-term sanatorium immediately.

Sam's situation was especially dire; her few months of residency in the Bay Area did not qualify her for hospitalization. At the time, only county residents qualified for health care. Residency was defined as living continuously in the state for three years with at least one year's continuous residence in the county. Given that many girls outed seasonally, most would have fallen in this precarious category and had to seek nonemergent and long-term care at OIA-run hospitals and sanatoriums. Fortunately, nonresidents were granted access to emergency aid.[32] However, Sam was in a "very bad state," and Royce hoped the two women could be sent to the Pyramid Lake Sanatorium.[33] Days later, Royce petitioned Dr. Snoddy at Pyramid Lake: "I earnestly beg you to give their cases favorable consideration." Royce gave Bay Area health providers the impression that both women would be immediately transferred to a government hospital, yet there were no beds secured, nor were there funds to transport either of them.[34] Sam and Dock continued to be hospitalized under emergency care.

On February 14, Sam was transferred to Fairmont Hospital, a facility reserved for the chronically ill and convalescent, including those with advanced tuberculosis.[35] Her transfer suggests that Sam may have stabilized but was still seriously ill. A week later, on February 21, Sam was sent back to Highland Hospital. That day, she gave birth to a baby girl named Anna May. Days later, and weeks after Royce's first petition, Superintendent Parrett wrote the matron that there was no room at Pyramid Lake Hospital for either woman. Parrett asked if he might be able to fund their continued hospitalization and requested that Royce send the rates if so. He further conceded that he had no means of transportation nor a suitable home for the women.[36] In response, Royce revealed that Sam's baby was premature by one month and in an incubator. Because Sam was both tubercular and apparently syphilitic, the child would need a "a long and thorough treatment if it lives." She pressed, "Let me know at once what to do with them." Royce also divulged, "We, (You, Dr. Snoddy and myself) are being severely criticized here, by employers of Ivy and health authorities, for allowing her to leave the Sanatorium. I did not know, of course, that she was sick or that she had been at Pyramid Sanatorium until the day before I took her to the Emergency Hospital."[37] Before outing, Sam had been a patient at Pyramid Lake. Understandably, Royce and her colleagues were under fire by Bay Area–based health officials for a severely mismanaged case of not one but two women and now an infant.

Parrett was hardly moved in his response. Instead, he reported that Sam did not belong to the Walker River Reservation.[38] Her residence in the vicinity of Coleville meant that she was an "unrestricted" Indian. Although Parrett claimed her family on the 1931 census, he believed the state was responsible for her care. He explained that if her status came to question, "the comptroller general might hold up payment for any care on her behalf," a risk he was not willing to take. In other words, Parrett stated, "her status would be for attention and care by the state of California, Inasmuch as any other indigent . . . person needing care . . . under the jurisdiction of the state." Parrett passed responsibility for the three patients to the State of California and to Royce. He admitted, "I can appreciate the situation and criticism which is bound to rise in cases of this kind," and he wrote that if the matron had made an arrangement for the care of Dock, Sam, and her baby, he would "do the best" to help in financing it. Yet he made no guarantees.[39] While Parrett ruminated on the technicalities, two women and an infant remained gravely ill with no recourse.

In March, Sam showed no signs of improvement, and Royce wrote to her relatives in Nixon, Nevada, "You may come at once if you want to." Royce informed her family, "Ivy Sam is in the hospital and is very sick."[40] It is unclear if the matron or any official, for that matter, had informed Sam's family of her condition before this point. It is very possible this letter was the first they had heard of her illness—two months too late. Meanwhile, Royce still attempted to locate an Indian agency responsible for Sam. She ached to be rid of the case and wrote to the Sacramento Indian Agency, declaring that Sam had "caused us untold trouble," and that if "she belongs in your jurisdiction and you can take her, we will be so glad for we have been placed in a most trying position because of her condition." Sam was deathly ill, and Royce was inconvenienced. Yet again, the matron was forwarded to the Walker River Indian Agency.[41] For a second time, Superintendent Parrett reflected on the technicalities of Sam's status. He offered no concrete support and ended by saying, "With reference to this class of Indians it is difficult to know how to proceed about some of these cases."[42]

On April 14, Sam's father, Pete Sam, wrote Royce from Smith, Nevada. He had finally received word of his daughter's illness and requested further information. "She wrote to me and said she was sick," Pete explained. "I wonder if you know anything about her. If you did will you please let me know at once."[43] Royce did not respond quickly. Two weeks later, on April 29—months after she was first hospitalized—Sam, a single mother with a sickly infant, passed away without her family by her side.

Later that same day, Royce responded to Sam's father, Pete, "I regret to tell you that your daughter Ivy Sam passed away at 5 o'clock this morning. Ever since we knew Ivy was sick we have tried to locate her folks, but were not able to do so until your letter, which I received only yesterday. Ivy either did not know where you were or did not want to tell us." Royce claimed, "We have repeatedly written to both Sacramento Indian Agency and Walker River Agency in endeavor to locate Ivy's people," although records do not substantiate this claim. Apparently, Royce had sent a wire to Pete Sam the previous day, indicating his daughter's condition, but he could not be located. In her closing lines, Royce requested, "We would like to know what you want regarding the care of the child. If we do not hear from you today, we will bury Ivy here."[44] Given that Royce's letter took days to reach Pete Sam, a same-day reply was clearly impossible. The Sam family would not be able to say their goodbyes, and a young woman was buried in a foreign place, without her family. Ivy Sam was buried May 1.

On May 4, Pete Sam wired a telegraph from Wellington, Nevada to Royce, asking that they send his daughter's body home. Royce again provided empty regrets. She responded, "We received your wire too late to send Ivy's body to Nevada. We waited for three days and thought we were not going to hear from you." In her response, Royce failed to mention that his daughter had already been buried. She continued, "You'll be glad to know that Ivy had good care during her sickness, and all possible to do, was done for her. I do not think she suffered at any time. The baby is having the best of care. Will you please let us know what to do with the baby, and Ivy's clothing and cash."[45] Pete Sam transferred work locations and responded from Topaz, California, on May 16. Rather than being justifiably upset with the matron, he extended his gratitude, writing, "I'll go out and see Mr. Snyder of the Stewart Institute and have him make arrangements to have Ivy's baby and clothing sent there. I thank you for the good care given my girl before she died and is now been given her baby."[46]

After Ivy Sam's death, Matron Royce, her OIA colleagues, and a local charity focused on the care of baby Anna May. Sallie Loveridge of the Associated Charities of the City of Oakland asked Superintendent Parrett of the Walker River Agency if Anna May could be sent home to live with her family. Parrett had an OIA field matron assess the home in Coleville, California, and the report was negative. Pete had no wife, and his school-age children would not be home to care for the infant. Moreover, there was no physician nearby for the baby's care and treatment. Parrett reported, "The family is very poor and have no means for support except a little work Pete Sam may obtain by working as a laborer. The family and home conditions are very unsanitary. The oldest boy . . . has tuberculosis and is in very poor health." Parrett described conditions of illness and economic hardship that were largely crafted by and made worse by the Indian Service. Yet the context was completely lost on him. He concluded, "Under such conditions, it would be almost criminal to place the baby in such environment."[47] On the basis of Parrett's conclusion, Anna May remained in Oakland. Another Indian baby had been separated from her family under the guise of it being "unfit."

In July, Ivy's sister Bernice Sam wrote Matron Royce inquiring about her niece and wondering if she could be sent to Stewart.[48] Meanwhile, Parrett continued to discredit the family, stating to Royce, "Relating to this child's people at Coleville, I cannot see how they could care for it at all." Instead, he believed it best for an arrangement between "the government and some home or institution" to care for the child.[49] A week later, the question of who should care for the baby became irrelevant. Anna May passed away on July 16, 1931, at Highland Hospital.

On July 20, Royce conveyed the news to Parrett: "She had the best care obtainable and everything possible was done for her. She never could've been well so it seems best for her to escape further suffering." Arrangements had been made to transfer the baby's bills to Parrett's office.[50] He was apparently fine with footing the bill for the baby's care, even if he had been unwilling to do the same for her mother.[51] It is unclear where the baby was buried or if any kind of services were held. One thing was certain, however: Royce had once again failed to notify the Sam family.

In August, Bernice Sam wrote Royce about her niece a second time: "You

[told] Pete Sam, my father that . . . Ivy had a baby girl down there. I'm going to tell you to send that baby down to Stewart Nevada. You let me [know] first and let me know how old is that baby. . . . Answer right away so please send her down."[52] Months after Anna May's complicated birth, the family still was left unaware of the basic details of the infant's brief life. Royce finally responded to Bernice Sam weeks later, offering no condolences: "When [the baby] was able to be taken from the hospital it was placed in a private home and had the very best of care possible right up to the time of [its] death. It was a little girl and its name was Anna May."[53] After one final letter regarding a bill, Ivy Sam's file ended.

Ivy Sam's short few months in the Bay Area Outing Program took a horrific turn. Her preexisting conditions of syphilis, tuberculosis, and pregnancy made for a complex health situation that was worsened by federal inaction and neglect. Upon entering the Bay Area, Sam was strong enough to work for two months as a domestic, and she apparently showed no signs of illness. Yet clearly something was seriously wrong. For months on end, she did not receive the long-term treatment she needed, nor was she able to see her family. During those same months, officials went back and forth over who had jurisdiction. Her status as a "restricted" Indian ultimately gridlocked the case. Royce and Parrett handled the case so poorly that their contemporaries criticized them. Although Sam received emergency care in the Bay Area, she was passed around from facility to facility until her untimely death. It is impossible to know if things would have worked out differently had Royce, Parrett, or any OIA official sent Sam to a specialist or a long-term hospital or sanatorium. We will never know if administrators could have made a difference. In this case they did not. No hospital bed was secured. No plan of action was made. When Sam passed away, her family were robbed of their goodbyes. Pete Sam never met his granddaughter Anna May. Instead, the very idea of sending her home with her family was deemed "criminal." Two lives were lost and a family shattered. The Bay Area Outing Program was invested in the "care" of outing women and girls, but only to a point. Moreover, this care regularly meant further surveillance and scrutiny. Productive laboring bodies were crucial to this system, but if labor could no longer be extracted from Native bodies, the outing program was no longer interested in them. Once Sam became deathly ill, she was no longer useful and, in turn, caused Royce "untold trouble." Certainly, the matron was out of her depth. Through months of correspondence and with lives on the line, neither she nor any of her colleagues took responsibility or action. Ultimately, that inaction proved fatal. Unfortunately, Sam was not the only Native woman to pass away under the auspices of the outing program.

Minnie Dock

In the 1920s, Minnie Dock Meyers, a Washoe and Paiute woman, arrived in the Bay Area from Schurz, Nevada. Though records are incomplete, it appears that both Dock and her older sister Rose Aguilar outed in the 1920s and became longtime residents of San Francisco. Dock settled in the Hayes Valley neighborhood, and Aguilar was based at her employer's home, adjacent to West Portal. Both sisters had their own families; Aguilar had four children, and Dock had three. Typical for Bay Area Indian families at the time, the eldest children, six and older, were enrolled at boarding school. Both Dock and Aguilar had children enrolled at Stewart Indian School, their alma mater. Both were single mothers working in the city and separated or divorced from their partners. In January 1930, their father passed away on the Walker River Reservation in Schurz, while they lived in the Bay Area.[54]

In February 1931, on the heels of her father's death, Dock became seriously ill and was hospitalized in San Francisco. Matron Royce petitioned Dr. Thomas Snoddy of the Pyramid Lake Hospital to admit both Dock and Ivy Sam. In response, Snoddy sent his regrets—there were no additional beds, and they were already over capacity.[55] Royce became irritated and looked for intervention from Superintendent Parrett of the Walker River Agency. Snoddy's refusal to admit Dock put Royce in "an embarrassing position" because she had promised the San Francisco County Hospital that they would admit Dock soon. As with Ivy Sam's case, Royce gave Dock's health providers the impression that she would be immediately transferred to a government hospital, but that was not the case. So Royce appealed to Parrett: "I'm wondering if you could take her at your Sanatorium. . . . The case is tuberculosis of the bone and the girl wants to go to a place near her home which is Schurz."[56] On this occasion, thankfully, Parrett quickly responded and made room for Dock at the Stewart sanatorium.[57]

Royce was grateful for Parrett's assistance after Ivy Sam's death. While she arranged for Dock's transportation, she expressed her gratitude to the superintendent: "Thank you so much for accepting Minnie. I have worried greatly over her case."[58] In the meantime, Dock's son Harry Meyers was also ill. The six-year-old seems to have contracted pneumonia while at the Stewart Indian School. Superintendent Snyder informed Royce that "his condition is improving. He is not dangerously ill at this time."[59] After some back-and-forth between OIA officials, Dock's transportation to the Stewart sanatorium was finally arranged. On Friday, March 13, she and an attendant boarded a train to Nevada. It appears that both Dock and her sister Rose furnished the transportation funds, amounting to $37—or roughly one month's outing wages. Rose Aguilar was reimbursed $20.09 for her sister's and the attendant's tickets. Minnie Dock was given $2.00 and later refunded $2.91 after the cost of her meals and tips. Further, the reimbursement of Minnie Dock's $9 sleeper ticket was still up for consideration at Parrett's discretion. While the outing program was willing to transport Native women to the Bay Area for outing work, it did not make itself responsible for their return ticket, even in the event of a medical crisis.

Despite being very unwell, Dock withstood the trip to Stewart, and Royce reported to her sister Rose that "the children who were sick at Stewart," meaning her nephew Harry and possibly his sibling, "were very much better."[60] Once at Stewart sanatorium, Dock sent a message of thanks to Royce, who responded on March 18, "I am so glad that you are at last where you so much wanted to be and I do hope you will get real well and strong once more. It is so nice that you can see your two children often."[61] Indeed, Dock's relocation to the Stewart sanatorium meant that she finally saw her children and her relatives. Dock's return to Nevada must have felt like a relief, but the joy was short-lived. On April 27, Minnie Dock died at thirty-one years of age. That day, Superintendent Snyder sent a telegram to this effect, indicating that the outing program should notify her sister Rose.[62]

Matters continued to worsen for the family. A month after his mother's death, Harry's health declined. Royce alerted Superintendent Snyder at Stewart that "in case of death of Harry Meyers, his father would like him buried beside his mother at Schurz."[63] Records do not indicate that the boy died, but this family was hit hard. Their father had died the year before, and in a matter of months Dock had also died, and her son was seriously ill twice, at least once reaching the brink of death. Minnie Dock's case demonstrates how access to health care and healthy living conditions was a privilege that Urban Indians could not rely on in the early twentieth century—its access was contingent on their labor productivity and usefulness to the outing program.

By contrast with Ivy Sam's case, at least a bed was secured for Minnie Dock, and she saw her children and family before she passed away. But these small acts should have been the standard rather than an exception to the rule. Although Dock resided in San Francisco and apparently qualified for long-term hospitalization, Bay Area–based physicians were eager to pass her on to another facility—in this case, an out-of-state institution. In this way, Dock's fate was similar to Ivy Sam's. In the interim, Royce was "embarrassed" for her inability to deliver on promises she had made.

It is difficult to know what more could have been done for Dock, yet it is fair to say that a hospital bed at Stewart sanatorium did not guarantee the best of care, or perhaps even adequate care. Though many OIA hospitals specialized in treating tuberculosis—on account of the rapid transmission of the disease on reservations and in boarding schools—such facilities may have simultaneously spread the disease. Moreover, as discussed in previous pages, they were subject to chronic inadequacies in qualified staffing and supplies. In short, these federal facilities may have been deadly. Although perhaps her case was better handled than Ivy Sam's, we still end with the same result—another Native woman and mother gone before her time. A final case also had a more promising start but a less-than-ideal ending.

Blanche Nixon

In 1929, Blanche Nixon Spott, a Klamath woman, arrived in the Bay Area at sixteen years of age. Although she maintained an official file with the outing program, Nixon came to the Bay Area by way of Ruth Roberts.[64] Roberts's husband was an accountant at a salmon cannery at Requa on the lower Klamath, where Ruth had accompanied him. During her time there, she befriended many local Native women and brought them to the Bay Area for work.[65] Roberts's unofficial job in many ways resembled that of an outing matron, but crucially, she was not a federal employee. Nixon's first official outing position arranged through the Bay Area Outing Program was at a Piedmont home in January of 1930, earning $30 a month. She went on a hiatus for some time and returned in 1935.[66]

Matron Van Every noted that Nixon was "pleasant, alert, cheerful" and had a "serene disposition." Nixon also had a "very good" natural ability. Aside from such favorable comments, which were more common than in many other outing files, Van Every's notes also indicate that Nixon had health issues. In February of 1935, Nixon had her teeth pulled and shortly thereafter suffered a knee injury requiring she recover in a convalescent home. That spring she was in a "long septic condition."[67] Another note of Van Every's indicated that "her health will never permit her to live in the Bay Region."[68] Indeed, Nixon suffered more health issues that made wage work impossible, and yet she remained in the Bay Area for this very purpose.

In the summer of 1935, Nixon had been employed at Ball Cannery in East Oakland but was hardly strong enough to endure the long hours of the demanding peach season. Her knee proved especially limiting. One day while at work, Nixon fainted. She was rushed to Highland Hospital and was diagnosed with active tuberculosis. At the time, Nixon was not legally eligible for further care at Fairmont Hospital in Oakland. Therefore, Roberts requested that Van Every assist with a plan.[69]

Given the case, Superintendent Boggess of the Hoopa Valley Indian Agency provided two options. First, though she was not a "ward"—meaning she technically did not have access to certain Indian services—Boggess offered Nixon a bed at the Indian Service Hospital at Hoopa. Second, he noted that if she were interested in the Southwest-based sanatoriums, she would need to furnish a physician's record of the case. Boggess gave a note of caution regarding the sanatoriums: "They are most all crowded and usually there is a waiting list." Tuberculosis was rampant in Indian Country, and yet the Indian Service was ill-equipped to manage the disease.[70] Further, though the BCG vaccination was developed in 1921, the Indian Health Service did not administer the inoculation until the year Nixon was hospitalized. Given the limitations, Nixon was, indeed, sent to the Hoopa Hospital for treatment. Thankfully, she was strong enough to withstand the rail trip home.[71]

On January 1, 1936, Nixon returned to the Bay Area for work. There is little correspondence about her case for most of the year, but by the fall, Nixon's health issues had returned. In September, Nixon came down with a cold and a low-grade temperature. Her physician noted she had "increased breath sounds" in the chest. By late October, the physician confirmed that Nixon had advanced active pulmonary tuberculosis.[72] On October 20, 1936, Roberts phoned Van Every to inform her of the diagnosis. Nixon's x-ray showed active tuberculosis in both lungs, requiring immediate hospitalization. Roberts conveyed that Nixon did not want to go to Fairmont Hospital, "since there had been so many unfavorable occurrences there in regard to tuberculosis treatment." Further, Roberts insisted that Nixon did not want to return to the "crowded" Hoopa Hospital. Roberts maintained that a return to Hoopa would be "injurious to her recovery." Instead, Nixon desired to be placed at the Stewart sanatorium in Nevada. Reportedly, a friend of hers was a former TB patient there and had "recovered nicely."[73] As Van Every continued on the case, Dr. Thompson, a physician Nixon had met through the organization called Friends of the Indian, furnished a medical report, which Van Every cross-referenced with a Dr. Eaton from the Oakland Clinic.[74] At the time, Nixon's hospitalization at a county hospital was still possible, but Van Every began to research other institutions.[75]

On October 21, the day after her conversation with Roberts, Van Every contacted three individuals about placing Nixon at tubercular institutions. First, Van Every petitioned Winifred Codman—who was the state chairman of the Daughters of the American Revolution's "Indian Citizenship" section. She asked whether Codman might assist with admitting Nixon to the Wish-I-Ah Sanitarium in Fresno.[76] Second, she wrote to Alida C. Bowler, superintendent of the Carson Indian Agency. Van Every petitioned to allow Nixon to enter the sanatorium at either Stewart or Schurz. She noted that while Nixon was full-blooded, she was not a ward. Van Every added compelling language, stating, "She is a woman of good character, willing to work, and is the support of her two children. She has been employed in Oakland since January of this year until the past two months."[77] Van Every's comments on Nixon's character, familial commitments, and willingness to work likely served to influence Nixon's admission—asserting that she was a worthy cause. Nonetheless, the fact remained that while she was indeed "willing to work," her health would not permit her to do so. Finally, Van Every sent a third letter. She wrote Superintendent Boggess for guidance on placing a non-ward in a government sanatorium, adding that Nixon desired a location in a higher altitude.[78]

On October 23, Dr. Eaton at the Oakland Clinic corroborated Dr. Thompson's findings and agreed that Nixon should be hospitalized. Because diagnostic services such as the x-rays initiated by Dr. Thompson and sputum tests administered by Dr. Eaton were largely unavailable in Indian Service facilities, Nixon tapped into superior medical care while in the Bay Area. Nevertheless, she was obliged to enter a federally run Indian Service sanatorium or hospital for long-term care, as other outing women had similarly experienced. A medical service worker at the Oakland Clinic informed Van Every that before Nixon could be admitted to a county hospital, it would be "necessary to ascertain what possibility there is for her to being readmitted to Hoopa."[79] As had been the case with Sam and Dock, yet again a local institution wanted to pass her off to an Indian hospital. Meanwhile, Van Every still awaited responses from her previous petitions.

The next day, an H. U. Sanders with the Health Division at Stewart wrote Van Every with unfortunate news: "I regret to inform you that we do not have a tuberculosis sanatorium here at Stewart. We have a general hospital only, and send our own tuberculosis patients to regular tuberculosis sanatorium elsewhere. I would suggest that you make application for admission to the Fort Bidwell Sanatorium."[80] Shortly thereafter, Winifred Codman replied the same. The representative of the Daughters of the American Revolution indicated that Wish-I-Ah Sanitarium was a Fresno County–based institution, smaller and more expensive than the recommended Weimar Joint Sanatorium. Weimar also had an Indian unit. The issue remained that Nixon was a non-ward, and Weimar was a paid institution at two dollars per day. Codman wrote that "if the money could be raised somewhere," and if Van

Every could "find out about financing it," she would write to her contacts and try to make arrangements. She added that if Nixon had been hospitalized at Hoopa before, they might pay for her stay at Weimar.[81]

Meanwhile, Boggess responded rather condescendingly to Van Every's request, stating, "You are informed that there are such institutions at Albuquerque, Phoenix and Winslow." In his letter he sent blank applications for admittance to the Southwest-based Indian Service sanatoriums. Boggess cautioned, "These institutions are usually full and if you have Blanche make out one of these [applications], I suggest that you write the strongest possible letter to the superintendent of the Sanitarium."[82] Again Boggess painted a rather bleak picture of the availability of and access to these federal sanatoriums.

Shortly after, on October 29, Van Every telegrammed Roy Nash, the superintendent of the Sacramento Indian Agency. At the recommendation of the Stewart staff, she wrote, "Is there a possibility of placing [a] non-ward Indian woman tubercular patient in Bidwell for immediate treatment." Nash responded quickly, first by telegram and then by patronizing letter, "As you are no doubt aware, no patients are accepted in the Indian service sanatoriums unless they are cases that the physician feels will be benefited by sanatorium care. In other words, advanced cases are not accepted." In short, if Nixon was deathly ill, Van Every need not bother. As Boggess had done, he enclosed the application blanks and maintained, "If the Indian is a non-ward, it will be necessary for Alameda County, or some charitable organization to pay the patient's transportation to the hospital if she's accepted."[83] Nash's unfeeling response revealed that many tubercular cases were in fact "too late," and that Nixon's admission was not a guarantee. Further, her non-ward status continued to play a role in her access to or exclusion from health care. Nixon was stuck in limbo; Alameda County–based clinicians were adamant about sending her to a federal Indian Service sanatorium, while Indian Service officials insisted on the contrary.

While Nixon remained in limbo, Dr. Thompson gave her a full medical examination, as required by the Indian Service sanatoriums. The completed Form 5-363c indicated that both of Nixon's parents had pulmonary tuberculosis, and that aside from her most recent bout, Nixon had been diagnosed with active tuberculosis in 1932. At the time, Nixon experienced a cough, expectoration, chest pain, and a hemorrhage. Rather dishearteningly, Dr. Thompson indicated whom to notify in case of death and details as to the "disposal of body." This rare document also commented on the practices of TB treatment within the US Indian Service. A thorough disclaimer detailed,

> NOTE advanced cases of pulmonary tuberculosis should not be sent to non-reservation sanatoria, since the trip is frequently long and arduous, and for the most part nothing can be done for patients except to make their last days more comfortable. They should be cared for on reservations where this is at all possible. Patients should be advised that other members of the family cannot be permitted to remain with them at the sanatorium, as the accommodations are limited and urgently needed for other sick patients. Particularly this is true in the case of young children, who should under no circumstances be sent with the patient. Their risk of contracting tuberculosis is very great, and the other patients must not have their rest disturbed. Prospective patients should be advised that upon arrival at the sanatorium they will in all probability be immediately put to bed, there to remain until their fever has fallen to normal and pulse rate and weight have improved. They must come prepared to obey implicitly the rules of the sanatorium and the instructions of the physician in charge.[84]

As Nixon remained hospitalized in the Bay Area, Van Every returned to searching for a facility that would take her. On November 4, she sent letters and copies of Form 5-363c to the US Indian Tubercular Sanatorium in Albuquerque, New Mexico, and Phoenix, Arizona.[85] Within a week, Phoenix sent its regrets—there was no bed available for Nixon.[86] Van Every pressed on and this time petitioned Dr. S. W. Cartwright at the Fort Bidwell Sanitorium, first through letter then by telegram.[87] On November 14 at 7:37 p.m., Dr. Cartwright telegrammed—there was room for Nixon![88] However, the telegram did not reach Van Every in time, and Nixon was already scheduled to return home. Three minutes after its arrival, Nixon departed on the 7:40 p.m. train to Crescent City, California, seemingly stable enough to make the trip home.

In the interim, Van Every also made one last petition to Boggess, updating him on the case. Van Every reported that Nixon had been "unwilling" to enter either one of the Alameda County hospitals, despite the social worker at the tubercular clinic being "willing to enter into the hospitalization plan with her." She was still awaiting word from Weimar, but Nixon was unable to afford the two-dollar-a-day fee. Van Every reported, "Blanche lately has not responded to the suggestions and advice of Mrs. Roberts and Dr. Thompson has urged that Mrs. Roberts not keep her much longer in her home." Indeed, when Nixon had not been hospitalized at Highland, she was staying at the Roberts's home in Oakland. Certainly, housing a young woman with active tuberculosis was inadvisable. Van Every conceded, "With these points in mind, the only feasible plan was to ask Blanche to go to her home."[89] This option was also likely inadvisable. That same day, Van Every belatedly received Dr. Cartwright's telegram and immediately wrote Nixon with the news.[90] Thereafter, Nixon was finally admitted to Fort Bidwell Sanitorium, traveling there directly from Crescent City. It must have been a relief to Van Every, but especially to Nixon. After months of back and forth, she finally received the care she needed.

A year later, Nixon was still a Fort Bidwell patient. On September 6, 1937, she wrote Van Every in search of dresses. She made her request in some embarrassment—she had no means nor anyone else to ask. Her letter to Van Every also revealed the inner workings of the sanatorium. Nixon wrote, "Doctor Cartwright was reassigned last June and we haven't had any doctor here all summer. However they are expecting one the latter part of this month. Our head nurse is also being transferred to Arizona so we are hoping a lot of things will be changed." Getting Nixon assigned to Fort Bidwell must have felt like a triumph after several dead ends. Yet, a year later, Nixon and her fellow patients lacked a physician on hand and, in short order, would not even have a nurse. This casual comment illuminates the circumstances that TB patients in the Indian Service experienced: uneven access to inconsistent care. Nixon added, "I seem unable to improve in health. Since I've been here. Although I'm up and can wander around. I get up a few hours in the morning and the rest of the day is spent in bed. I am the oldest patient here as this is more or less a children's hospital. And there are times I really get dreadfully lonesome."[91] Nixon's health seemed to be on an uncertain trajectory, and she was feeling isolated and alone. Later that year, Van Every mailed Nixon a Christmas gift and some cookies. In April 1938, she finally mailed Nixon a brown dress.

Several years later, Nixon was still hospitalized for tuberculosis. The year 1940 found her at the Weimar Joint Sanatorium, about fifty miles northeast of Sacramento. Years earlier, payment for her treatment at Weimar had been an issue, but apparently this was no longer the case. That, or Nixon had found some means to furnish the two-dollar monthly charge for her stay. While Nixon was unable to engage in domestic work, Van Every began to sell her crafts in the Bay Area. In particular, she began selling her beaded moccasins. On November 4, 1940, Van Every wrote, "Several people have admired the little shoes which you gave me when I was visiting you last month. . . . I think of you often and I am always thankful that I get to see you from year to year. Remember me to Madeline and Betty."[92] Ever the maternalist, Van Every was generous in expressing her care for Nixon and seems to have made annual visits over the years.

In the following weeks, the two corresponded about more moccasin orders. Business was "booming," and Nixon agreed to make eighteen pairs of moccasins at $0.35 each for a total of $6.30. This was a fraction of what she earned while outing but sufficient to cover three months of her care at Weimar.[93] On New Year's Eve, Van Every wrote again, requesting more moccasins for another order. This time, she reached Nixon by way of her hometown, Crescent City, California.[94] Perhaps Nixon was home for the holidays.

On January 9, 1941, Nixon wrote from the Hoopa Hospital, where she described having been able to visit her children briefly before setting off for a new sanatorium. She wrote, "I was only home for two weeks however I got to see both of the children before coming here. I am here waiting for my transfer to go through. The doctor seems to think I will be leaving before long."[95] Later in the month, Van Every wrote to Nixon at the Phoenix Indian Sanatorium in Arizona. She included $1.40 in payment for a recent order of "cute as can be" moccasins. Apparently, Nixon was again awaiting transfer, for Van Every added, "Please let me know when you will be going to Weimar or the other San [sanitorium] you have in mind."[96] In early February, Nixon responded with a note of gratitude: "Thank you so much for the money you sent for the moccasins. It is so nice of you Miss Van Every to make the sales for me. I certainly do appreciate it. The weather down here is just grand, nice and warm. But I'm sure dreading the summer, judging from what the others tell me. The sanatorium here is just grand at least what I've seen of it is. There are three patients here, that I knew at Bidwell. I am in the ward with one of the little girls."[97]

In a final note, Van Every wrote Nixon, "I hope that you are enjoying Arizona and that you will come back to see us soon looking as brown as your Southern Indian friends. I will miss not getting to Weimar to see you on our annual visit."[98] Van Every's friendly, if clumsy, letter was the final document in Nixon's outing file. Ultimately, Nixon's experience appears to have been a success story—the successful placement of an outing woman in proper tubercular care. Unfortunately, the story still did not end well. On September 1, 1943, after two years and seven months at the Phoenix Indian Sanatorium, Nixon passed away. She was just thirty years old.[99]

Compared to her peers, Nixon fared well in her ability to enter a proper tubercular institution—several, for that matter. Perhaps the fact that her case occurred years after Sam's and Dock's meant that she had access to more effective treatments that offered her a fighting chance. It also seems likely that other factors played into her case. First, Ruth Roberts was the route through which Nixon came to the Bay Area, and she may have been a useful advocate. While Van Every and Roberts were cordial, the former felt the latter interfered with her official work as outing matron. Van Every undoubtedly resented the competition, as Roberts placed Native women in Bay Area homes. Nonetheless, Roberts's involvement in the case may have encouraged Van Every to save face and work diligently toward a solution. Second, the fact that Van Every found Nixon to be "pleasant," "cheerful," and "serene" suggests her favorable assessment of the young woman. Had Nixon not been in Van Every's good graces, the matron may have felt less compelled to come to her aid. Third, the matron may have known about Sam's and Dock's poorly handled cases, motivating her to act quickly.

Still, the odds were stacked against Nixon. Both of her parents had pulmonary tuberculosis, and she personally had battled it from a young age.

Further, as Van Every noted, Nixon's health would never permit her to live in the Bay region, much less work. The archive is silent on Nixon's experience of working in the Bay Area and on what her wages afforded her. Perhaps she sent money home to her children or enjoyed an occasional movie at the theater. Nixon's situation indicates the best-case scenario of access to tubercular care, and yet that care remained insufficient. Nixon did not want to be treated at Fairmont Hospital for the many "unfavorable occurrences" there with TB patients—perhaps she heard about Sam's experience there in 1931. Nixon and her peers found themselves in limbo—although they had access to emergent services in the Bay Area, they were excluded from long-term treatment. For nonemergency care, they depended on the matron's ability to secure a federal or federally funded bed. Nixon's non-ward status made this much more complicated. Finally, although she secured a bed, the situation at Indian Service hospitals and sanatoriums proved lacking—they were usually overcrowded, with waiting lists. At Fort Bidwell, Nixon and her peers went a whole summer with no physician on duty, on the verge of losing even their nurse. The turnover rate was high, and patients had uneven access to inconsistent care.

The three lives explored in this chapter reveal some of the most atrocious aspects of the Bay Area Outing Program. In Ivy Sam's case, she and her baby were quite literally left for dead. Sam had complex preexisting conditions, but her situation was worsened by federal inaction and neglect. For months, she did not receive the care she needed, nor could she see her family. Officials debated her "restricted" status while two lives were lost. Minnie Dock fared better than Sam, for she was able to secure a bed at the Stewart sanatorium and see her children and family before she passed away. Like Sam, however, physicians eagerly passed her off to another facility—this in spite of the fact that she was a Bay Area resident and should have had access to Bay Area–based long-term care.

Compared with the cases of her peers, Nixon's seems to present a different trajectory. Certainly, Matron Van Every seemed more sympathetic to Nixon's humanity than Matron Royce had been with Sam and Dock. Ultimately,

Nixon received extended care at several tubercular institutions. Nonetheless, she still dealt with the same jurisdictional limbo that Sam and Dock had experienced years prior. Certainly, Van Every acted quickly and did so more successfully than her predecessor Royce. But she had to knock on a number of doors just to secure one hospital bed. This process reveals how access to these overcrowded Indian sanatoriums and hospitals was a privilege, not a right, even as they offered little more than comfort care. As several federal studies revealed, these institutions were chronically understaffed and had little equipment or means to deliver proper patient care. While the rest of the country advanced toward containment and treatment of tuberculosis, the Indian Medical Service appeared frozen. Ultimately, Nixon's experience was the best-case scenario of access to tubercular care in the outing program, but her care was still qualified by the limitations of the federal Indian health care system and a larger unwillingness at all levels of government to accept responsibility for Indian lives.

As critically ill patients, Sam, Dock, and Nixon all found themselves in a jurisdictional limbo. Officials argued over their status—whether they were an "unrestricted" Indian or a "ward." These debates gridlocked their cases and led to their exclusion from Bay Area–based health care. Local hospitals responsible for their emergent care were desperate to hand them off to federal Indian facilities, while OIA officials often hoped that state or county governments would take responsibility for their care and transport. Clearly, few wanted to take responsibility for these women, and yet their lives were literally in the hands of federal officials. This lack of care in many cases extended to the outing program as well—even in a medical crisis, the program would not furnish funds to transport women to a medical facility, once one had been secured. Sam's, Dock's, and Nixon's experiences in the Bay Area Outing Program are a chilling demonstration of federal neglect.

Conclusion

WHEN THE INDIAN RELOCATION ACT OF 1956 encouraged and coerced Native people off the reservation and into urban areas, federal officials believed that the city would assimilate Native peoples. Just as with countless policies before—like the Dawes Act and Indian boarding schools—they believed they could transform us, that we would cut ties with our tribal communities, become absorbed and rendered invisible. But the city, as Tommy Orange puts it, made us new. In *There There*, he writes, "Getting us to cities was supposed to be the final, necessary step in our assimilation, absorption, erasure, completion of a five hundred year old genocidal campaign. But the city made us new, and we made it ours."[1]

Instead of shedding our cultures and blending in, we shared our languages, dances, and experiences. In the city, we met other Natives, created community, and gave birth to intertribal babies. Native people went on to earn college degrees, create nonprofits, and succeed in ways they weren't supposed to. No one expected Indian people to thrive in the city.

Although many believe that Urban Indians and Urban Indian communities were created with the advent of the Indian Relocation Act, there is a history that precedes the Relocation Act, one that has been described in the chapters of this book. The history of the Bay Area Outing Program affirms that an Urban Indian community, while small, existed decades before Public Law 959. This community was largely made up of Native American women. Many Native women who outed in the Bay Area grew to love the city and worked hard to create new futures for their children. Some continued careers in domestic work but ultimately broke the cycle of domesticity. Their children were not forced into domestic labor or boarding schools. Many attended public school, graduated from college, and forged new careers. With them grew pan-Indian families and intertribal communities that would come to welcome newly arrived relocatees.

In the early twentieth century, Native domestic workers organizing on their day off created one of the first Native hubs in the San Francisco Bay Area. The concept of the "hub" emerges from Renya Ramirez's geographical and virtual concept of Urban Indian belonging. Ramirez argues that the hub "suggests how landless Native Americans maintain a sense of connection to their tribal homelands and urban spaces through participation in cultural circuits and maintenance of social networks, as well as shared activity with other Native Americans in the city and on the reservation."[2] Indeed, Native women who outed in the Bay Area did not sever ties with their families and tribal communities. They returned home for gatherings, ceremonies, and family-oriented seasonal labor. Through the hub, women sustained connections with their tribal communities and shared their cultures and experiences with other Native people in the Bay Area.

Native women's leadership and organizing through the Four Winds Club is one prominent example of the hub in action. Socials, dances, and feeds created space for local Indian children, Native college students, and Native military personnel. In these spaces, Native people embraced one another in their common experience as Urban Indians. They shared songs and dances and began to create a truly intertribal community. These efforts lend credit to Ramirez's argument that Native women in particular are "central" to sustaining Urban Indian community life. Native women specifically assert their own notions of culture, community, identity, and belonging.[3] The hub that Native domestic workers created strengthened Native identity in the Bay Area and provided a space of belonging for other Urban Indians. I would argue that Native domestic workers not only sustained the early twentieth-century Urban Indian community but also actively created the Bay Area Indian community as we know it today.

The Bay Area Indian Community and the Founding Generation

As Susan Lobo has argued in her seminal study of the Bay Area Indian Community, California Indian people have always been in what is now the San Francisco Bay Area. They traveled, traded, intermarried, and enjoyed the fruits of their land that millions of people now call "home." In the eighteenth century, Ohlone peoples were especially affected by Spanish colonization and missionization. In these institutions, however, Ohlone peoples continued their songs, cultural practices, and languages. Many blended Catholicism with their Indigenous culture and to this day rightfully protect and revere the missions their ancestors built. Today, the Ohlone community continues to thrive throughout the Bay Area, in cities like Niles, Sunol, San Lorenzo, and Oakland. In the East Bay in recent years, community members fought to protect their ancestral shellmounds, developed a land trust, and championed the revival of Ohlone food traditions. The Ohlone remember that their ancestors have been on this land since time immemorial. The Bay Area always has been and always will be Native.

The early twentieth century brought forth a new kind of intertribal community. As early as 1911, Indian girls from Stewart Indian School were sent to labor in homes across the Bay Area through the school's outing program. This early iteration did not have a home base in the Bay, and because it stemmed from Stewart, it was largely composed of Washoe, Paiute, and Shoshone students. However, in 1918, with the advent of the Bay Area Outing Program, girls from all across the West began to seek outing work and new experiences in the big city. City lights, streetcars, music, and motion pictures promised a vibrant urban life and attracted Native girls and women. Simultaneously, veterans of World War I and those who enlisted during the interwar years also came to live and work in the Bay Area.[4] Shortly thereafter, in 1922, the Santa Fe Indian Village was established, just outside of Richmond, California. The hundred or so Laguna and Acoma families that lived there performed the same traditions they would have enacted at home—including a tribal council, their language, dances, and traditional feasts.[5] During World War II, many Native people in the armed forces were stationed in or at least passed through the greater Bay Area.[6] This was the beginning of the intertribal foundation of the Bay Area Urban Indian community. This mostly young population were often unmarried with their whole lives ahead of them. Some returned home to rural areas and reservations, but others stayed in the city and became the "founding generation of the Bay Area Indian community."[7]

Decades before Indian Relocation, this population, while small, was actively carving out a space for other Urban Indians in the Bay Area. In these early years, Native people found each other at local bars or, more frequently, through organizations like the Four Winds Club, operated out of Oakland's YWCA. This hub started as early as the 1920s as an extension of the Y. In the early years, it was a central meeting place for Native women in the Bay Area, particularly outing women. Members of the club met on Thursdays, when domestic workers had their day off. By the mid-1930s, the Four Winds Club established a lively social calendar, hosting afternoon tea, socials, and dinners. While the organization was very much a product of the Y and managed by outing matrons, Indian women made it their own. In addition to creating a community space for outing women and girls, the Four Winds Club grew to include Indians from all over the Bay Area, including college students and military personnel. By World War II, the club grew even further and became an organization for both Native women and Native men. Eventually, as Lobo notes, "these first inter-tribal migrants to the city formed voluntary associations."[8] In addition to the Four Winds, local Native people began to create organized sports, including basketball, bowling, and softball teams. Decades after its humble beginnings, the new generation of the Four Winds Club organized to establish a long-lasting community that would embrace the incoming influx of Native people.

In 1954, under the Indian Relocation policy, Indian people from across the country migrated to the San Francisco Bay Area. Relocation was part and parcel to Termination policy, in which the government literally terminated and dismantled tribes across the nation. The goal of both policies was assimilation. Policymakers believed that if Indian people were taken from the reservation and sent to urban areas, assimilation would be complete. One of the initial relocation sites on the West Coast was Oakland. Here, the relocatee population largely comprised young and unmarried people, many from Plains and Southwest tribes. Government assistance through the Bureau of Indian Affairs (BIA) was only temporary; it usually consisted of a few months of assistance in locating and paying for housing and sometimes—especially later in the program—assistance in job training. As relocatees settled in the Bay Area, the BIA encouraged nonclustered housing to facilitate assimilation. Such dispersed housing was considered "a step toward 'melting into'" the population at large. Lobo argues that BIA assistance was "inadequate" to meet the "complex, diverse and immense" needs of relocatees, who were far from home in a foreign environment. Temporary, inadequate assistance and isolation meant that newly relocated Indian people experienced great need, compounded by culture shock. For many relocates, this was their first experience living off of reservations, out of state, or in urban areas. Moving into the city was like "stepping off into the unknown and actual arrival to the city was often a sudden jolt of urban reality."[9] The Native community expanded very quickly from its foundations established in earlier decades. Genny Mitchell, an elder in the community, explained that in the 1950s, the Four Winds Club "outgrew itself."[10] An increased Urban Indian population required a larger community space. This new space drew from the "founding generation" to create the Intertribal Friendship House.

The Intertribal Friendship House, affectionately known as IFH, was founded in 1955. The inaugural building was situated on Telegraph Avenue in Oakland. This Native hub was one of the first of its kind in the United States, providing not only a main community space but also a variety of social services, as well as cultural and recreational programs.[11] Mitchell recollects that IFH had a vibrant weekly calendar and pulled people from the Four Winds because "it was what people needed then." The center was open three or four nights a week, with Saturday activities and Sunday services. Ruth Sarracino Hopper, who grew up in the Santa Fe Indian Village, recalls that IFH "was a good place for gathering and welcoming for all Indian people." It was one of the "hot spots," in addition to Indian bars and the Oakland YWCA. They had rock 'n' roll dances on Friday nights and regular socials.[12] One of the most notable was the Singles Supper Club. On Wednesday nights in the late '50s, dozens of diners paid fifty cents for a meal and a chance to meet other eligible singles. One woman called it a "dating bureau."[13] Similar feeds, for romance or otherwise, have continued to this day.

By the 1960s, a new pan-Indian consciousness within the Bay Area American Indian community had begun to emerge. As the Bay Area Indian population grew, so did specialized organizations that responded to everyday Urban Indian needs, addressing housing, food, education, economic stability, and cultural expression. Some of the organizations that still exist today include the Native American Health Center, the American Indian Child Resource Center, International Indian Treaty Council, Hintil Kuu Ca, and California Indian Legal Services. In the absence of ethnic neighborhoods, these organizations and their events "provided the locational nodes in the developing community network."[14] Lobo's concept of "nodes" echoes Ramirez's hubs. Indian community centers, organizations, and events sustained tribal connections in a decidedly urban environment. Indeed, while Urban Indians made the Bay Area their home, their ties to their tribal communities were not broken. Rather, as Lobo argues, "one simply extends the territory." The Bay Area Indian "community is characterized by a geographic mobility as people move in and out of the city, make return visits to their rural home territories or reservations, or sometimes return there for good."[15] Just like Native women in the outing program, this next generation of Indian people journeyed back and forth from their communities and reservations. In the city, the hubs provided. For a community spread out across the bay, these Native hubs were and are essential to fostering and maintaining the Bay Area Indian community.

Over time, the Bay Area Indian community grew increasingly diverse in its tribal representation, age, and occupation. Socioeconomic diversity also occurred, as Indian people gained seniority in their workplaces and took advantage of opportunities in higher education that became available after the mid-'60s. Some moved out of the inner city to suburbs, where they enjoyed greater access to better public schools and safer communities.[16] This new generation of Indian people in the Bay Area gained access to new opportunities. The children of Native domestic workers tapped into these prospects and created new futures for themselves and their families. Long after the Bay Area Outing Program, some Native women continued laboring as domestic workers. After all, it was what they were trained for, and work was not hard to find. However, in the city, their children were not forced into domestic labor or into boarding schools. Instead, many attended public school and graduated from college. These children contributed to the growing Urban Indian community, participating in sports leagues, powwows, and centers like IFH. All of these things had come into existence with the help their mothers, who had organized the first intertribal hub in the San Francisco Bay Area. Indeed, the same women who came to labor in the early twentieth century created and sustained community and fostered Indian identity in the growing intertribal urban environment. Those Thursday meetings in the 1920s, 1930s, and 1940s developed into a thriving Bay Area Indian community for generations to come. Their efforts serve as a testament to the failure of assimilation and open resistance to it.

This project has explored the rich and complicated lives of Native women who experienced the weight of federal assimilation efforts through the Bay Area Outing Program. I interrogated the overarching question, Within the confines of domestic labor, how did Native women comply, resist, and negotiate their circumstances? The chapters in this study revealed that the Bay Area Outing Program was structurally oppressive, requiring regular surveillance of the lives and bodies of Native girls and women. Women who came to the city to work were constrained by scales of containment. Many ran away, only to return for the security of wage work. Outing matrons imposed strict regulations on live-in domestic workers—but rarely their employers. Amid the demands of domestic work, some young women were criminalized and incarcerated in Bay Area detention centers. Others resisted the threat of Indian child removal. Others still were faced with life-threatening illnesses and found themselves subject to the fickle benevolence of outing matrons, federal negligence, and a murderously inadequate Indian health care system. Women were drawn to the Bay Area Outing Program to experience city life and provide for their families, yet they often found that the program was invested in their dispossession. This study has chronicled a history of gendered, racialized labor and its effects on Native women and their families. Through their own voices and actions, I demonstrated how Native women navigated this system of oppression. Some reworked potential and possibility into these systems. Close examination of those who frustrated the system reveals that Native women challenged their liminal standing and unsettled domesticity.

Notes

Preface

1 "Tahoe" is the anglicized mispronunciation of the Washoe word for lake, *dáʔaw*. I am grateful to linguist Ryan Bochnak for assistance with the spelling of *daʔawʔá·gaʔ* and for being a great Washoe teacher.

Prologue

1 Bagwell, *Oakland*, 81; Johnson, *The Second Gold Rush*, 14–17; Gutman, *A City for Children*, 17–19.
2 Gutman, *A City for Children*, 69.
3 Gutman, *A City for Children*, 39.
4 Gutman, *A City for Children*, 72.
5 "The Great 1906 San Francisco Earthquake," Earthquake Hazards Program of the U.S. Geological Survey (USGS), accessed September 30, 2023, https://earthquake.usgs.gov/earthquakes/events/1906calif/18april.
6 Bagwell, *Oakland*, 179.
7 Bagwell, *Oakland*, 201.
8 Bagwell, *Oakland*, 205.
9 "27 Indian Girls from the Reservation Welcomed by Oakland Housewives," *Oakland Tribune*, June 6, 1919, home ed. This article mentions Mrs. Helen C. Sheahan from Carson Indian School as the girls' chaperone.
10 Bagwell, *Oakland*, 221.
11 Bagwell, *Oakland*, 178–85.
12 Bagwell, *Oakland*, 164–67. See also O'Donoghue, "'End of the Line': How We

Lost the Key System," East Bay Yesterday, accessed October 9, 2023, https://soundcloud.com/user-736747354/end-of-the-line-how-we-lost-the-key-system.

Introduction

1 The Tribune misspelled Belma's surname as "Barbar." It is in fact "Barber." A 1920 census record indicates that by the age of eight years old, Barber was an enrolled student at Stewart Indian School. 1920 United States Federal Census—Belma Barber, United States Census, Carson, Ormsby, Nevada, roll T625_1004, page 1B, enumeration district 68, records of the Bureau of the Census, record group 29, National Archives, Washington, DC.

2 Trennert, "From Carlisle to Phoenix," 267. Though Pratt established outing in the federal Indian boarding school model, the concept of placing Indian children in religious homes as a means to educate them stemmed from American colonial period practices.

3 For instance, Glenn, *Issei, Nisei, War Bride*; Romero, *Maid in the U.S.A.*; Parreñas, *Servants of Globalization*; Hondagneu-Sotelo, *Doméstica.*

4 See above note as well as Rollins, *Between Women*; Palmer, *Domesticity and Dirt*; Tucker, *Telling Memories among Southern Women*; Katzman, *Seven Days a Week.*

5 Glenn, *Issei, Nisei, War Bride*, 99. For a brief time, Chinese and Japanese male servants were common in California, but the lion's share of the field was and continues to be composed of women.

6 Glenn, *Forced to Care.*

7 Hondagneu-Sotelo, *Doméstica*, 22–23.

8 Haskins and Lowrie, *Colonization and Domestic Service.*

9 Hansen, *Distant Companions.*

10 Glenn, *Forced to Care*, 86.

11 The conditions of domestic work are consistently difficult and often exploitative, especially for immigrant and undocumented workers. Even where workers seemingly have a good rapport with their employers, scholars reveal that feelings of anger and resentment are commonplace. Mary Romero found that while working in white middle-class women's homes, Chicana domestic workers experienced humiliation and exploitation. They quickly learned that their employers were not "comrades" or their "sisters." Instead, Chicana workers found themselves starved for respect and positive social interaction. Romero, *Maid in the U.S.A.* Domestics across the board experience low wages, as well as non- and

underpayment of wages. While the job is difficult and arduous, it is especially so for live-in workers. Even during breaks and off time, live-in domestics are expected to respond to employers' needs as they arise. Glenn asserts that with live-in positions, "there [is] no clear line between work and non-work time." Glenn, *Issei, Nisei, War Bride*, 141. In Hondagneu-Sotelo's study, domestics felt that live-in work was depressing, and their employers frequently abused or took advantage of them. For one woman, live-in work necessitated "social isolation, morning-to-midnight work schedules, and additions to cleaning tasks without commensurate raises in pay." Hondagneu-Sotelo, *Doméstica*, 65. Despite their poor working conditions, many domestic workers feel compelled to remain for the sake of a good reference. Whereas in most sectors, long-term employment means higher wages over time, for domestic workers, it is often the opposite.

12 Wolfe, "Settler Colonialism and the Elimination of the Native," 388.

13 Lobo, *Urban Voices*; Ramirez, *Native Hubs*; Rosenthal, *Reimagining Indian Country*; LaPier and Beck, *City Indian*; Thrush and Cronon, *Native Seattle*; Miller, *Indians on the Move*. For an international account, see Thrush, *Indigenous London*.

14 Rosenthal, *Reimagining Indian Country*, 19–23.

15 Miller, *Indians on the Move*, 33.

16 Miller, *Indians on the Move*, 37.

17 Miller, *Indians on the Move*, 67–89.

18 Miller, *Indians on the Move*, 1.

19 Ramirez, *Native Hubs*, 47.

20 Miller, *Indians on the Move*, 37.

21 Meriam, *The Problem of Indian Administration*, 389. The federal report, published in 1928 and administered by the Brookings Institution, surveyed conditions on Indian reservations in twenty-six states.

22 Whalen, *Native Students at Work*; Haskins, *Matrons and Maids*.

23 Markwyn's thesis provides an excellent overview of the late 1920s and early 1930s outing program as administered by Matron Bonnie Royce. Her particular attention to Native community illuminates how Native women coped with physically isolating work and imagined new futures for themselves. Markwyn, "'It Was a Place for the Girls to Meet.'" Jacobs's article turned subchapter on outing extends into the 1940s and Matron Van Every's role in the program. It offers a comparative view of Native women's experiences to those of Aboriginal women in Australia. Jacobs considers white women maternalists like outing matrons and outing employers as key players in the process of settler colo-

nialism. Her analysis examines how Native women experienced conflict with their employers and often defied the matrons. Jacobs also focuses on women who became pregnant while outing, paying close attention to single mothers. Jacobs, "Working on the Domestic Frontier." This thread of analysis continues in her subsequent article, "Diverted Mothering," which explores processes of Indian child removal in the outing program.

24 Jacobs, "Working on the Domestic Frontier," 165–99; Jacobs, "Diverted Mothering among American Indian Domestic Servants," 179–92; Markwyn, "'It Was a Place for the Girls to Meet.'"

25 Adams, *Education for Extinction*; Child, *Boarding School Seasons*; Lomawaima, *They Called It Prairie Light*; Lomawaima and McCarty, *"To Remain an Indian."* For a Canadian context, see Graham, *The Mush Hole.*

26 For more on carcerality and criminality in Native communities and in California, see Ross, *Inventing the Savage*; Chavez-Garcia, *States of Delinquency*; Lumsden, "Reproductive Justice, Sovereignty, and Incarceration," 33–46; Teran, "The Violent Legacies of the California Missions," 19–32.

27 Trouillot, *Silencing the Past*, 48.

28 Risling Baldy, *We Are Dancing for You*, 24.

29 I did not make this decision lightly and a great deal of thought went into it. I am reminded of Deborah Miranda's work on telling histories of violence. That storytelling is "testimony, education, community action, resistance." That storytelling has the power to heal. Miranda, "'Saying the Padre Grabbed Her,'" 107.

ONE / Domestic Labor in California, 1769–1940

1 Reséndez, *The Other Slavery*; Hackel, *Children of Coyote, Missionaries of Saint Francis*; Miranda, *Bad Indians*; Bauer, *We Were All Like Migrant Workers Here*; Hurtado, *Indian Survival on the California Frontier*; Sandos, *Converting California*; Silliman, *Lost Laborers in Colonial California*; Forbes, *Native Americans of California and Nevada*; Rawls, *Indians of California*; Magliari, "Free State Slavery"; Magliari, "Free Soil, Unfree Labor."

2 Trennert, "From Carlisle to Phoenix," 267–91; Jacobs, *White Mother to a Dark Race*; Haskins, *Matrons and Maids*; Valoma, *Scrape the Willow until It Sings*; Keliiaa, "Unsettling Domesticity," 87–90.

3 Paxton, "Learning Gender," 174–86; Trennert, "From Carlisle to Phoenix," 267–91; Olund, "Public Domesticity during the Indian Reform Era," 153–66; Lomawaima, "Estelle Reel, Superintendent of Indian Schools," 5–32; Prucha,

Americanizing the American Indians; Lomawaima and McCarty, *"To Remain an Indian"*; Lomawaima, "Domesticity in the Federal Indian Schools," 227–40; Trennert, "Educating Indian Girls at Nonreservation Boarding Schools," 281.

4 In this chapter I use the term "slavery" or "enslavement" to discuss the various forms of Indian enslavement in the Spanish, Mexican, and American periods. In doing so, I also take up California Indian scholar Stephanie Lumsden's treatise to frustrate the language of the colonial archive. Lumsden argues, "The failure of historians to deploy the language of slavery consistently in their analyses of California Indian genocide upholds the narrative of the settler state and erases the violence of captivity while replacing it with the sanitized langue of state benevolence." Lumsden, "What's in a Name?"

5 Wolfe, "Settler Colonialism and the Elimination of the Native," 388.

6 Wolfe, "Settler Colonialism and the Elimination of the Native," 388.

7 Hixson, *American Settler Colonialism*, 1.

8 Hixson, *American Settler Colonialism*, 5.

9 Veracini, *Settler Colonialism*, 75.

10 Reed, "We Are a Part of the Land and the Land Is Us," 27–49.

11 Arvin, Tuck, and Morrill, "Decolonizing Feminism," 8–34.

12 Baldy, *We Are Dancing for You*, 12.

13 Baldy, *We Are Dancing for You*, 13.

14 Jacobs, *White Mother to a Dark Race*, 4.

15 Jacobs, *White Mother to a Dark Race*, 149.

16 Jacobs, *White Mother to a Dark Race*, 193–92 (emphasis added). The destructive process for reaching Indian "assimilation" or "protection" outweighed any supposed benefits these children were to receive. Compared to "traditional" colonialism, Jacobs argues that "settler colonialism was anything but benign and may have been even more deadly to Indigenous people than more classic types of extractive colonialism."

17 Wolfe, "Land, Labor, and Difference," 867.

18 Interestingly, Wolfe's footnotes argue that the "pure" settler colonialism of the Australian and North American varieties "should be distinguished from so-called colonial settler societies that depended on indigenous labor," as found in southern Africa or South Asia.

19 Glenn, *Forced to Care*, 43.

20 Glenn's *Forced to Care* offers a thorough analysis of the gendered and racialized reality of caring labor, which has induced women, and especially poor and minority women, to assume the responsibility of caring for family members.

21 Kaplan, "Manifest Domesticity," 582.

22 Kaplan, "Manifest Domesticity," 583.

23 Jacobs, "Working on the Domestic Frontier," 166.

24 Jacobs, "Working on the Domestic Frontier," 190.

25 Haskins, "Domestic Service and Frontier Feminism," 124.

26 Haskins, "Domestic Service and Frontier Feminism," 142.

27 Stoler, *Carnal Knowledge and Imperial Power*, 7.

28 Pratt, "Arts of the Contact Zone," 33–40.

29 Conor, *Skin Deep*, 114.

30 Haskins, "On the Doorstep."

31 Haskins, "On the Doorstep," 18.

32 Also known in Spanish as *neofitos*.

33 Sandos, *Converting California*, 95.

34 Sandos, *Converting California*, 101.

35 Hackel, *Children of Coyote, Missionaries of Saint Francis*, 285.

36 Hurtado, *Intimate Frontiers*, 22.

37 According to Sherburne Cook, "Secularization of the missions created a vast population of wandering, vagrant Indians." Cook, *Conflict between the California Indian and White Civilization*, 471. While perhaps not "wandering," these Indians that had been born and raised within the structure of the mission system had no other means aside from entering into the market of labor exploitation. Moreover, as California Indian policy developed, the issue of "vagrancy" meant that Indians not employed could be arrested or punished and forced to labor.

38 Hackel, *Children of Coyote, Missionaries of Saint Francis*, 370.

39 Castillo, "The Impact of Euro-American Exploration and Settlement," 105.

40 Silliman, *Lost Laborers in Colonial California*, 12.

41 Forbes, *Native Americans of California and Nevada*, 54. Interestingly, these rancho demands mirror Indian education policy decades later, which institutionalized Native women domestic workers and Native men ranch hands through Indian boarding schools. Moreover, Hurtado notes that those who did not become "peons" for Mexican rancheros moved to California's interior, where they lived more freely with independent Indian communities. Hurtado, *Indian Survival on the California Frontier*, 32–54. See also Haas, *Saints and Citizens* and Tac, *Pablo Tac, Indigenous Scholar*.

42 Silliman, *Lost Laborers in Colonial California*, 69.

43 Forbes, *Native Americans of California and Nevada*, 54.

44 Sánchez, *Telling Identities*, 173.

45 Silliman, *Lost Laborers in Colonial California*, 13.

46 Silliman, *Lost Laborers in Colonial California*, 22–23. According to Bakken (cited in Silliman, pg. 24), at Rancho Cañon de Santa Ana, Bernardo Yorba retained twenty-six Indians as domestic servants, over one hundred as livestock workers, and fourteen for wool combing, tanning, and household entertainments. They were paid in silver dollars.

47 Silliman, *Lost Laborers in Colonial California*, 23–24.

48 Forbes, *Native Americans of California and Nevada*, 59.

49 Hurtado, *Intimate Frontiers*, 39–40.

50 Phillips, *Indians and Indian Agents*, 39; Forbes, *Native Americans of California and Nevada*, 60.

51 Hurtado, *Indian Survival on the California Frontier*, 49.

52 Hurtado, *Indian Survival on the California Frontier*, 55.

53 Hurtado, *Intimate Frontiers*, 41.

54 Hurtado, *Intimate Frontiers*, 42.

55 Phillips, *Indians and Indian Agents*, 34.

56 Bauer, "Native Californians in the Nineteenth Century," 196.

57 Rawls, *Indians of California*, 81.

58 Rawls, *Indians of California*, 88.

59 Magliari, "Free State Slavery," 157.

60 Mexican, Chinese, or other nonwhite immigrants were unable to petition Indian wards or "apprentices."

61 Hurtado, "'Hardly a Farm House—A Kitchen without Them,'" 245–70.

62 Rawls, *Indians of California*, 99.

63 Hurtado, *Indian Survival on the California Frontier*, 169–92.

64 Rawls, *Indians of California*, 87.

65 Magliari, "Free State Slavery," 168; Chandler and Quinn, "Emma Is a Good Girl."

66 Magliari, "Free State Slavery," 174.

67 Magliari, "Free State Slavery," 177.

68 Magliari, "Free State Slavery," 177.

69 Michael Magliari argues that in rural households, young married white women settlers played a major role in the demand for bound Indian labor. In fact, Henry Bailey admitted, "All the early female settlers of California were overworked" and "found little respite from never-ending household cares and grind of cooking, washing, scouring, milking, churning and all the other tread wheel

attachments of the time." Magliari, "Free State Slavery," 176. White women played a significant role in the settler colonial project.

70 Magliari, "Free State Slavery," 184–85.

71 Mr. Chase desired an Indian servant early on, but his wife, untrusting of her husband in his early forties, refused the idea. Her refusal underlies fear that her husband might make sexual advances on the girl and take advantage of her.

72 Chandler and Quinn, "Emma Is a Good Girl," 35.

73 Chandler and Quinn, "Emma Is a Good Girl," 37.

74 Chandler and Quinn, "Emma Is a Good Girl," 35.

75 Glancy, *Fort Marion Prisoners and the Trauma of Native Education*, 103.

76 Adams, *Education for Extinction*, 36–49. Hampton is where Pratt, along with Hampton's founder and principal, Samuel Armstrong, crafted the infamous "before" and "after" institutionalization images of Native children.

77 Child, *Boarding School Seasons*, 5–6.

78 Lomawaima and Ostler, "Reconsidering Richard Henry Pratt," 79–100. New research suggests that Pratt may not have been the architect that scholars previously believed him to be. He both deplored and attacked the Office of Indian Affairs for its use of Indian schools as a means to train Native people into subservience and control.

79 Adams, *Education for Extinction*, 19–20.

80 National Native American Boarding School Healing Coalition, "Indian Boarding Schools in the United States." This number includes a mix of schools, including faith-based institutions, those that received federal funding, those operated by the modern Bureau of Indian Education, and those still open today.

81 Adams, *Education for Extinction*, 58. This number is not inclusive of day schools, which accounted for nearly four thousand students in 1900.

82 Adams, *Education for Extinction*, 27. It is important to note that Canada operated its own system of Indian "residential" schools, which operated similarly to US Indian boarding schools but are technically distinct. For more information, see the Truth and Reconciliation Commission of Canada and its final report. Truth and Reconciliation Commission of Canada, accessed April 4, 2024, www.rcaanc-cirnac.gc.ca/eng/1450124405592/1529106060525.

83 Ziibiwing Center of Anishinabe Culture & Lifeways, *American Indian Boarding Schools*, 10.

84 Lomawaima and McCarty, *"To Remain an Indian,"* 4.

85 Lomawaima and McCarty, *"To Remain an Indian,"* 4.

86 Adams, *Education for Extinction*, 100–120.

87 Adams, *Education for Extinction*, 331–32.

88 Krupat, *Changed Forever*, xvii.

89 Reel, *Course of Study for the Indian Schools of the United States*, 151.

90 Littlefield and Knack, *Native Americans and Wage Labor*, 117.

91 Whalen, *Native Students at Work*, 163.

92 Whalen, *Native Students at Work*, 64.

93 Trennert, "Educating Indian Girls at Nonreservation Boarding Schools," 286.

94 Bonnell, "Chemawa Indian Boarding School."

95 Gilbert, *Education beyond the Mesas*.

96 Katanski, *Learning to Write "Indian."*

97 Lomawaima and McCarty, *"To Remain an Indian,"* 52–53.

98 Littlefield and Knack, *Native Americans and Wage Labor*.

99 Krupat, *Changed Forever*, xviii. At Carlisle, students had to request or agree to an outing assignment, but it is not clear that they understood they had a choice.

100 Littlefield and Knack, *Native Americans and Wage Labor*.

101 Trennert, *The Phoenix Indian School*, 72.

102 Whalen, *Native Students at Work*, 58–59.

103 Williams, *Assimilation, Resilience, and Survival*.

104 Haskins, *Matrons and Maids*.

105 Lomawaima, *They Called It Prairie Light*; Lomawaima, "Estelle Reel, Superintendent of Indian Schools," 5–31; Lomawaima and McCarty, *"To Remain an Indian"*; Child, *Boarding School Seasons*; Adams, *Education for Extinction*; Trennert, "Educating Indian Girls at Nonreservation Boarding Schools"; Jacobs, *White Mother to a Dark Race*; Whalen, *Native Students at Work*; Haskins, *Matrons and Maids*.

106 For more on Victorian morality and womanhood, see Lomawaima, "Domesticity in the Federal Indian Schools," 227–40; McClintock, *Imperial Leather*; Trennert, "Victorian Morality and the Supervision of Indian Women Working in Phoenix," 113–28; Olund, "Public Domesticity during the Indian Reform Era," 153–66; Paxton, "Learning Gender," 182.

107 Haskins, *Matrons and Maids*, 166.

108 Haskins, *Matrons and Maids*, 164.

109 Trennert, "Victorian Morality and the Supervision of Indian Women Working in Phoenix," 123–24.

110 Piatote, *Domestic Subjects*, 87.

111 Trennert, "From Carlisle to Phoenix," 280.

112 Whalen, "Labored Learning," 156.

113 Native girls and women often worked collectively to resist the assimilation doctrine. Runaways often traveled in groups and worked together to resist policies meant to control and marginalize them.

114 Lomawaima, *They Called It Prairie Light*, 96.

TWO / The Bay Area Outing Program

1 Outing Certificate—Stella Healey, 1931, NARA, Healey, Stella.

2 Family History, May 22, 1934, NARA, Healey, Stella.

3 Asst. Superintendent to Stella Healey, August 24, 1928, NARA, Healey, Stella.

4 Frederic Snyder to Alice Gibson, August 19, 1931, NARA, Healey, Stella.

5 The Office of Indian Affairs (OIA) was later renamed the Bureau of Indian Affairs (BIA).

6 Whalen, "Labored Learning," 153.

7 Child, *Boarding School Seasons*, 5–6; Glancy, *Fort Marion Prisoners and the Trauma of Native Education*. In Pratt's outing program at Carlisle, employers were to treat outing participants "like family." In the West, however, outing focused more on labor extraction. Western patrons of outing were not concerned with education but rather with cheap labor, and western-based Indian boarding schools and outing programs delivered.

8 Trennert, "From Carlisle to Phoenix"; Whalen, *Native Students at Work*.

9 Haskins, *Matrons and Maids*.

10 Trennert, "From Carlisle to Phoenix," 268; Bauer, "The Economy of Indian Education in California," 91–113; Littlefield, "Indian Education and the World of Work in Michigan," 100–121; Child, *Boarding School Seasons*.

11 Child, *Boarding School Seasons*, 79–80.

12 Practice cottages were established at various boarding schools. Students took turns living in the house to learn more about homemaking. Some practice cottages also included baby dolls so girl students could learn to care for a baby's feeding, bathing, and laundering. For more on practice cottages, or "industrial" or "model" cottages for Native children, see Buffalohead and Molin, "'A Nucleus of Civilization,'" 59–94; Lomawaima, "Estelle Reel, Superintendent of Indian Schools"; Simonsen, "'Object Lessons': Domesticity and Display in Native American Assimilation," 75–99; Trennert, "Educating Indian Girls at Nonreservation Boarding Schools," 271–90; Orata and Galloway, "Promoting Boy-Girl Relationships through the Practice Cottage," 321–23.

13 Whalen, *Native Students at Work*, 163.

14 Trennert, "From Carlisle to Phoenix," 282–83.

15 Lomawaima, *They Called It Prairie Light*.

16 United States, *Annual Reports of the Department of the Interior*.

17 Bauer, *We Were All Like Migrant Workers Here*, 14.

18 Bauer, *We Were All Like Migrant Workers Here*, 3.

19 Beck, *Unfair Labor?*

20 Child, *My Grandfather's Knocking Sticks*.

21 O'Neill and Hosmer, *Native Pathways*.

22 O'Neill, *Working the Navajo Way*.

23 Raibmon, *Authentic Indians*.

24 Bauer, *We Were All Like Migrant Workers Here*.

25 Littlefield and Knack, *Native Americans and Wage Labor*, 14.

26 Littlefield and Knack, *Native Americans and Wage Labor*, 36.

27 Littlefield and Knack, *Native Americans and Wage Labor*, 42.

28 Knack, "Nineteenth-Century Great Basin Wage Labor," 168.

29 Knack, "Nineteenth-Century Great Basin Wage Labor," 162.

30 Knack, "Nineteenth-Century Great Basin Wage Labor," 150–53.

31 Knack, "Nineteenth-Century Great Basin Wage Labor," 150.

32 Knack, "Nineteenth-Century Great Basin Wage Labor," 174.

33 Knack, "The Dynamics of Southern Paiute Women's Roles," 148–52.

34 Patterson, "Evolving Gender Roles in Pomo Society," 128–44.

35 *Survey of Conditions of the Indians in the United States*. See especially Bishop Subagency and Hoopa Agency.

36 Littlefield and Knack, *Native Americans and Wage Labor*, 18. While illuminating, these census statistics missed other forms of labor and women's wages earned from seasonal agricultural labor, crafts, etc.

37 Arguably, a shortage of farms in the Bay Area influenced the absence of male workers in the Bay Area Outing Program. However, in the early twentieth century, large swaths of agricultural land existed just outside of the city. In effect, the program could have integrated male outing labor similarly to Sherman's outing program. Ultimately, it did not.

38 "Escaped Indian Girl Located in Oakland: Minnie Rook Will Be Returned to School," *San Francisco Call*, September 26, 1911.

39 "Ishi Host at Reception to Indian Maids: Builds Primitive Fires; Sings Songs to Entertain Fair Carson Students. First Native Girls He Ever Saw; They Warble Love Notes; He Grows Sad," *San Francisco Call*, August 26, 1912.

40 Anthropologist Alfred Kroeber sent his protégé T. T. Waterman to capture Ishi. In 1911, Ishi was found at a slaughterhouse in Oroville, California. He was promptly arrested and then turned over to the anthropologists. For a critical account of Ishi's life and legacy, see Bauer, "Stop Hunting Ishi," 46–50.

41 "Situation Wanted," *Berkeley Daily Gazette*, June 16, 1913.

42 For more information on Japanese domestic workers in the Bay Area, see Evelyn Nakano Glenn, *Issei, Nisei, War Bride*.

43 "Lost Indian Girl Sought by Police," *Berkeley Daily Gazette*, October 22, 1914. In fact, there is no such thing as the "Carson Indian Reservation." The author of this article confused "reservation" for "school." Today there exists federally recognized reservation land in Carson City, Nevada, known as the "Carson colony" of the Washoe Tribe of Nevada and California. However, this land acquisition occurred decades after publication of said article.

44 Southworth and Ben-Joseph, *Streets and the Shaping of Towns and Cities*, 109–13. The neighborhood was developed after the 1906 earthquake at a distance from the central city. Over time, it became enveloped by it. Original homes in the area were built on a lot-by-lot basis, suggesting that the home's 1918 build was financed by the Office of Indian Affairs.

45 Some archival documents lacked specific data about a woman's outing employment. However, if the file contained an application for outing employment, that address was included in the map. If an employment address was missing, we used "catchall" addresses, including the outing matron's offices throughout the Bay Area, such as on Market Street in San Francisco and Webster Street in Oakland. While less common, some addresses represented in this map include outing placements at schools and hospitals.

46 Sells's reference to mining towns alludes to the lawlessness and chaos brought forth by California's Gold Rush (1848–55) and Nevada's Comstock Lode (1859–81). As described in the introduction, these events brought forth thousands of fortune-seeking settlers notorious for unruliness and disorder. Saloons, gambling houses, brothels, and other businesses catering to such a clientele helped create an unsavory and dangerous environment. Sells's reference to "degrading moral conditions" was code for promiscuity, prostitution, and sex. Commissioner Sells, therefore, sought to remove Native women from these demoralizing environments.

47 Jacobs, "Working on the Domestic Frontier," 176.

48 Lomawaima, "Domesticity in the Federal Indian Schools," 230.

49 Cahill, *Federal Fathers and Mothers*.

50 Jacobs, *White Mother to a Dark Race*, 282.

51 Jacobs, "Working on the Domestic Frontier," 173–74.

52 Paxton, "Learning Gender," 179.

53 Bonnie V. Royce to Ivora Nelson, September 17, 1929, NARA, Nelson, Ivora.

54 As an interesting point of comparison, the Phoenix outing program, which grew from Phoenix Indian School, controlled all Native women in the Phoenix area, including nonstudent, reservation-based women. As Robert Trennert has found, Phoenix outing matron Chingren had the power to place, punish, or jail local Native women. Trennert, "Victorian Morality and the Supervision of Indian Women Working in Phoenix," 124.

55 Irene Tungate to John Collier, August 6, 1933, NARA, Tungate Spinks, Irene. Tungate continued in domestic work for nearly a decade after her appeal to Collier. In 1942 she completed a training to become a hospital attendant.

56 O'Neill, "Testing the Limits of Colonial Parenting," 578.

57 Williams, *Assimilation, Resilience, and Survival*, 77.

58 Lois Godawa to Mildred Van Every, August 15, 1942, NARA, Godawa, Lois.

59 Odem, *Delinquent Daughters*, 40–42.

60 Glenn, *Issei, Nisei, War Bride*, 99–109. See also Katzman, *Seven Days a Week*.

61 Mr. Harry H. Meyers to Mildred Van Every, November 28, 1940, NARA, Meyers, Dorothy.

62 Jacobs, "Working on the Domestic Frontier," 175.

63 Helen Kibby to Mildred Van Every, August 20, 1939, NARA, Kibby, Helen.

64 "Commensurate" as in wages relative to other Native women doing similar domestic work and/or relative to Native women's established pay rate based on their skill set.

65 Freda Eleck to Mildred Van Every, January 20, 1936, NARA, Eleck, Freda.

66 Freda Eleck to Mildred Van Every, February 11, 1936, NARA, Eleck, Freda.

67 Specifically, the form in 1936 lists "Graduate of Stewart, Haskell Inst., Sherman Inst. or Chemawa," thus illuminating the official ties between these Indian boarding school institutions and the young women they transferred among them for domestic employment.

68 Application for Girls, February 17, 1936, NARA, Eleck, Freda.

69 Eleck, Freda, 1937, NARA, Eleck, Freda.

70 Index Outing System—Hazel Emm, 1935, NARA, Hazel Emm.

71 Dorris C. Taft to Jeannette Traxler, November 13, 1933, NARA, Hazel Emm.

72 Outing Certificate—Kathryn Jones, June 1931, NARA, Jones, Kathryn.

73 Lettie Holland to Bonnie V. Royce, August 7, 1930, NARA, Jones, Kathryn.

74 Supt. McNeilly to Bonnie V. Royce, February 23, 1932, NARA, Egan, Lucy.

75 Williams, *Assimilation, Resilience, and Survival*, 92. Williams argues that this kind of labor "reinforced white, middle-class gender norms, perpetuated the assimilationist policies of previous years, and reversed the school's previous policy of reducing the number of hours students engaged in vocational and industrial labor" (94). Into the 1960s and '70s, despite BIA mandates otherwise, girl students still received domestic training at Stewart (160, 184).

76 For more on Victorian morality and womanhood, see Lomawaima, "Domesticity in the Federal Indian Schools," 227–40; McClintock, *Imperial Leather*; Trennert, "Victorian Morality and the Supervision of Indian Women Working in Phoenix," 113–28; Olund, "Public Domesticity during the Indian Reform Era," 153–66; Paxton, "Learning Gender," 182.

77 Lomawaima, "Estelle Reel, Superintendent of Indian Schools," 8. This half-day plan started with Pratt and became entrenched in official boarding school policy.

78 Interview with Esther Wasson, December 7, 2013. Victoria Patterson and Robert Trennert have both found that Indian women in outing regularly sent remittances home to their families living on impoverished reservations. In fact, for the Phoenix outing program, Trennert maintains that financial benefits were the main reason Indian women joined the program. Trennert, "Victorian Morality and the Supervision of Indian Women Working in Phoenix," 118; Patterson, "Indian Life in the City" 409–10.

79 Application to Bay Region Employment Agencies for Employment, February 1936, NARA, Eleck, Freda.

80 Outing Certificate—Kathryn Jones, June 1931, NARA, Jones, Kathryn.

81 Reel, *Course of Study for the Indian Schools of the United States*, 190. For more analysis on Reel, see Lomawaima, "Estelle Reel, Superintendent of Indian Schools," 5–31; Lomawaima and McCarty, *"To Remain an Indian"*; Glenn, *Forced to Care* 42–57; Slivka, "Art, Craft, and Assimilation," 225–42.

82 Lomawaima, "Estelle Reel, Superintendent of Indian Schools," 149.

83 Reel, *Course of Study for the Indian Schools of the United States*, 151.

84 Harriet Cleveland to Bonnie V. Royce, March 4, 1932, NARA, Cleveland, Harriet.

85 Bonnie V. Royce to Harriet Cleveland, March 8, 1932, NARA, Cleveland, Harriet.

86 Index Outing System—Harriet Cleveland, 1932, NARA, Cleveland, Harriet.

87 Mildred Van Every to Helen Williams, February 28, 1941, NARA, Williams, Helen.

88 Helen Williams to Mildred Van Every, January 31, 1941, NARA, Williams, Helen.

89 Assistant Superintendent S. E. Beahm to Alice Davies Endriss, August 17, 1925, NARA, Paradice, Ruby. Beahm's mention of "drop out" here suggests that in

the early years of the outing program, not all women enrolled in public school while working throughout the year.

90 Contract—Josephine Natchez, June 1930, NARA, Natchez, Josephine.

91 In practice, placing Indian children to work as live-in domestics in the private homes of American citizens meant that the Office and later Bureau of Indian Affairs was effectively transferring the responsibility of the "Indian problem" from federal hands to private hands. In this way, the OIA/BIA reneged on its responsibilities to Indian communities.

92 Contract—Josephine Natchez, June 1930, NARA, Natchez, Josephine.

93 Lomawaima, "Domesticity in the Federal Indian Schools," 231.

94 Contract—Josephine Natchez, June 1930, NARA, Natchez, Josephine.

95 Haskins, "'The Matter of Wages Does Not Seem to Be Material,'" 336.

96 In her comparative study on outing wages, Haskins found that by the late 1920s, there was a growing dissatisfaction regarding wage withholding among outing girls. By 1930, the SF-based Indian Defense Association of Central and Northern California intervened. The secretary there wrote directly to the commissioner of Indian Affairs regarding several complaints. Apparently, Matron Royce "arbitrarily takes away their earnings and doles them out to them as what money she thinks they should have. These girls want to know what their rights are in the matter." Ultimately the complaints were dismissed. Haskins, "'The Matter of Wages Does Not Seem to Be Material,'" 344–45.

97 Bonnie V. Royce to Frederic Snyder, Supt. of Carson Indian School, October 12, 1931, NARA, Natchez, Josephine.

98 Rosalie Patterson to Mildred Van Every, December 28, 1936, NARA, Patterson Pike, Rosalie. Like most women in the program, Patterson was troubled by the tension between her need for money and her desire to further her education. While considering a cosmetology program in Oakland, she was discouraged by the lower wages that would preclude her from sending remittances home. Dismayed, she contended, "I just have to continue sending mother money."

99 Jacobs, *White Mother to a Dark Race*, 334.

100 Index Outing System—Elaine Johnson, 1933, NARA, Johnson, Elaine.

101 Index Outing System—Grace Boone, 1932, NARA, Boone, Grace.

102 Though the outing program began in 1916, no wages were recorded until roughly 1926.

103 Stigler, "Domestic Servants in the United States."

104 Pratt's contemporary and colleague, anthropologist and historian George Bird Grinnell, argued that outing wages were a lesson in thrift. He wrote, "The

money earned by a child during his outing belongs to him absolutely, yet he is not free to spend it as he wishes." Haskins, "'The Matter of Wages Does Not Seem to be Material,'" 335.

105 Contract—Lucy Egan, June 11, 1930, NARA, Egan, Lucy.

106 Lucy Egan to Bonnie V. Royce, August 9, 1930, NARA, Egan, Lucy.

107 Bonnie V. Royce to Lucy Egan, August 15, 1930, NARA, Egan, Lucy.

108 Haskins, "'The Matter of Wages Does Not Seem to Be Material,'" 334.

109 Index Outing System—Persia McCarty, 1933, NARA, McCarty, Persia. Persia's Outing Index indicates "Wintoona," which might be a misspelling of "Wintun," a Northern California tribe.

110 Index Outing System—Theresa Williams, 1935, NARA, Williams, Theresa.

111 Index Outing System—Thana Thompson Mitchell, 1933, NARA, Thompson Mitchell, Thana.

112 Bonnie V. Royce to Mr. Allen Thompson, March 9, 1933, NARA, Thompson Mitchell, Thana.

113 Index Outing System—Thana Thompson Mitchell, NARA, Thompson Mitchell, Thana.

114 Mildred Van Every to Mabel Whipple, May 1, 1939, NARA, Whipple, Mabel.

115 Delphine Holbrook and Phyllis Washoe to Mr. Blish, August 27, 1929, NARA, Holbrook, Delphine.

116 Bonnie V. Royce to Frederic Snyder, October 11, 1929, NARA, Holbrook, Delphine.

117 Velma Fred to Bonnie V. Royce, June 24, 1929, NARA, Fred, Velma.

118 Bonnie V. Royce to Velma Fred, July 10, 1929, NARA, Fred, Velma. The Community Chest was a nongovernmental locally based fundraising and philanthropic organization. For instance, in 1941 the Oakland and Berkeley Community Chest funds supported 34 percent of funding of the Salvation Army Home. For more info, see Schionneman, "Maternal Care for Low-Income Families in Berkeley and Oakland, California."

119 Clara Shaw to Bonnie V. Royce, August 29, 1929, NARA, Shaw, Clara.

120 Bertha Daniels against Mrs. S. West, 101 Oakmont Ave. Piedmont. for Wages from December 1931 to July 1932. At $15 per Month., 1932, NARA, Daniels, Bertha.

121 Sue Andrews Morgan to Mildred Van Every, July 19, 1935, NARA, Andrews Morgan, Sue.

122 Leona Godawa to Bonnie V. Royce, November 21, 1932, NARA, Godawa, Leona.

123 Leona Godawa to Bonnie V. Royce, October 28, 1932, NARA, Godawa, Leona.

124 The year the Four Winds Club started is debatable. Victoria Patterson attri-

butes the creation of the organization to Mildred Van Every, who started working for the outing program around 1934. However, the *Oakland Tribune* documents Four Winds Club activities as early as 1932. In a 1946 article, moreover, the same paper reported that the club was organized in 1926. Finally, Genny Mitchell understood that the club began in 1924. Regardless, it is clear that the Four Winds Club was initially affiliated with the YWCA and that it thrived under Mildred Van Every. Patterson, "Indian Life in the City," 410; "Indian Work Leader Here," *Oakland Tribune*, January 18, 1932; "Wild in a Nice Way," *Oakland Tribune*, February 24, 1946. Lobo *Urban Voices*, 12.

125 Lomawaima and McCarty's "safety zone" theory aptly notes that in some cases, reformers allowed Indigenous cultural representation that was deemed "safe" because it seemed to pose no threat to American identity. Such a fascinating tableau would have certainly been acceptable. For more on this theory, see Lomawaima and McCarty, *"To Remain an Indian."*

126 "Four Winds," *Oakland Tribune*, November 28, 1934.

127 "City Club Plans Dance," *Oakland Tribune*, February 6, 1935.

128 "Y.W. Plans Industrial Girls' Work," *Oakland Tribune*, October 28, 1938.

129 Patterson, "Indian Life in the City," 409–410.

130 Lobo, *Urban Voices*, 12.

131 *Oakland Tribune*, December 18, 1944.

132 "Wild in a Nice Way," *Oakland Tribune*, February 24, 1946.

133 Lobo, *Urban Voices*, 12.

134 Piatote, *Domestic Subjects.*

135 Jacobs, *White Mother to a Dark Race*, 334.

136 Piatote, *Domestic Subjects*, 87.

THREE / "Indian Girls Prefer Park to Housework"

1 For the purposes of this chapter, I use the term "runaway" to indicate women who ran away from the Bay Area Outing Program. At times I use the term "deserters," as this was the official term used for runaways by the Office of Indian Affairs/Bureau of Indian Affairs—a term with decidedly criminalized connotations. I occasionally use the terms "escape" or "escapee" to highlight the carceral, confining nature of boarding schools and outing programs. Notably, I do not consider the women in this chapter in the framework of murdered or missing Indigenous women or girls (MMIW). Many of the young women mentioned in this chapter express their departure and often report back when

they have returned home. That is not to say that cases of MMIW did not occur in national outing programs, only that more research on this topic is needed.

2 See Lomawaima, *They Called It Prairie Light*; Trennert, *The Phoenix Indian School*; and Child, *Boarding School Seasons*.

3 What we know today as juvenile detention centers.

4 Miller, *Indians on the Move*, 16–27. In his analysis of the reservation as confinement, Miller highlights firsthand accounts from Native activists. Carlos Montezuma argued, "Reservations are prisons where our people are kept to live and die, where equal possibilities, equal education, and equal responsibilities are unknown." Henry Roe Cloud shared similar sentiments on reservation confinement and its ability to narrow the circumstances of Native people. Qtd. in Miller, *Indians on the Move*, 22–23. Mishuana Goeman finds that both boarding schools and reservations fall within the settler "logic of containment." She writes, "Boarding schools' link with prisons is that of containing and surveillance of aberrant bodies." And further states, "It is important to remember that many reservations were set up as places of containment, some even requiring passes to leave, and other 'landless' Natives were arrested." Goeman, "Land as Life," 81–82.

5 Ross, "Introduction," 3.

6 Odem, *Delinquent Daughters*.

7 The Bay Area Outing Program was highlighted in several local newspapers of the time, including coverage of an early iteration of outing in the Bay Area run by Stewart Indian School. See "Escaped Indian Girl Located in Oakland: Minnie Rook Will Be Returned to School," *San Francisco Call*, September 26, 1911; "Want Summer Homes for Indian Girls," *Berkeley Daily Gazette*, May, 22 1912; "Ishi Host at Reception to Indian Maids," *San Francisco Call*, August 26, 1912; "Situation Wanted," *Berkeley Daily Gazette*, June 16, 1913; "Lost Indian Girl Sought by Police," *Berkeley Daily Gazette*, October 22, 1914; "They Will Prove Studies in Housework," *Oakland Tribune*, June 7, 1927.

8 Indigenous women's sexuality was a dilemma to colonizers, who treated Native women as sexual objects yet regarded their sexual independence as a threat to the patriarchal family and evidence that they were out of control. Barman, "Taming Aboriginal Sexuality," 241. For more on Indigenous women, settlers, and sexuality see Barman, 237–66; Conor, *Skin Deep*.

9 Lomawaima, *They Called It Prairie Light*, 121.

10 Williams, *Assimilation, Resilience, and Survival*, 32.

11 Child, *Boarding School Seasons*, 87–92.

12 Williams, *Assimilation, Resilience, and Survival*, 34–35.

13 Child, *Boarding School Seasons*, 85.

14 Whalen, *Native Students at Work*, 48.

15 Child, *Boarding School Seasons*, 84. See also Vučković, *Voices from Haskell.*

16 Ross, *Inventing the Savage*. Ross asserts that "criminal" was other than Euro-American. For more on the criminalization of Native American peoples, especially women, see Perry, "Nobody Trusts Them!," 411–44; Lumsden, "Reproductive Justice, Sovereignty, and Incarceration," 33–46; Ogden, "Prisoner W-20170/Other"; Teran, "The Violent Legacies of the California Missions," 19–32.

17 Chavez-Garcia, *States of Delinquency*, 33–35.

18 Native women were under the guardianship of the outing matron. But legally, all minors in California were subject to parens patriae. This doctrine gave the state power over all children and youths identified as delinquents.

19 Odem and Schlossman, "Guardians of Virtue," 192–93. Girls with hymens that doctors perceived as broken were segregated to prevent "moral corruption."

20 Medical Examination—Detention Home, Alameda County, CA, January 10, 1935, NARA, Elliott, Rosita.

21 Chavez-Garcia, *States of Delinquency*, 117–26. Native youths were often tried as adults and incarcerated in California prisons such as San Quentin.

22 "Two Indian Girls Reported Missing," *Berkeley Daily Gazette*, July 31, 1922.

23 "Indian Girls Are Reported Missing," *Berkeley Daily Gazette*, August 25, 1922.

24 Under the typical structures of the outing program, Native women and girls received wages for their live-in domestic work on top of room and board. It is possible the *Tribune* misreported on this fact. However, perhaps this early in the program, girls' labor was unpaid. Therefore, it is not surprising that they would want to run away.

25 Index Outing System—Vivian Cooper, 1932, NARA, Cooper, Vivian.

26 Bonnie V. Royce to Lucy Keenan, Public Health Nurse, June 10, 1929, NARA, Cooper, Vivian.

27 Bonnie V. Royce to Lucy Keenan, Public Health Nurse, July 13, 1929, NARA, Cooper, Vivian.

28 Vivian Cooper to Bonnie V. Royce, August 6, 1929, NARA, Cooper, Vivian.

29 According to Margaret Jacobs, in some years these Native women's wages in the Bay Area Outing Program were as much as 47 percent below the national average.

30 Hunter's file describes her as a "digger" Indian. This enduring term dated from

the nineteenth century and was often attributed to Native people from Northern California.

31 Index Outing System—Bernice Hunter, 1935, NARA, Hunter, Bernice.

32 "Moron" was a technical term of the eugenics movement, coined in 1910 by the eugenicist Henry Goddard. It linked intelligence and criminal behavior.

33 Bonnie V. Royce to Frederic Snyder, February 10, 1932, NARA, Hunter, Bernice.

34 Index Outing System—Bernice Hunter, 1935, NARA, Hunter, Bernice.

35 Bernice Hunter to Mildred Van Every, July 5, 1935, NARA, Hunter, Bernice.

36 Index Outing System—Bernice Hunter, 1935, NARA, Hunter, Bernice.

37 Index Outing System—Ida Moore, 1931, NARA, Moore, Ida.

38 Ida Moore to Bonnie V. Royce, February 22, 1931, NARA, Moore, Ida.

39 Ida Moore to Bonnie V. Royce, March 30, 1932, NARA, Moore, Ida.

40 Bonnie V. Royce to Ida Moore, March 4, 1932, NARA, Moore, Ida.

41 Agustin Maldonado to Bonnie V. Royce, March 22, 1932, NARA, Moore, Ida.

42 Index Outing System—Martha Graham, 1933, NARA, Graham, Martha.

43 Martha Graham to Bonnie V. Royce, November 25, 1930, NARA, Graham, Martha.

44 Index Outing System—Martha Graham, 1933, NARA, Graham, Martha.

45 Thereafter, the Graham family leaned on the outing program to sell their crafts. In December 1933, Martha's father sent a basket to Traxler to sell for five dollars on behalf of the family. It was not uncommon for families to sell their arts and crafts in lieu of their daughters' labor.

46 Index Outing System—Della Smart, 1931, NARA, Smart, Della.

47 Bonnie V. Royce to Frederic Snyder, August 26, 1931, NARA, Smart, Della.

48 Bonnie V. Royce to Mr. and Mrs. Bob Wright, August 26, 1931, NARA, Smart, Della.

49 Crabtree's file also lists an illegible tribe, possibly "Malibu" or "Maidu."

50 Index Outing System—Loretta Crabtree, 1935, NARA, Crabtree, Loretta.

51 Evelyn Joaquin to Mildred Van Every, December 1936, NARA, Crabtree, Loretta.

52 Loretta Crabtree to Mildred Van Every, December 7, 1936, NARA, Crabtree, Loretta.

53 Mildred Van Every to Edith Murphy, December 21, 1936, NARA, Crabtree, Loretta.

54 Edith Murphy to Mildred Van Every, December 24, 1936, NARA, Crabtree, Loretta.

55 Mildred Van Every to Loretta Crabtree, January 6, 1937, NARA, Crabtree, Loretta. The "medical certificate" Van Every mentioned refers to health clearances. While seemingly interested in the general health of the Native woman or girl in question, these clearances were purely intended to police Native women's sexuality and gauge whether they had venereal diseases.

56 Index Outing System—Marjorie Peters, 1936, NARA, Peters, Marjorie.

57 Significantly, Peters's file contains a rare Government Request for Transportation form. The receipt indicates payment made for Peters's travel from San Francisco to Eureka, California. The Hoopa Valley Agency was responsible for payment. In many cases, outing girls were required to pay for their own transportation home. This rare occurrence seems to suggest the urgency of her health issue. Government Request for Transportation Memorandum, July 17, 1935, NARA, Peters, Marjorie. In late September 1935, a field nurse from Hoopa wrote Van Every to report, "As you probably know, [Peters] has returned home." Dorothy Owens to Mildred Van Every, September 26, 1935, NARA, Nixon, Blanche.

58 Doctor's Note—H. G. Leland, November 4, 1935, NARA, Peters, Marjorie.

59 Mildred Van Every to Supt. O. M. Boggess, March 13, 1936, NARA, Peters, Marjorie.

60 Re. Marjorie Peters, March 20, 1936, NARA, Peters, Marjorie.

61 Bonnie V. Royce to Frederic Snyder, July 3, 1923, NARA, Sam, Sadie.

62 Bonnie V. Royce to Frederic Snyder, July 3, 1923, NARA, Sam, Sadie.

63 Index Outing System—Winifred Nelson, 1932, NARA, Nelson, Winifred.

64 Index Outing System—Winifred Nelson, 1932, NARA, Nelson, Winifred.

65 Bonnie V. Royce to Mrs. George Nelson, January 4, 1933, NARA, Nelson, Winifred.

66 Bonnie V. Royce to Supt. O. M. Boggess, January 4, 1933, NARA, Nelson, Winifred.

67 Undoubtedly, Royce confiscated these letters and transcribed them. I made an educated assumption on the date of Nelson's first letter. Her reference to New Year's Eve and mention of Saturday indicate the letter was most likely written on January 7, 1933.

68 Winifred Nelson to Sister, January 7, 1933, NARA, Nelson, Winifred.

69 Bonnie V. Royce to Supt. O. M. Boggess, January 20, 1933, NARA, Nelson, Winifred.

70 Winifred Nelson to Sister, January 18, 1933, NARA, Nelson, Winifred.

71 Winifred Nelson to Sister, January 19, 1933, NARA, Nelson, Winifred. At this point in the outing program, Nelson was walking over a mile each way from Royce's home in Piedmont.

72 Bonnie V. Royce to Supt. O. M. Boggess, January 20, 1933, NARA, Nelson, Winifred.

73 Several years later, in September 1935, a field nurse at Hoopa wrote Van Every with an update about Nelson. Apparently, she was working locally and undergoing some medical treatments. The nurse wrote, "We are having a little difficulty in getting Winifred Nelson to come in for her treatments. She has been

working part-time in a little restaurant and does not like to be bothered with the shots." This appears to be the last mention of Nelson in the outing files. Dorothy Owens to Mildred Van Every, September 26, 1935, NARA, Nixon, Blanche.

74 Index Outing System—Bernice Nelson, 1933, NARA, Nelson, Bernice.

75 Mrs. George Nelson to Jeannette Traxler, February 13, 1934, NARA, Nelson, Bernice.

76 Jeannette Traxler to Mrs. George Nelson, February 16, 1934, NARA, Nelson, Bernice.

77 Re: Bernice Nelson, M. Van Every Notes, 1934, NARA, Nelson, Bernice.

78 Ogden, "Prisoner W-20170/Other," 156.

79 Ivora was Bernice and Winifred Nelson's older sister.

80 Index Outing System—Thana Thompson Mitchell, 1933, NARA, Thompson Mitchell, Thana.

81 Thana Thompson Mitchell to Bonnie V. Royce, undated, NARA, Thompson Mitchell, Thana.

82 Thana Thompson Mitchell to Bonnie V. Royce, April 14, 1930, NARA, Thompson Mitchell, Thana.

83 Bonnie V. Royce to Mr. and Mrs. Allen Thompson, October 1, 1930, NARA, Thompson Mitchell, Thana.

84 Mr. Allen Thompson to Bonnie V. Royce, May 19, 1930, NARA, Thompson Mitchell, Thana.

85 Index Outing System—Thana Thompson Mitchell, 1933, NARA, Thompson Mitchell, Thana

86 Bonnie V. Royce to Mr. and Mrs. Allen Thompson, October 18, 1930, NARA, Thompson Mitchell, Thana.

87 Bonnie V. Royce to Mr. Allen Thompson, February 2, 1931, NARA, Thompson Mitchell, Thana.

88 Bonnie V. Royce to Mr. Allen Thompson, February 2, 1931, NARA, Thompson Mitchell, Thana.

FOUR / Breaking the Family

1 Indian child removal was often seen as a necessary means to assimilate Indian children. Margaret Jacobs has done extensive research on the topic of Indian child removal and argues it is a "key practice of colonialism." Jacobs, "The Great White Mother," 193. For more on Indian child removal, see Jacobs, "Breaking and Remaking Families"; and Jacobs, *A Generation Removed*.

2 Jacobs, "Diverted Mothering among American Indian Domestic Servants," 179–92.

3 Wong, "Diverted Mothering," 69.

4 Lisa Emmerich's study on the Save the Babies campaign reveals that technologically advanced, large-scale baby fairs and baby shows were a focal point. At these popular events, Native women dressed their babies in the finest "citizen's" dress and competed for the best baby award. At these events, Native women were lectured on "civilized" family life and health care. While such contests targeted Native American communities, "better baby" contests could be found across the United States as part of a national infant welfare movement, which also sought to combat high rates of infant mortality and morbidity. Emmerich, "'Save the Babies!'" For more on Indian baby shows, see Klann, "Babies in Baskets."

5 Emphasis in original.

6 "Congress on Indian Progress," 4–5.

7 In 1917, a year after this statement, Cato Sells declared: "The Indian is no longer a vanishing race." The mortality rate for Indian children under the age of three had declined by more than 50 percent from 1914 figures. Sells's statistics could have been hyperbole or perhaps by 1917 were more accurate. It is also possible that the improvement reflected the efficacy of the Save the Babies campaign. Emmerich, "'Save the Babies!'" 404.

8 *Indian Babies*, 27.

9 *Indian Babies*, 28.

10 *Indian Babies*, 28.

11 Emmerich, "'Save the Babies!'" 397.

12 Intentions aside, the Save the Babies campaign failed. For example, field matrons did not have, nor were they required to have, any special qualifications or training for their work. Crucially, the movement failed to remedy poverty or cultural instability. Emmerich argues the campaign "was little more than an assimilationist Band-Aid." Emmerich, "'Save the Babies!'" 404.

13 Jacobs, "Breaking and Remaking Families." In this study, Jacobs found that white women had a particular penchant for adopting Native children. Some believed they were fulfilling a higher purpose, others that they were saving the children from a life of destitution. Indian adoption was terribly informal and the belief that Indian children were free for the taking prevailed.

14 I use the term "reproductive capacity," as employed by Stephanie Lumsden. Lumsden, "Reproductive Justice, Sovereignty, and Incarceration," 33–46.

15 Given that sexual relations in employers' homes were imaginable, it is possible

that these health clearances were especially in the interest of male homeowners—men who might take their liberties with the help and become sexually involved with outing workers.

16 For more on (settler) colonialism and sexual assault, especially as a weapon, see Behrendt, "Consent in a (Neo)Colonial Society," 353–67; Hurtado, *Indian Survival on the California Frontier*; Deer, *The Beginning and End of Rape*; Miranda, "'Saying the Padre Had Grabbed Her,'" 93; McClintock, *Imperial Leather*; Conor, *Skin Deep*.

17 For more on domestic workers and sexual violence, especially with regard to migrant domestic workers, see Ahsan, "Abuse and Violence against Foreign Domestic Workers," 221–38; Conor, *Skin Deep*; KAFA, "Dreams for Sale"; Zahreddine et al., "Psychiatric Morbidity," 619–28; Ghaddar, Khandaqji, and Ghattas, "Justifying Abuse of Women Migrant Domestic Workers in Lebanon," 493–99; Hantzaroula, "Public Discourses on Sexuality and Narratives of Sexual Violence," 283–310.

18 For more on this, see Weiss, "Absent Men," 342–56; Graunke, "'Just Like One of the Family,'" 138; Human Rights Watch, *World Report 2019*; Jones, *Labor of Love, Labor of Sorrow*. Among domestic workers, live-in workers suffer the worst working conditions. Graunke asserts that live-in domestic workers are especially at risk of sexual abuse for the mere fact of their "constant and intimate interactions with their employers."

19 Outing records give little detail on Dyer's life. The US Census provides more: In 1920, Agnes and her husband, Henry West, lived in a boarding home on Filbert Street in San Francisco. That census indicates she was twenty-one years old and working as a maid. Though the census indicates the pair as "white," her husband was born in Hawaii, and his native tongue is listed as "Amoy," a language from the southeastern coast of China. West's World War I draft card indicates he was Malaysian. A decade later, in 1930, Agnes West was widowed and working as a live-in housemaid for the McDonald family on Lyon Street in San Francisco. The family had a live-in Japanese cook. In 1937, a Carson Agency Indian Census Roll categorized West, her three daughters, and her son as all living off reservation. In 1940, Agnes West rented an apartment in the Cow Hollow neighborhood of San Francisco. She lived there with her three daughters. At the time, the youngest, Cynthia, was nine years old, Alice was eleven, and her oldest, Helen, was seventeen. 1920 United States Federal Census—Agnas West, United States Census, San Francisco Assembly District 31, San Francisco, California, roll T625_136, page 21A, enumeration district 154,

accessed April 24, 2021, https://www.ancestry.com; U.S., World War I Draft Registration Cards, 1917–1918—Henry West, National Archives, Washington, DC, M1509, 4,582 rolls, accessed April 24, 2021; 1930 United States Federal Census—Agnes West, United States Census, San Francisco, California, page 6A, enumeration district 0325, FHL microfilm 2339941, accessed April 24, 2021, https://www.ancestry.com; 1937 Indian Census—Agnes West, National Archives, Washington, DC, Indian Census Rolls, 1885–1940, M595, 692 rolls; 1940 United States Federal Census—Agnes West, United States Census, San Francisco, California, roll m-t0627-00317, page 63A, enumeration district 38-486, accessed April 24, 2021, https://www.ancestry.com.

20 Elizabeth Peterson, The Children's Agency to Bonnie V. Royce, August 28, 1931, NARA, Dyer, Agnes.

21 Elizabeth Peterson, The Children's Agency to Bonnie V. Royce, August 28, 1931, NARA, Dyer, Agnes.

22 Adamson's account indicates Alice as the oldest child, yet the 1940 US Census indicates Helen West as her oldest. It is unclear why the discrepancy exists.

23 Esther Adamson to Mrs. J. R. McDonald, December 9, 1932, NARA, Dyer, Agnes.

24 Sadie Sam to Bonnie V. Royce, August 1927, NARA, Sam, Sadie.

25 Sadie Sam to Bonnie V. Royce, October 1927, NARA, Sam, Sadie.

26 Sadie Sam to Bonnie V. Royce, November 10, 1928, NARA, Sam, Sadie.

27 Amy Bethel to Mildred Van Every, January 7, 1942, NARA, Bethel, Amy.

28 Amy Bethel to Mildred Van Every, June 22, 1942, NARA, Bethel, Amy.

29 Amy Bethel to Mildred Van Every, June 22, 1942, NARA, Bethel, Amy.

30 Glenn, "Racial Ethnic Women's Labor," 86–108.

31 Slang for money.

32 Index Outing System—Maude Mitchell, 1934, NARA, Mitchell, Maude.

33 Mrs. Frank S. Baxter to Ross B. Wiley, Education Division for Alida C. Bowler, Supt. of Carson Indian School, October 30, 1936, NARA, Mitchell, Maude.

34 Mildred Van Every to Alida C. Bowler, Supt. of Carson Indian Agency, November 30, 1936, NARA, Mitchell, Maude.

35 Mitchell's case is similar to one Sarah Haley examined in the context of paroled Black women forced into domestic labor in Georgia. Mattie Price became pregnant as a domestic and had a falling out with her warder, particularly because as a new mother, she would be unable to care for her ward's children. Haley argues, "[Price] defied the expectations of docile servant . . . refusing to privilege her mistresses' children to the detriment of her own." Haley, "'Like I Was a Man,'" 70–71.

36 Frederic Snyder to Daniel E. Robertson, May 15, 1925, NARA, Wasson, Gertrude.

37 John Wasson to Bonnie V. Royce, July 6, 1925, NARA, Wasson, Gertrude.

38 John Wasson to Bonnie V. Royce, July 6, 1925, NARA, Wasson, Gertrude.

39 Bonnie V. Royce to Norma Wasson, October 27, 1926, NARA, Wasson, Gertrude.

40 Elizabeth Peterson, The Children's Agency to Bonnie V. Royce, January 24, 1931, NARA, Wasson, Gertrude.

41 Elizabeth Peterson, The Children's Agency to Bonnie V. Royce, January 24, 1931, NARA, Wasson, Gertrude.

42 Jacobs, "Diverted Mothering among American Indian Domestic Servants," 188.

43 Mrs. Mary Paige, Infant Shelter to Bonnie V. Royce, July 14, 1931, NARA, Wasson, Gertrude.

44 F. Baringer to Director, Indian Bureau, June 10, 1932, NARA, Wasson, Gertrude.

45 Frederic Snyder to Bonnie V. Royce, July 2, 1932, NARA, Wasson, Gertrude.

46 Mrs. Mary Paige, Infant Shelter to Bonnie V. Royce, July 14, 1931, NARA, Wasson, Gertrude.

47 Bonnie V. Royce to F. Baringer, July 22, 1932, NARA, Wasson, Gertrude.

48 Ida Sinai, The Children's Agency to Bonnie V. Royce, August 17, 1932, NARA, Wasson, Gertrude.

49 Historically, the practice of fostering and adoption of Native children was extensive even in the nineteenth century. However, after World War II, the BIA officially established the Indian Adoption Project and began adopting Indian children into non-Native, typically white American homes. As evidenced in this chapter, state child welfare and private adoption agencies also contributed to removal. These children grew up experiencing abuse, trauma, and loss of cultural identity that led many to substance abuse. The endemic of shattered families and children severed from their culture rallied Native Americans across the nation to fight for a solution. In 1978, the Indian Child Welfare Act (ICWA) was enacted in response to the crisis. For more on this history, see Chandler and Quinn, "Emma Is a Good Girl"; Jacobs, *A Generation Removed*; Bual, "Native American Rights & Adoption by Non-Indian Families," 270; *Indian Child Welfare Act of 1978: Hearings*; *Indian Child Welfare Act of 1978: Questions and Answers*; Stevenson, "Vibrations across a Continent," 218.

50 Daisy Plummer to Bonnie V. Royce, November 25, 1927, NARA, Plummer, Daisy.

51 Daisy Plummer to Bonnie V. Royce, May 20, 1929, NARA, Plummer, Daisy.

52 Daisy Plummer to Bonnie V. Royce, January 14, 1930, NARA, Plummer, Daisy.

53 Daisy Plummer to Bonnie V. Royce, March 25, 1930, NARA, Plummer, Daisy.

54 Bonnie V. Royce to Ray Parrett, June 21, 1930, NARA, Plummer, Daisy.

55 Bonnie V. Royce to Ray Parrett, June 21, 1930, NARA, Plummer, Daisy.

56 Green's insistence on a "public" place suggests that she was both aware and wary of private domestic placements, which rendered workers vulnerable in the home. Josephine and Thelma Green to Bonnie V. Royce, April 5, 1930, NARA, Green, Josephine.

57 Bonnie V. Royce to Josephine and Thelma Green, April 7, 1930, NARA, Green, Josephine.

58 Josephine and Thelma Green to Bonnie V. Royce, April 8, 1930, NARA, Green, Josephine.

59 Amy Braden, The Salvation Army, SF to Bonnie V. Royce, February 10, 1932, NARA, Green, Josephine.

60 Amy Braden, The Salvation Army, SF to Bonnie V. Royce, February 17, 1932, NARA, Green, Josephine.

61 Josephine Green to Bonnie V. Royce, undated, NARA, Green, Josephine.

62 In 1891, Dr. J. R. Townsend and his wife founded the Children's Home Society of California (CHS) to help homeless and abandoned children, prioritizing adoption over institutions. Though it was founded in the Los Angeles area, within a year CHS had expanded into the Bay Area. By the mid-twentieth century, the organization was influential in the establishing of public and county adoption agencies. By 1966, CHS had become the largest private adoption agency in the world.

63 March 29 Notes, March 29, 1934, NARA, Green, Josephine.

64 April 7 Notes, April 12, 1934, 7, NARA, Green, Josephine.

65 Index Outing System—Avis Hooper, 1933, NARA, Hooper, Avis.

66 Sam Hooper to Bonnie V. Royce, March 7, 1928, NARA, Hooper, Avis.

67 Bonnie V. Royce to Sam Hooper, March 15, 1928, NARA, Hooper, Avis.

68 Bonnie V. Royce to Sam Hooper, April 11, 1928, NARA, Hooper, Avis.

69 Avis Hooper to Bonnie V. Royce, September 25, 1928, NARA, Hooper, Avis.

70 Genevieve Martinelli to Bonnie V. Royce, October 23, 1928, NARA, Hooper, Avis.

71 Bonnie V. Royce to McNeilly, February 16, 1929, NARA, Hooper, Avis.

72 Sam Hooper to Bonnie V. Royce, February 23, 1929, NARA, Hooper, Avis.

73 Bonnie V. Royce to Sam Hooper, March 12, 1929, NARA, Hooper, Avis.

74 Avis Hooper to Bonnie V. Royce, October 2, 1930, NARA, Hooper, Avis.

75 Bonnie V. Royce to Avis Hooper, October 7, 1930, NARA, Hooper, Avis.

76 Mildred Van Every to Supt. L. B. Patterson, October 26, 1934, NARA, Hooper, Avis.

77 Avis Hooper to Jeannette Traxler, March 16, 1934, NARA, Hooper, Avis.

78 Mildred Van Every to Commanding Officer, Presidio of San Francisco, October 18, 1934, NARA, Hooper, Avis; D. P. Frissell, Presidio of San Francisco to Mildred Van Every, October 19, 1934, NARA, Hooper, Avis.

79 Mildred Van Every to Supt. Emmett E. McNeilly, October 18, 1934, NARA, Hooper, Avis.

80 While You Were Out, October 25, 1934, NARA, Hooper, Avis.

81 Mildred Van Every to Supt. L. B. Patterson, October 26, 1934, NARA, Hooper, Avis.

82 Mildred Van Every to Supt. Emmett E. McNeilly, November 13, 1934, NARA, Hooper, Avis.

83 Supt. L. B. Patterson to Louisa Dalen, March 4, 1935, NARA, Hooper, Avis.

84 1940 United States Federal Census, United States Census, Elko, Nevada, roll m-to627-02277, page 6B, enumeration district 4-4, NARA, Washington, DC.

85 Ernest C. Mueller to Mildred Van Every, January 20, 1944, NARA, Penrose, Lillian.

86 Ernest C. Mueller to Mildred Van Every, February 5, 1944, NARA, Penrose, Lillian.

87 The Booth Memorial Hospital in Oakland was a Salvation Army hospital.

88 At the time, California State Welfare prohibited out-of-state girls from receiving services without remuneration. Therefore, Penrose's labor would act as payment. In the early twentieth century, the state began to formalize its welfare administration. For more on this, see Leiby, "State Welfare Administration in California," 303–18.

89 Mildred Van Every to Supt. Don C. Foster, February 9, 1944, NARA, Penrose, Lillian. Not long after Penrose's case, Mildred Van Every transitioned from the Bay Area to work for the Sacramento region. There, she was regularly involved in the placement of Native children, especially related to Indian tribes of Northern California.

90 Re: Lillian Penrose, M. Van Every Notes, April 13, 1944, NARA, Penrose, Lillian.

91 Consent Form, April 29, 1944, NARA, Penrose, Lillian.

92 Muriel Smith, Social Worker to Mildred Van Every, NARA, Penrose, Lillian.

93 Muriel Smith, Social Worker to Mildred Van Every, May 8, 1944, NARA, Penrose, Lillian.

94 Mildred Van Every to Supt. Ralph M. Gelvin, May 10, 1944, NARA, Penrose, Lillian.

95 Dr. Donald J. Hunt to Mildred Van Every, June 3, 1944, NARA, Penrose, Lillian.

96 Supt. Ralph M. Gelvin to Mildred Van Every, September 28, 1944, NARA, Penrose, Lillian.

97 Supt. Ralph M. Gelvin to Mildred Van Every, September 28, 1944, NARA, Penrose, Lillian.

98 After World War II, it was common for young veterans to petition Matron Van Every for assistance with seeking employment or enrolling in college. Furthermore, in one instance, an elderly Native man petitioned the matron to assist with securing aid.

99 Supt. Alida C. Bowler to Mildred Van Every, September 25, 1934, NARA, Pensotti, Joseph.

100 Supt. Alida C. Bowler to Mildred Van Every, September 25, 1934, NARA, Pensotti, Joseph.

101 Carl M. Moore to Frederic Snyder, November 1, 1930, NARA, Pensotti, Joseph.

102 Bonnie V. Royce to Frederic Snyder, November 19, 1930, NARA, Pensotti, Joseph.

103 Supt. Alida C. Bowler to Mildred Van Every, September 25, 1934, NARA, Pensotti, Joseph.

104 Supt. Alida C. Bowler to Mildred Van Every, November 25, 1934, NARA, Pensotti, Joseph.

FIVE / Containment, Sexual Surveillance, and Bodily Regulation

1 Vučković, *Voices from Haskell*, 180.

2 Two scholars offer a deeper understanding of containment particularly in the context of settler colonialism and the domestic sphere. Mishuana Goeman's "logics of containment" describes the colonial spatial restructuring of both land and bodies. Land as property, for instance, falls into these logics, "a process that contains Indigenous bodies and land into colonial categorizations." Goeman argues for a transnational feminism that unsettles these logics of containment. Sarah Haley's concept of the "domestic carceral sphere" is helpful in considering the outing home as carceral. While framed in the forced domestic labor of paroled Black women in Georgia, Haley's concept nonetheless underscores the white home as carceral. Within the domestic carceral space, Black women were contained and exploited for their labor. Haley argues the domestic carceral sphere "restored white women's historical role as domestic managers with full control over black female workers" and domestic carceral servitude "reinforced patriarchal notions of white women's dependency and

white supremacist structures of racial subordination." Aikau et. al, "Indigenous Feminisms Roundtable," 96; Haley, "'Like I Was a Man,'" 67.

3 Theobald, *Reproduction on the Reservation.*

4 DeJong, *"If You Knew the Conditions,"* 18–19.

5 See Keller, "'In the Fall of the Year We Were Troubled with Some Sickness,'" 32–51; Rindfleisch, "'A Very Considerable Mortality,'" 2–13; Adams, "'A Very Serious and Perplexing Epidemic of Grippe,'" 1–35; Vučković, *Voices from Haskell*; DeJong, "'Unless They Are Kept Alive,'" 256–82.

6 DeJong, *"If You Knew the Conditions,"* 102.

7 Brandt, *No Magic Bullet.*

8 Sarka, "The Role of the United States," 5.

9 Sarka, "The Role of the United States," 57.

10 Shah, *Contagious Divides*, 87.

11 Sarka, "The Role of the United States," 29.

12 Sherman, *The Power of Plagues*, 316.

13 To address this "girl problem," World War I authorities created the Committee on the Protective Work for Girls (CPWG), aimed at preventing sex delinquency among young women. This initiative hired "protective officers," who essentially patrolled the streets, policed young women, and enforced rules. Odem, *Delinquent Daughters*, 121–23.

14 Sarka, "The Role of the United States," 57–58.

15 Shah, *Contagious Divides*, 110.

16 Odem, *Delinquent Daughters*, 96–97.

17 Odem, *Delinquent Daughters*, 124. See also Odem and Schlossman, "Guardians of Virtue."

18 Odem, *Delinquent Daughters*, 145.

19 This blame demonstrated a weak understanding of how venereal disease were contracted. According to Nayan Shah, though not domestic workers, Chinese women were similarly pathologized—in fact more so. In the late nineteenth century, Chinese women were regarded as syphilitic prostitutes responsible for transmitting disease among white men. Chinese prostitutes—real or imagined—embodied syphilis and threatened the integrity of marriage and purity of reproduction. Shah, *Contagious Divides*, 105–9.

20 Shah, *Contagious Divides*, 89.

21 Whalen, *Native Students at Work*, 117.

22 Whalen, *Native Students at Work*, 118.

23 Trennert, "From Carlisle to Phoenix," 282.

24 Haskins, *Matrons and Maids*, 33.

25 Trennert, "Victorian Morality," 124.

26 For instance, many O'odham women practiced a form of marriage that was less fixed than Anglo-American marriage. Should a Native woman choose to leave her partner for another, she did so freely. Generally, Native women and their families and community found legal—that is, Anglo—marriage unnecessary. Haskins, *Matrons and Maids*, 100–101.

27 Haskins, *Matrons and Maids*, 55.

28 They wanted a space very similar to what the Oakland YWCA and affiliated organizations like the Four Winds Club provided for outing girls in the Bay Area.

29 Haskins, *Matrons and Maids*, 50–51.

30 Haskins, *Matrons and Maids*, 67.

31 Some cases of single outing mothers were taken to court, and almost always white offenders—the fathers of their children—evaded any charges or financial responsibility. At least one of the court cases involved a young outing woman who intended to testify against a white man on a charge of rape.

32 Haskins, *Matrons and Maids*, 85–86.

33 Haskins, *Matrons and Maids*, 99.

34 Theobald, *Reproduction on the Reservation*, 78.

35 Theobald, *Reproduction on the Reservation*, 94–95.

36 Dr. Eagleton to Ray R. Parrett, Superintendent of Walker River Agency, October 21, 1933, NARA, Emm, Hazel.

37 Physician's Note Re: Alice Nix, December 28, 1933, NARA, Marshall Nix, Alice.

38 Complement Fixation Test for Syphilis (Wassermann Test), October 16, 1930, NARA, Martin, Marcie. The Wassermann test, developed in 1906, is an antibody test for syphilis, taking its name from the bacteriologist August Paul von Wassermann. This test was widely used despite its tendency to produce false positives when detecting other diseases.

39 Presumably Martin promised to be good because she left her previous outing position in 1931 "without consent or knowledge" of the employers. Though she returned to the Gurnett household in 1932, this infraction seems to have colored her perceived character.

40 Marcie Martin to Matron Bonnie V. Royce, February 9, 1934, NARA, Martin, Marcie.

41 Jeannette Traxler to Marcie Martin, February 15, 1934, NARA, Martin, Marcie.

42 Re: Patricia Ince, M. Van Every Notes, 1935, NARA, Ince, Patricia. In her notes, Van Every refers to Circular 3051 from the Commissioner of Indian Affairs,

which details the processes of quarantining Indians with contagious or infectious diseases. Although boarding schools were by nature hotbeds for disease, school officials often blamed their Indian students for the spread of contagions.

43 Records indicate that women had to be county residents in order to receive care at local clinics. While emergency services were accessible, women in need of long-term care were often sent to their respective tribal hospital or sanatorium.

44 Theobald, *Reproduction on the Reservation*, 107.

45 Theobald, *Reproduction on the Reservation*, 116–17.

46 Medical Examination—Detention Home, Alameda County, CA, January 10, 1935, NARA, Elliott, Rosita.

47 Odem and Schlossman, "Guardians of Virtue," 192.

48 Avery to Carrie Spencer, October 9, 1925, NARA, Spencer, Carrie. Spencer's file is striking, as it includes fond letters from fellow Indian girls. Correspondence between girls is rarely present in these federal records. In fact, it only remains because it was withheld from recipients. Indeed, the matron at the Salvation Army Home forwarded this letter to Royce, for it would not do Spencer "any good." Spencer never saw it.

49 Carrie Spencer to Royce, November 19, 1925, NARA, Spencer, Carrie.

50 Supt. Parrett to Cecil Mosbacher, Bureau of Children's Aid, April 23, 1926, NARA, Spencer, Carrie.

51 Leave of Absence, October 15, 1926, NARA, Spencer, Carrie,

52 Leonidas Swain to Royce, December 20, 1926, NARA, Spencer, Carrie.

53 Chavez-Garcia, *States of Delinquency*, 143–44.

54 Chavez-Garcia, *States of Delinquency*, 136–44.

55 L. L. Goen to Royce, July 14, 1928, NARA, Spencer, Carrie.

56 Royce to L. L. Goen, July 17, 1928, NARA, Spencer, Carrie.

57 L. L. Goen to F. O. Butler, August 2, 1928, NARA, Spencer, Carrie.

58 L. L. Goen to Royce, December 19, 1928, NARA, Spencer, Carrie.

59 Royce to L. L. Goen, January 2, 1929, NARA, Spencer, Carrie. Savings Deposit Account with Mercantile Trust Company of California, November 23, 1926, NARA, Spencer, Carrie. Spencer had a total of $59.73 in her account, but Royce sent Goen only $55.00—or $4.73 less than what was owed to Spencer.

60 Re: Patricia Ince, Outing Notes, March 1, 1934, NARA, Ince, Patricia.

61 Jeannette Traxler to Supt. O. M. Boggess, March 9, 1934, NARA, Ince, Patricia.

62 Etta H. Porter to Jeannette Traxler, March 21, 1934, NARA, Ince, Patricia.

63 Supt. O. H. Lipps to Jeannette Traxler, March 23, 1934, NARA, Ince, Patricia.

64 Dr. George Uhl to Mildred Van Every, January 24, 1935, NARA, Ince, Patricia.

65 Mildred Van Every to Etta H. Porter, January 26, 1935, NARA, Ince, Patricia.

66 Hosings were a form of punishment in which girls were hosed down with water. Odem, *Delinquent Daughters*, 147.

67 Chavez-Garcia, *States of Delinquency*, 130.

68 Mildred Van Every to Roy Nash, January 28, 1935, NARA, Ince, Patricia.

69 Schionneman, "Maternal Care for Low-Income Families," 77–83.

70 Schionneman, "Maternal Care for Low-Income Families," 77–83.

71 Mildred Van Every to Roy Nash, January 28, 1935, NARA, Ince, Patricia.

72 Roy Nash to Mildred Van Every, January 30, 1935, NARA, Ince, Patricia.

73 Keisner's outing file lists her as Wiyot, but her sister's outing file indicates the family is Miwok. The California Indian Census Rolls indicate the family is of the "Eel River" tribe and therefore Wiyot. Indians of California Census Rolls—Lila M Keisner, May 18, 1928, National Archives, Washington, DC, microfilm roll 1.

74 Re: Lila Keisner, Outing Notes, 1931, NARA, Keisner, Lila.

75 Hazel Keisner to Bonnie V. Royce, April 14, 1931, NARA, Keisner, Lila.

76 Lila Keisner to Bonnie V. Royce, October 12, 1931, NARA, Keisner, Lila.

77 Lila Keisner to Jeannette Traxler, October 29, 1931, NARA, Keisner, Lila.

78 Jeannette Traxler to Lila Keisner, November 2, 1931, NARA, Keisner, Lila.

79 Lila Keisner to Jeannette Traxler, November 3, 1931, NARA, Keisner, Lila.

80 Lila Keisner to Bonnie V. Royce, January 6, 1932, NARA, Keisner, Lila.

81 Lila Keisner to Jeannette Traxler, January 26, 1932, NARA, Keisner, Lila.

82 Lila Keisner to Bonnie V. Royce, October 13, 1932, NARA, Keisner, Lila.

83 Lila Keisner to Bonnie V. Royce, October 21, 1932, NARA, Keisner, Lila.

84 Bonnie V. Royce to Lila Keisner, October 24, 1932, NARA, Keisner, Lila.

85 Bonnie V. Royce to Henry Keisner, August 1, 1933, NARA, Keisner, Lila.

86 The fact that Keisner's personal letter to her father is present in these records indicates that the matron may have confiscated it. It is entirely possible that Henry Keisner never received this particular correspondence. Lila Keisner to Henry Keisner, November 27, 1933, NARA, Keisner, Lila.

87 At this time, Lila's sister Ann began working in the outing program and was apparently recently married. Jeannette Traxler to Henry Keisner, January 13, 1934, NARA, Keisner, Lila.

88 Jeannette Traxler to O. M. Boggess, February 5, 1934, NARA, Keisner, Lila.

89 Re: Keisner-Lila, Outing Notes, March 1934, NARA, Keisner, Lila.

90 Henry Keisner to Jeannette Traxler, February 7, 1934, NARA, Keisner, Lila.

91 Re: Keisner-Lila, Outing Notes, March 1934, NARA, Keisner, Lila.

92 Lossing was the first college-trained woman officer in the United States. Her hire was part of the feminization of the early criminal justice system, which often resulted in harsher punishments for women. Odem and Schlossman, "Guardians of Virtue," 189–92.

93 Chavez-Garcia, *States of Delinquency*, 62–73.

94 Re: Keisner-Lila, Outing Notes, 1931, NARA, Keisner, Lila.

95 Re: Lila Keisner, March and April, Outing Notes, March 1934, NARA, Keisner, Lila.

96 Jeannette Traxler to Supt. O. M. Boggess, March 26, 1934, NARA, Keisner, Lila.

97 Chavez-Garcia, *States of Delinquency*, 142–43.

98 Re: Lila Keisner, March and April, Outing Notes, March 1934, NARA, Keisner, Lila.

99 The New Deal established this work relief program for unemployed young men, many of whom were on government assistance.

100 Re: Lila Keisner, April and June, Outing Notes, April 1934, NARA, Keisner, Lila.

101 Re: Lila Keisner, April, Outing Notes, April 1934, NARA, Keisner, Lila.

102 Supt. O. M. Boggess to Jeannette Traxler, April 13, 1934, NARA, Keisner, Lila.

103 Mildred Van Every to Supt. O. M. Boggess, April 23, 1934, NARA, Keisner, Lila.

104 Re: Lila Keisner, April, Outing Notes, April 1934, NARA, Keisner, Lila.

105 Re: Lila Keisner, April and June, Outing Notes, April 1934, NARA, Keisner, Lila.

106 Supt. O. M. Boggess to Mildred Van Every, June 26, 1934, NARA, Keisner, Lila.

SIX / The Failure of Indian Health Care

1 Cook, "The Epidemic of 1830–1833," 322.

2 McMillen, "'The Red Man and the White Plague,'" 615.

3 DeJong, *"If You Knew the Conditions,"* 18–19.

4 DeJong, *"If You Knew the Conditions,"* 13–14.

5 The report includes a 1903 study, the findings of which were published in the "Report of the Commissioner of Indian Affairs–Annual Report of the Commissioner of Indian Affairs, 1904"; United States, *Contagious and Infectious Diseases among the Indians*; Moorehead, *The American Indian in the United States*; National Tuberculosis Association et al., *Tuberculosis among the North American Indians.*

6 Meriam, Work, and Brookings Institution, *The Problem of Indian Administration*, 190.

7 Meriam, Work, and Brookings Institution, *The Problem of Indian Administration*, 244–45.

8 Hiscock and American Public Health Association, *An Appraisal of the Public Health Program*, 46.

9 Mountin, "Summary of a Study of Health."

10 Ira Hiscock's report notes the Arequipa Sanatorium in Marin County received many of its patients by way of San Francisco. This sanatorium was reserved for the treatment of early cases of tuberculosis in wage-earning women and married women of "equivalent financial status." Records do not indicate this resource was made available to outing women, perhaps because their cases were often advanced, or because they were of a distinct social class. Lynn Downey's scholarship on Arequipa indicates the facility was open to women of color and served Asian American and African American tubercular patients. Neither her study nor outing records indicate that Native women were ever hospitalized there. Downey, *Arequipa Sanatorium*.

11 Hiscock and American Public Health Association, *An Appraisal of the Public Health Program*, 47.

12 It must the stated that while large and modern, the San Francisco tubercular hospital was, as Susan Craddock argues, "inadequate" as a curative institution. Indeed, in 1930, Hiscock determined that the tubercular services were about 72 percent of what they needed to be. That being said, it was far advanced when compared to most Indian Service facilities. Craddock, *City of Plagues*, 235–36.

13 Craddock, *City of Plagues*, 239.

14 Meriam, Work, and Brookings Institution, *The Problem of Indian Administration*, 297.

15 Meriam, Work, and Brookings Institution, *The Problem of Indian Administration*, 257.

16 Vučković, *Voices from Haskell*, 179–210.

17 See Keller, "'In the Fall of the Year We Were Troubled with Some Sickness'"; Keller, *Empty Beds*; Rindfleisch, "'A Very Considerable Mortality,'" 2–13; Adams, "'A Very Serious and Perplexing Epidemic of Grippe,'" 1–35; Vučković, *Voices from Haskell*; DeJong, "'Unless They Are Kept Alive,'" 256–82.

18 Craddock, *City of Plagues*, 240.

19 McMillen, *Discovering Tuberculosis*, 1–14.

20 DeJong, *"If You Knew the Conditions,"* 27–31.

21 Meriam, Work, and Brookings Institution, *The Problem of Indian Administration*, 193.

22 Meriam, Work, and Brookings Institution, *The Problem of Indian Administration*, 201–6.

23 Sanford, "What Is Killing Our Indians?," 10.

24 McMillen, "The Red Man and the White Plague," 620–27.

25 McMillen, "The Red Man and the White Plague," 612.

26 Sherman, *The Power of Plagues*, 349–50.

27 DeJong, *"If You Knew the Conditions,"* 85.

28 DeJong, *"If You Knew the Conditions,"* 102.

29 According to census records and family letters, her name was in fact "Iva." Apparently, Royce did not catch the error or felt it negligible. However, in keeping with the continuity of the records and letters that reference her, I use "Ivy."

30 Sam's exact age is difficult to ascertain. Three separate records indicate a birth year of 1909, 1910, and 1913. I have decided to use the date Sam indicated on her Application for Older Girls form. Application for Older Girls, October 31, 1930, NARA, Sam, Ivy; "Index Outing System—Ivy Sam," November 15, 1930, NARA, Sam, Ivy; U.S., Indian Census Rolls, 1885–1940—Iva Sam, April 1, 1931, National Archives, Washington, DC, Walker River Agency, roll M595_632, page 100, line 7.

31 Because the Indian Medical Service was ill-equipped to detect tuberculosis, patients were often diagnosed only after a painful and traumatic hemorrhage, when it was usually too late. DeJong, *"If You Knew the Conditions,"* 37.

32 Schionneman, "Maternal Care for Low-Income Families," 24–25.

33 Bonnie V. Royce to Ray Parrett, February 2, 1931, NARA, Sam, Ivy.

34 Bonnie V. Royce to Dr. Thomas B. Snoddy, February 9, 1931, NARA, Sam, Ivy.

35 Schionneman, "Maternal Care for Low-Income Families," 29.

36 Ray Parrett to Bonnie V. Royce, February 24, 1931, NARA, Sam, Ivy.

37 Bonnie V. Royce to Ray Parrett, February 28, 1931, NARA, Sam, Ivy.

38 Ivy Sam may not have belonged to the Walker River Reservation; however, she was under Parrett's jurisdiction. On April 1, a month after sending this letter, Parrett himself conducted the 1931 US Indian Census. He listed the Sam family as residents of the Bishop Reservation under the Walker River Agency. Although he knew she was hospitalized in the Bay Area, he counted Ivy Sam in the census. U.S., Indian Census Rolls, 1885–1940—Iva Sam, April 1, 1931, National Archives, Washington, DC, Walker River Agency, roll M595_632, page 100, line 7.

39 Ray Parrett to Bonnie V. Royce, March 2, 1931, NARA, Sam, Ivy.

40 Bonnie V. Royce to Mabel Sam, March 15, 1931, NARA, Sam, Ivy.

41 Bonnie V. Royce to Edward Swengel, Acting Supt. Sacramento Indian Agency, March 16, 1931, NARA, Sam, Ivy.

42 Ray Parrett to Bonnie V. Royce, March 23, 1931, NARA, Sam, Ivy.

43 Pete Sam to Bonnie V. Royce, April 14, 1931, NARA, Sam, Ivy.

44 Bonnie V. Royce to Pete Sam, April 29, 1931, NARA, Sam, Ivy.

45 Pete Sam to Bonnie V. Royce, May 4, 1931, NARA, Sam, Ivy.

46 Pete Sam to Bonnie V. Royce, May 16, 1931, NARA, Sam, Ivy.

47 Ray Parrett to Sallie Loveridge, Assoc. Charities of the City of Oakland, June 17, 1931, NARA, Sam, Ivy.

48 Bernice Sam to Bonnie V. Royce, July 4, 1931, NARA, Sam, Ivy.

49 Ray Parrett to Bonnie V. Royce, July 8, 1931, NARA, Sam, Ivy.

50 Bonnie V. Royce to Ray Parrett, July 20, 1931, NARA, Sam, Ivy.

51 Ray Parrett to Sallie Loveridge, Assoc. Charities of the City of Oakland, July 25, 1931, NARA, Sam, Ivy.

52 Bernice Sam to Bonnie V. Royce, August 4, 1931, NARA, Sam, Ivy.

53 Bonnie V. Royce to Bernice Sam, August 14, 1931, NARA, Sam, Ivy.

54 Ray Parrett to Bonnie V. Royce, January 30, 1930, NARA, Dock, Minnie; Ray Parrett to Bonnie V. Royce, January 12, 1931, NARA, Dock, Minnie.

55 Dr. Thomas B. Snoddy to Bonnie V. Royce, February 9, 1931, NARA, Dock, Minnie.

56 Bonnie V. Royce to Frederic Snyder, March 2, 1931, NARA, Dock, Minnie.

57 Frederic Snyder to Bonnie V. Royce, March 5, 1931, NARA, Dock, Minnie.

58 Bonnie V. Royce to Frederic Snyder, March 7, 1931, NARA, Dock, Minnie.

59 Frederic Snyder to Bonnie V. Royce, March 11, 1931, NARA, Dock, Minnie.

60 Bonnie V. Royce to Rose Aguilar, March 18, 1931, NARA, Dock, Minnie.

61 Bonnie V. Royce to Minnie Dock, March 18, 1931, NARA, Dock, Minnie.

62 Frederic Snyder to Bonnie V. Royce, April 27, 1931, NARA, Dock, Minnie.

63 Bonnie V. Royce to Frederic Snyder, June 2, 1931, NARA, Dock, Minnie.

64 Some outing records indicated that Nixon was Yurok, others that she was Tolowa. But Arizona State records indicate that she was Klamath. It's possible that she was all three tribes.

65 "UON Researcher Presents at University of California," University of Newcastle, Australia, April 6, 2017.

66 Index Outing System—Blanche Nixon, January 1930, NARA, Nixon, Blanche.

67 Re: Blanche Nixon, April 1, Outing Notes, April 1, 1935, NARA, Nixon, Blanche.

68 Index Outing System—Blanche Nixon, 1935, NARA, Nixon, Blanche.

69 Ruth Roberts to Mildred Van Every, August 18, 1935, NARA, Nixon, Blanche.

70 Supt. O. M. Boggess to Miss F. R. Knapp, Oakland YWCA, August 25, 1935, NARA, Nixon, Blanche.

71 Dorothy Owens to Mildred Van Every, September 26, 1935, NARA, Nixon, Blanche.

72 Dr. K. J. Thompson to Mildred Van Every, October 21, 1936, NARA, Nixon, Blanche.

73 Re: Blanche Nixon, October Outing Notes, October 1936, NARA, Nixon, Blanche.

74 For more on the reformist organization Friends of the Indian, see Prucha, *Americanizing the American Indians*, and Mathes, *The Women's National Indian Association.*

75 Re: Blanche Nixon, October Outing Notes, October 1936, NARA, Nixon, Blanche.

76 Mildred Van Every to Winifred Codman, October 21, 1936, NARA, Nixon, Blanche.

77 Mildred Van Every to Alida C. Bowler, October 21, 1936, NARA, Nixon, Blanche.

78 Mildred Van Every to Supt. O. M. Boggess, October 21, 1936, NARA, Nixon, Blanche.

79 Katharine Page, Medical Social Worker, Oakland Clinic to Mildred Van Every, October 23, 1936, NARA, Nixon, Blanche.

80 H. U. Sanders to Mildred Van Every, October 24, 1936, NARA, Nixon, Blanche.

81 Winifred Codman to Mildred Van Every, October 25, 1936, NARA, Nixon, Blanche.

82 Supt. O. M. Boggess to Mildred Van Every, October 27, 1936, NARA, Nixon, Blanche.

83 Roy Nash to Mildred Van Every, October 29, 1936, NARA, Nixon, Blanche.

84 Application—Form 5-363 c, November 2, 1936, NARA, Nixon, Blanche.

85 Mildred Van Every to U.S. Indian Tubercular Sanitorium, Albuquerque, NM, November 4, 1936, NARA, Nixon, Blanche; Mildred Van Every to U.S. Indian Tubercular Sanitorium, Phoenix, AZ, November 4, 1936, NARA, Nixon, Blanche.

86 M. K. Mihran to Mildred Van Every, November 10, 1936, NARA, Nixon, Blanche.

87 Mildred Van Every to Dr. S. W. Cartwright, November 10, 1936, NARA, Nixon, Blanche; Mildred Van Every to Dr. S. W. Cartwright, November 14, 1936, NARA, Nixon, Blanche.

88 Dr. S. W. Cartwright to Mildred Van Every, November 14, 1936, NARA, Nixon, Blanche.

89 Mildred Van Every to Supt. O. M. Boggess, November 18, 1936, NARA, Nixon, Blanche.

90 Mildred Van Every to Blanche Nixon, November 18, 1936, NARA, Nixon, Blanche.
91 Blanche Nixon to Mildred Van Every, September 6, 1937, NARA, Nixon, Blanche.
92 Mildred Van Every to Blanche Nixon, November 4, 1940, NARA, Nixon, Blanche.
93 Mildred Van Every to Blanche Nixon, November 18, 1940, NARA, Nixon, Blanche; Mildred Van Every to Blanche Nixon, November 30, 1940, NARA, Nixon, Blanche.
94 Mildred Van Every to Blanche Nixon, December 31, 1940, NARA, Nixon, Blanche.
95 Blanche Nixon to Mildred Van Every, January 9, 1941, NARA, Nixon, Blanche.
96 Mildred Van Every to Blanche Nixon, January 24, 1941, NARA, Nixon, Blanche.
97 Blanche Nixon to Mildred Van Every, February 6, 1941, NARA, Nixon, Blanche.
98 Mildred Van Every to Blanche Nixon, March 25, 1941, NARA, Nixon, Blanche.
99 Arizona, U.S., Death Records, 1887–1960—Blanche Nixon, September 3, 1943, Arizona Department of Health Services.

Conclusion

1 Orange, *There There*, 8.
2 Ramirez, *Native Hubs*, 3.
3 Ramirez, *Native Hubs*, 3–4.
4 Lobo, *Urban Voices*, 10.
5 Lobo, *Urban Voices*, 14.
6 Lobo, "Oakland's American Indian Community."
7 Lobo, "Oakland's American Indian Community," 8.
8 Lobo, "Oakland's American Indian Community," 8.
9 Lobo, "Oakland's American Indian Community," 9. See also Ramirez's *Native Hubs*, chapter 3.
10 Lobo, *Urban Voices*, 12.
11 Lobo, *Urban Voices*, 49.
12 Lobo, *Urban Voices*, 14.
13 Lobo, *Urban Voices*, 42.
14 Lobo, "Oakland's American Indian Community," 10.
15 Lobo, *Urban Voices*, 6–7.
16 Lobo, *Urban Voices*, 14.

Bibliography

Adams, David Wallace. *Education for Extinction: American Indians and the Boarding School Experience, 1875–1928*. Lawrence: University Press of Kansas, 1995.

Adams, Mikaëla M. "'A Very Serious and Perplexing Epidemic of Grippe': The Influenza of 1918 at the Haskell Institute." *American Indian Quarterly* 44, no. 1 (2020): 1–35. https://doi.org/10.5250/amerindiquar.44.1.0001.

Aikau, Hokulani K., Maile Arvin, Mishuana Goeman, and Scott Morgensen. "Indigenous Feminisms Roundtable." *Frontiers* 36, no. 3 (2015): 84–106.

Arizona Department of Health Services, Phoenix. Arizona Genealogy Birth and Death Certificates. Ancestrylibrary.com.

Arvin, Maile, Eve Tuck, and Angie Morrill. "Decolonizing Feminism: Challenging Connections between Settler Colonialism and Heteropatriarchy." *Feminist Formations* 25, no. 1 (2013): 8–34.

Bagwell, Beth. *Oakland: The Story of a City*. Oakland, CA: Oakland Heritage Alliance, 1996.

Barman, Jean. "Taming Aboriginal Sexuality: Gender, Power, and Race in British Columbia, 1850–1900." *BC Studies: The British Columbian Quarterly*, no. 115/6 (1997): 237–66.

Bauer, William, Jr. "The Economy of Indian Education in California, 1902–1945." In *Indian Subjects: Hemispheric Perspectives on the History of Indigenous Education*, 91–113. Santa Fe, NM: SAR Press, 2014..

———. "Native Californians in the Nineteenth Century." In *A Companion to California History*, edited by William Deverell and David Igler, 192–214. Newark: John Wiley & Sons, 2008.

———. "Stop Hunting Ishi." *Boom* 4, no. 3 (2014): 46–50.

———. *We Were All Like Migrant Workers Here: Work, Community, and Memory on California's Round Valley Reservation, 1850–1941*. Chapel Hill: University of North Carolina Press, 2009.

Beck, David R. M. *Unfair Labor? American Indians and the 1893 World's Columbian Exposition in Chicago*. Lincoln: University of Nebraska Press, 2019.

Behrendt, Larissa. "Consent in a (Neo)Colonial Society: Aboriginal Women as Sexual and Legal 'Other.'" *Australian Feminist Studies* 15, no. 33 (2000): 353–67.

Bonnell, Sonciray. "Chemawa Indian Boarding School: The First One Hundred Years 1880 to 1980." Master's thesis, Dartmouth College, 1997.

Brandt, Allan M. *No Magic Bullet: A Social History of Venereal Disease in the United States since 1880*. Enlarged edition. New York: Oxford University Press, 1987.

Bual, Harman. "Native American Rights & Adoption by Non-Indian Families: The Manipulation and Distortion of Public Opinion to Overthrow ICWA." *American Indian Law Journal* 6, no. 2 (2018).

Buffalohead, W. Roger, and Paulette Fairbanks Molin. "'A Nucleus of Civilization': American Indian Families at Hampton Institute in the Late Nineteenth Century." *Journal of American Indian Education* 35, no. 3 (1996): 59–94.

Cahill, Cathleen D. *Federal Fathers and Mothers: A Social History of the United States Indian Service, 1869–1933*. Illustrated edition. Chapel Hill: University of North Carolina Press, 2013.

Castillo, Edward D. "The Impact of Euro-American Exploration and Settlement." In *Handbook of North American Indians*, Vol. 8, *California*, edited by Robert F. Heizer, 99–127. Washington, DC: Smithsonian Institution, 1978.

Chandler, Robert J., and Ronald J. Quinn. "Emma Is a Good Girl." *Californians* 8, no. 5 (January/February 1991): 34–37.

Chavez-Garcia, Miroslava. *States of Delinquency: Race and Science in the Making of California's Juvenile Justice System*. Berkeley: University of California Press, 2012.

Child, Brenda. *Boarding School Seasons: American Indian Families, 1900–1940*. Lincoln: University of Nebraska Press, 2000.

———. *My Grandfather's Knocking Sticks: Ojibwe Family Life and Labor on the Reservation*. St. Paul: Minnesota Historical Society Press, 2014.

"Congress on Indian Progress." *Indian's Friend* 28, no. 1 (September 1915): 4–5.

Conor, Liz. *Skin Deep: Settler Impressions of Aboriginal Women*. Crawley, Western Australia: UWA Publishing, 2016.

Cook, Sherburne. *Conflict between the California Indian and White Civilization*. Originally published 1976. Berkeley: University of California Press, 2023. eBook.

———. "The Epidemic of 1830–1833 in California and Oregon." *University of California Publications in American Archaeology and Ethnology* 43, no. 3 (1955): 303–26.

Craddock, Susan. *City of Plagues: Disease, Poverty, and Deviance in San Francisco.* Minneapolis: University of Minnesota Press, 2000.

Deer, Sarah. *The Beginning and End of Rape: Confronting Sexual Violence in Native America.* Minneapolis: University of Minnesota Press, 2015.

DeJong, David H. *"If You Knew the Conditions": A Chronicle of the Indian Medical Service and American Indian Health Care, 1908–1955.* Lanham, MD: Lexington Books, 2008.

———. "'Unless They Are Kept Alive': Federal Indian Schools and Student Health, 1878–1918." *American Indian Quarterly* 31, no. 2 (2007): 256–82.

Downey, Lynn. *Arequipa Sanatorium: Life in California's Lung Resort for Women.* Norman: University of Oklahoma Press, 2019.

Emmerich, Lisa E. "'Save the Babies!' American Indian Women, Assimilation Policy, and Scientific Motherhood, 1912–1918." In *Writing the Range: Race, Class, and Culture in the Women's West,* edited by Susan Armitage and Elizabeth Jameson, 393–409. Norman: University of Oklahoma Press, 1997.

Forbes, Jack D. *Native Americans of California and Nevada.* Revised edition. Happy Camp, CA: Naturegraph, 1982.

Ghaddar, Ali, Sanaa Khandaqji, and Jinane Ghattas, "Justifying Abuse of Women Migrant Domestic Workers in Lebanon: The Opinion of Recruitment Agencies." *Gaceta Sanitaria* 34, no. 5 (2020) 493–99.

Gilbert, Matthew Sakiestewa. *Education beyond the Mesas: Hopi Students at Sherman Institute, 1902–1929.* Lincoln: University of Nebraska Press, 2010.

Glancy, Diane. *Fort Marion Prisoners and the Trauma of Native Education.* Lincoln: University of Nebraska Press, 2014.

Glenn, Evelyn Nakano. *Forced to Care: Coercion and Caregiving in America.* Cambridge, MA: Harvard University Press, 2012.

———. *Issei, Nisei, War Bride: Three Generations of Japanese American Women in Domestic Service.* Philadelphia: Temple University Press, 1986.

———. "Racial Ethnic Women's Labor: The Intersection of Race, Gender and Class Oppression." *Review of Radical Political Economics* 17, no. 3 (September 1, 1985): 86–108. https://doi.org/10.1177/048661348501700306.

Goeman, Mishuana. "Land as Life: Unsettling the Logics of Containment." In *Native Studies Keywords,* edited by Stephanie Nohelani Teves, Andrea Smith, and Michelle H. Raheja, 71–89. Tucson: University of Arizona Press, 2015.

Graham, Elizabeth. *The Mush Hole: Life at Two Indian Residential Schools*. Waterloo, Ontario: Heffle, 1997.

Graunke, Kristi. "'Just Like One of the Family': Domestic Violence Paradigms and Combating On-the-Job Violence against Household Workers in the United States." *Michigan Journal of Gender and Law* 9, no. 1 (January 1, 2002): 131–205.

Gutman, Marta. *A City for Children: Women, Architecture, and the Charitable Landscapes of Oakland, 1850–1950*. Chicago: University of Chicago Press, 2014.

Haas, Lisbeth. *Saints and Citizens: Indigenous Histories of Colonial Missions and Mexican California*. Berkeley: University of California Press, 2013.

Hackel, Steven. *Children of Coyote, Missionaries of Saint Francis: Indian-Spanish Relations in Colonial California, 1769–1850*. Chapel Hill: University of North Carolina Press, 2005.

Haley, Sarah. "'Like I Was a Man': Chain Gangs, Gender, and the Domestic Carceral Sphere in Jim Crow Georgia." *Signs: Journal of Women in Culture and Society* 39, no. 1 (2013): 53–77.

Hansen, Karen Tranberg. *Distant Companions: Servants and Employers in Zambia, 1900–1985*. Ithaca, NY: Cornell University Press, 1989.

Hantzaroula, Pothiti. "Public Discourses on Sexuality and Narratives of Sexual Violence of Domestic Servants in Greece (1880–1950)." *Journal of Mediterranean Studies* 18, no. 2 (2009): 283–310.

Haskins, Victoria. "Domestic Service and Frontier Feminism: The Call for a Woman Visitor to 'Half-Caste' Girls and Women in Domestic Service, Adelaide, 1925–1928." *Frontiers: A Journal of Women Studies* 28, no. 1/2 (2007): 124–64.

———. *Matrons and Maids: Regulating Indian Domestic Service in Tucson, 1914–1934*. Tucson: University of Arizona Press, 2012.

———. "'The Matter of Wages Does Not Seem to Be Material': Native American Domestic Workers' Wages under the Outing System in the United States, 1880s–1930s." In *Towards a Global History of Domestic and Caregiving Workers*, edited by Dirk Hoerder, Elise Van Nederveen Meerkerk, and Silke Neunsinger. Boston: Brill, 2015. http://ebookcentral.proquest.com/lib/ucsc/detail.action?docID=2063827.

———. "On the Doorstep: Aboriginal Domestic Service as a 'Contact Zone.'" *Australian Feminist Studies* 16, no. 34 (March 1, 2001): 13–25. https://doi.org/10.1080/08164640120038881.

Haskins, Victoria K., and Claire Lowrie, eds. *Colonization and Domestic Service: Historical and Contemporary Perspectives*. New York: Routledge, 2014.

Hiscock, Ira V., and American Public Health Association. *An Appraisal of the Public*

Health Program, San Francisco, California, for the Fiscal Year 1929–1930, for the Committee on Administrative Practice of the American Public Health Association. N.p., 1930. https://catalog.hathitrust.org/Record/102801947.

Hixson, Walter L. *American Settler Colonialism: A History.* New York: Palgrave Macmillan, 2013.

Hondagneu-Sotelo, Pierrette. *Doméstica: Immigrant Workers Cleaning and Caring in the Shadows of Affluence.* Berkeley: University of California Press, 2007.

Human Rights Watch. *World Report 2019: Human Rights Trends around the Globe.* New York: Human Rights Watch, 2019. https://www.hrw.org/world-report/2019.

Hurtado, Albert L. "'Hardly a Farm House—A Kitchen without Them': Indian and White Households on the California Borderland Frontier in 1860." *Western Historical Quarterly* 13, no. 3 (July 1, 1982): 245–70. https://doi.org/10.2307/969413.

———. *Indian Survival on the California Frontier.* New Haven, CT: Yale University Press, 1990.

———. *Intimate Frontiers: Sex, Gender, and Culture in Old California.* Albuquerque: University of New Mexico Press, 1999.

Indian Babies: How to Keep Them Well. Washington, DC: Dept. of the Interior, Office of Indian Affairs, 1916. http://hdl.handle.net/2027/uc2.ark:/13960/t3kw5kr2m.

Indian Child Welfare Act of 1978: Hearings before the Subcommittee on Indian Affairs and Public Lands of the Committee on Interior and Insular Affairs, House of Representatives, Ninety-Fifth Congress, Second Session, on S. 1214 . . . Hearings Held in Washington, D.C., February 9 and March 9, 1978. Washington, DC: US GPO, 1981.

Indian Child Welfare Act of 1978: Questions and Answers. Washington, DC: Department of Health, Education, and Welfare, Office of Human Development Services, Administration for Native Americans, 1979.

Jacobs, Margaret D. "Breaking and Remaking Families: The Fostering and Adoption of Native American Children in Non-native Families in the American West, 1880–1940." In *On the Borders of Love and Power: Families and Kinship in the Intercultural American Southwest,* edited by David Wallace Adams and Crista DeLuzio, 19–46. Berkeley: University of California Press, 2012.

———. "Diverted Mothering among American Indian Domestic Servants, 1920–1940." In *Indigenous Women and Work: From Labor to Activism,* edited by Carol Williams, 179–92. Urbana: University of Illinois Press, 2012. Oxford Academic, Illinois Scholarship Online.

———. *A Generation Removed: The Fostering and Adoption of Indigenous Children in the Postwar World.* Lincoln: University of Nebraska Press, 2014.

———. "The Great White Mother: Maternalism and American Indian Child Removal in the American West, 1880–1940." In *One Step Over the Line: Toward a History of Women in the North American Wests*, edited by Elizabeth Jameson and Sheila McManus, 191–213. Edmonton: University of Alberta Press, 2008.

———. *White Mother to a Dark Race: Settler Colonialism, Maternalism, and the Removal of Indigenous Children in the American West and Australia, 1880–1940.* Lincoln: University of Nebraska Press, 2009.

———. "Working on the Domestic Frontier: American Indian Domestic Servants in White Women's Households in the San Francisco Bay Area, 1920–1940." *Frontiers: A Journal of Women Studies* 28, no. 1 (2007): 165–99.

Johnson, Marilynn S. *The Second Gold Rush: Oakland and the East Bay in World War II*. Berkeley: University of California Press, 1993.

Jones, Jacqueline. *Labor of Love, Labor of Sorrow: Black Women, Work, and the Family from Slavery to the Present*. New York: Basic Books, 1985.

KAFA, "Dreams for Sale: The Exploitation of Domestic Workers from Recruitment in Nepal and Bangladesh to Working in Lebanon." KAFA Violence & Exploitation, 2014. https://www.idwfed.org/en/resources/dreams-for-sale-the-exploitation-of-domestic-workers-from-recruitment-in-nepal-and-bangladesh-to-working-in-lebanon.

Kaplan, Amy. "Manifest Domesticity." *American Literature* 70, no. 3 (September 1998): 581–606.

Katanski, Amelia V. *Learning to Write "Indian": The Boarding-School Experience and American Indian Literature*. Norman: University of Oklahoma Press, 2005.

Katzman, David M. *Seven Days a Week: Women and Domestic Service in Industrializing America*. New York: Oxford University Press, 1978.

Keliiaa, Caitlin. "Unsettling Domesticity: Native Women and US Indian Policy in the San Francisco Bay Area." In *Counterpoints: A San Francisco Bay Area Atlas of Displacement & Resistance*, illustrated edition, edited by Anti-eviction Mapping Project, 87–90. Oakland, CA: PM Press, 2021.

Keller, Jean A. *Empty Beds: Indian Student Health at Sherman Institute, 1902–1922*. East Lansing: Michigan State University Press, 2002.

———. "'In the Fall of the Year We Were Troubled with Some Sickness': Typhoid Fever Deaths at Sherman Institute, 1904." In *Medicine Ways: Disease, Health, and Survival among Native Americans*, edited by Clifford E. Trafzer, 32–51. Walnut Creek, CA: Altamira Press, 2001.

Klann, Mary. "Babies in Baskets: Motherhood, Tourism, and American Identity in Indian Baby Shows, 1916–1949." *Journal of Women's History* 29, no. 2 (2017): 38–61.

Knack, Martha C. "The Dynamics of Southern Paiute Women's Roles." In *Women and Power in Native North America*, edited by Laura F. Klein and Lillian A. Ackerman, 146–58. Norman: University of Oklahoma Press, 1995.

———"Nineteenth-Century Great Basin Wage Labor." In *Native Americans and Wage Labor: Ethnohistorical Perspectives*. Norman: University of Oklahoma Press, 1996.

Krupat, Arnold. *Changed Forever*. Vol. 1: *American Indian Boarding-School Literature*. Albany: State University of New York Press, 2018. ProQuest.

LaPier, Rosalyn R., and David R. M. Beck. *City Indian: Native American Activism in Chicago, 1893–1934*. Lincoln: University of Nebraska Press, 2015.

Leiby, James. "State Welfare Administration in California, 1930–1945." *Southern California Quarterly* 55, no. 3 (1973): 303–18. https://doi.org/10.2307/41170488.

Littlefield, Alice. "Indian Education and the World of Work in Michigan, 1893–1933." In *Native Americans and Wage Labor: Ethnohistorical Perspectives*, edited by Alice Littlefield and Martha C. Knack, 100–121. Norman: University of Oklahoma Press, 1996.

Littlefield, Alice, and Martha C. Knack, eds. *Native Americans and Wage Labor: Ethnohistorical Perspectives*. Norman: University of Oklahoma Press, 1996.

Lobo, Susan. "Oakland's American Indian Community: History, Social Organization and Factors That Contribute to Census Undercount." Preliminary Report for the Joint Statistical Agreement. Washington, DC: Center for Survey Methods Research—Bureau of the Census, May 1990.

———, ed. *Urban Voices: The Bay Area American Indian Community*. Tucson: University of Arizona Press, 2002.

Lomawaima, K. Tsianina. "Domesticity in the Federal Indian Schools: The Power of Authority over Mind and Body." *American Ethnologist* 20, no. 2 (1993): 227–40.

———. "Estelle Reel, Superintendent of Indian Schools, 1989–1910: Politics, Curriculum, and Land." *Journal of American Indian Education* 35, no. 3 (1996): 5–31.

———. *They Called It Prairie Light: The Story of Chilocco Indian School*. Reprint edition. Lincoln: University of Nebraska Press, 1995.

Lomawaima, K. Tsianina, and T. L. McCarty. *"To Remain an Indian": Lessons in Democracy from a Century of Native American Education*. New York: Teachers College Press, 2006.

Lomawaima, K. Tsianina, and Jeffrey Ostler. "Reconsidering Richard Henry Pratt: Cultural Genocide and Native Liberation in an Era of Racial Oppression." *Journal of American Indian Education* 57, no. 1 (2018): 79–100.

Lumsden, Stephanie. "Reproductive Justice, Sovereignty, and Incarceration: Prison Abolition Politics and California Indians." *American Indian Culture and Re-*

search Journal 40, no. 1 (January 1, 2016): 33–46. https://doi.org/10.17953/aicrj.40.1.lumsden.

———. "What's in a Name? An Examination of Historians' Reluctance to Use the Word Slavery in the Context of California Indian Genocide." *Center for the Study of Women* (blog), October 18, 2018. https://csw.ucla.edu/2018/10/18/whats-in-a-name-an-examination-of-historians-reluctance-to-use-the-word-slavery-in-the-context-of-california-indian-genocide.

Magliari, Michael. "Free Soil, Unfree Labor." *Pacific Historical Review* 73, no. 3 (2004): 349–90. https://doi.org/10.1525/phr.2004.73.3.349.

———. "Free State Slavery: Bound Indian Labor and Slave Trafficking in California's Sacramento Valley, 1850–1864." *Pacific Historical Review* 81, no. 2 (2012): 155–92. https://doi.org/10.1525/phr.2012.81.2.155.

Markwyn, Abigail Margaret. "'It Was a Place for the Girls to Meet': Community, Native Americans, and the Berkeley Outing Center, 1927–1933." PhD diss., University of Wisconsin–Madison, 2000.

Mathes, Valerie Sherer, ed. *The Women's National Indian Association: A History*. Illustrated edition. Albuquerque: University of New Mexico Press, 2015.

McClintock, Anne. *Imperial Leather: Race, Gender, and Sexuality in the Colonial Contest*. New York: Routledge, 1995.

McMillen, Christian W. *Discovering Tuberculosis: A Global History, 1900 to the Present*. New Haven, CT: Yale University Press, 2015.

———. "'The Red Man and the White Plague': Rethinking Race, Tuberculosis, and American Indians, ca. 1890–1950." *Bulletin of the History of Medicine* 82, no. 3 (2008): 608–45.

Meriam, Lewis, Hubert Work, and Brookings Institution. *The Problem of Indian Administration*. Baltimore: Johns Hopkins Press, 1928. https://catalog.hathitrust.org/Record/009063777.

Miller, Douglas K. *Indians on the Move: Native American Mobility and Urbanization in the Twentieth Century*. Chapel Hill: University of North Carolina Press, 2019.

Miranda, Deborah A. *Bad Indians: A Tribal Memoir*. Berkeley: Heyday, 2013.

———. "'Saying the Padre Had Grabbed Her': Rape Is the Weapon, Story Is the Cure." *Intertexts* 14, no. 2 (2010): 93–112.

Moorehead, Warren K. *The American Indian in the United States. Period 1850–1914. The Present Condition of the American Indian; His Political History and Other Topics: A Plea for Justice*. 1914. Facsimile of the first edition. Whitefish, MT: Kessinger, 2007.

Mountin, Joseph W. "Summary of a Study of Health and Hospital Services in Alameda County, Calif." *Public Health Reports (1896–1970)* 45, no. 52 (1930): 3179–94. https://doi.org/10.2307/4579896.

National Archives, Washington, DC. Indian Census Rolls, 1885–1940. Records of the Bureau of Indian Affairs, RG 75. https://www.ancestry.com.

———. Indians of California Census Rolls. Records of the Bureau of Indian Affairs, RG 75.

———. U.S., World War I Draft Registration Cards, 1917–1918. https://www.ancestrylibrary.com.

National Archives and Records Administration (NARA), San Bruno. Relocation, Education, and Employment Assistance Case Files 1926–1946, RG 75.

National Native American Boarding School Healing Coalition. "Indian Boarding Schools in the United States." 2023. https://boardingschoolhealing.org/list.

National Tuberculosis Association, Committee on Tuberculosis among the North American Indians, George M. Kober, United States, and Congress. *Tuberculosis among the North American Indians: Report of a Committee of the National Tuberculosis Association Appointed on October 28, 1921, on Tuberculosis among the North American Indians . . .* Washington, DC: Government Printing Office, 1923.

Odem, Mary E. *Delinquent Daughters: Protecting and Policing Adolescent Female Sexuality in the United States, 1885–1920*. 2nd ed. Chapel Hill: University of North Carolina Press, 1995.

Odem, Mary E., and Steven Schlossman. "Guardians of Virtue: The Juvenile Court and Female Delinquency in Early 20th-Century Los Angeles." *Crime & Delinquency* 37, no. 2 (1991): 186–203. https://doi.org/10.1177/0011128791037002003.

Ogden, Stormy. "Prisoner W-20170/Other." In *Sharing Our Stories of Survival: Native Women Surviving Violence*, edited by Sarah Deer, 149–66. Tribal Legal Studies. Walnut Creek, CA: Altamira Press, 2007. ProQuest.

Olund, Eric N. "Public Domesticity during the Indian Reform Era; or, Mrs. Jackson Is Induced to Go to Washington." *Gender, Place & Culture* 9, no. 2 (2002): 153–66. https://doi.org/10.1080/09663960220139662.

O'Neill, Colleen. "Testing the Limits of Colonial Parenting: Navajo Domestic Workers, the Intermountain Indian School, and the Urban Relocation Program, 1950–1962." *Ethnohistory* 66, no. 3 (July 1, 2019): 565–92. https://doi.org/10.1215/00141801-7517958.

———. *Working the Navajo Way: Labor and Culture in the Twentieth Century*. Illustrated edition. Lawrence: University Press of Kansas, 2005.

O'Neill, Colleen, and Brian C. Hosmer. *Native Pathways: American Indian Culture *and Economic Development in the Twentieth Century*. Boulder: University Press of Colorado, 2004.

Orange, Tommy. *There There*. New York: Knopf, 2018.

Orata, Pedro T., and Olive Galloway. "Promoting Boy-Girl Relationships through the Practice Cottage." *Journal of Home Economics* 30, no. 5 (May 1938): 321–23. https://reader.library.cornell.edu/docviewer/digital?id=hearth4732504_30_005#page/35/mode/1up.

Palmer, Phyllis. *Domesticity and Dirt: Housewives and Domestic Servants in the United States, 1920–1945*. Philadelphia: Temple University Press, 1991.

Parreñas, Rhacel Salazar. *Servants of Globalization: Women, Migration and Domestic Work*. Stanford, CA: Stanford University Press, 2001.

Patterson, Victoria D. "Evolving Gender Roles in Pomo Society." In *Women and Power in Native North America*, edited by Laura F. Klein and Lillian A. Ackerman, 126–45. Norman: University of Oklahoma Press, 1995.

———. "Indian Life in the City: A Glimpse of the Urban Experience of Pomo Women in the 1930s." *California History* 71, no. 3 (1992): 402–11.

Paxton, Katrina A. "Learning Gender: Female Students at the Sherman Institute, 1907–1925." In *Boarding School Blues: Revisiting American Indian Educational Experiences*, edited by Clifford E. Trafzer, Jean A. Keller, and Lorene Sisquoc, 174–186. Lincoln: Bison Books, 2006.

Perry, Barbara. "Nobody Trusts Them! Under- and Over-policing Native American Communities." *Critical Criminology* 14, no. 4 (November 1, 2006): 411–44. https://doi.org/10.1007/s10612-006-9007-z.

Phillips, George Harwood. *Indians and Indian Agents: The Origins of the Reservation System in California, 1849–1852*. Norman: University of Oklahoma Press, 1997.

Piatote, Beth H. *Domestic Subjects*. New Haven, CT: Yale University Press, 2013.

Pratt, Mary Louise. "Arts of the Contact Zone." *Profession* (1991): 33–40.

Prucha, Francis Paul, ed. *Americanizing the American Indians: Writings by the "Friends of the Indian," 1880–1900*. New edition. Lincoln: University of Nebraska Press, 1978.

Raibmon, Paige. *Authentic Indians: Episodes of Encounter from the Late-Nineteenth-Century Northwest Coast*. Durham, NC: Duke University Press, 2005.

Ramirez, Renya K. *Native Hubs: Culture, Community, and Belonging in Silicon Valley and Beyond*. Durham, NC: Duke University Press, 2007.

Rawls, James J. *Indians of California: The Changing Image*. Reprint edition. Norman: University of Oklahoma Press, 1986.

Reed, Kaitlin. "We Are a Part of the Land and the Land Is Us: Settler Colonialism,

Genocide & Healing in California." *Humboldt Journal of Social Relations* 1, no. 42 (October 7, 2020): 27–49. https://doi.org/10.55671/0160-4341.1131.
Reel, Estelle. *Course of Study for the Indian Schools of the United States: Industrial and Literary*. Washington, DC: Government Printing Office, 1901.
"Report of the Commissioner of Indian Affairs—Annual Report of the Commissioner of Indian Affairs, 1904," 1904. https://babel.hathitrust.org/cgi/pt?id=osu.32435064041965&seq=3.
Reséndez, Andrés. *The Other Slavery: The Uncovered Story of Indian Enslavement in America*. Boston: Houghton Mifflin Harcourt, 2016.
Rindfleisch, Bryan. "'A Very Considerable Mortality': Federal Indian Health Policy and Disease at the Hayward Indian School and Lac Courte Oreilles Reservation." *Wisconsin Magazine of History* 94, no. 4 (2011): 2–13.
Risling Baldy, Cutcha. *We Are Dancing for You: Native Feminisms and the Revitalization of Women's Coming-of-Age Ceremonies*. Seattle: University of Washington Press, 2018.
Rollins, Judith. *Between Women: Domestics and Their Employers*. Philadelphia: Temple University Press, 1985.
Romero, Mary. *Maid in the U.S.A.* New York: Routledge, 2002.
Rosenthal, Nicolas G. *Reimagining Indian Country: Native American Migration and Identity in Twentieth-Century Los Angeles*. Chapel Hill: University of North Carolina Press, 2014.
Ross, Luana. "Introduction: Settler Colonialism and the Legislating of Criminality." *American Indian Culture and Research Journal* 40, no. 1 (January 1, 2016): 1–18. https://doi.org/10.17953/aicrj.40.1.ross.
———. *Inventing the Savage: The Social Construction of Native American Criminality*. Austin: University of Texas Press, 1998.
Sánchez, Rosaura. *Telling Identities: The Californio Testimonios*. New edition. Minneapolis: University of Minnesota Press, 1995. https://www.jstor.org/stable/10.5749/j.ctttskkk.
Sandos, James A. *Converting California: Indians and Franciscans in the Missions*. New Haven, CT: Yale University Press, 2008.
Sanford, D. A. "What Is Killing Our Indians?" *Indian's Friend* 14, no. 1 (September 1901): 10.
Sarka, George. "The Role of the United States Public Health Service in the Control of Syphilis during the Early 20th Century." PhD diss., University of California, Los Angeles, 2013. https://escholarship.org/uc/item/4qv4b0hj#main.

Schionneman, Louise Marie. "Maternal Care for Low-Income Families in Berkeley and Oakland, California." PhD diss., University of California, Berkeley, 1941. https://catalog.hathitrust.org/Record/101650221.

Shah, Nayan. *Contagious Divides: Epidemics and Race in San Francisco's Chinatown*. Berkeley: University of California Press, 2001.

Sherman, Irwin W. *The Power of Plagues*. Washington, DC: ASM Press, 2006.

Silliman, Stephen W. *Lost Laborers in Colonial California: Native Americans and the Archaeology of Rancho Petaluma*. Tucson: University of Arizona Press, 2004.

Simonsen, Jane E. "'Object Lessons': Domesticity and Display in Native American Assimilation," *American Studies* 43, no. 1 (2002): 75–99.

Slivka, Kevin. "Art, Craft, and Assimilation: Curriculum for Native Students during the Boarding School Era." *Studies in Art Education* 52, no. 3 (2011): 225–42.

Smith, Stacey L. *Freedom's Frontier: California and the Struggle over Unfree Labor, Emancipation, and Reconstruction*. Chapel Hill: University of North Carolina Press, 2013.

Southworth, Michael, and Eran Ben-Joseph. *Streets and the Shaping of Towns and Cities*. Washington, DC: Island Press, 2003.

Stevenson, Allyson. "Vibrations across a Continent: The 1978 Indian Child Welfare Act and the Politicization of First Nations Leaders in Saskatchewan." *American Indian Quarterly* 37, no. 1 (2013): 218–36.

Stigler, George. "Domestic Servants in the United States, 1900–1940." *National Bureau of Economic Research Occasional Paper* 24 (1946): 12–20.

Stoler, Ann Laura. *Carnal Knowledge and Imperial Power: Race and the Intimate in Colonial Rule*. Berkeley: University of California Press, 2010.

Survey of Conditions of the Indians in the United States. Vol. 12. Part 29: California. Washington, DC: United States Government Printing Office, 1934. ProQuest.

Tac, Pablo. *Pablo Tac, Indigenous Scholar: Writing on Luiseño Language and Colonial History, c.1840*. Edited by Lisbeth Haas. Berkeley: University of California Press, 2011.

Teran, Jackie. "The Violent Legacies of the California Missions: Mapping the Origins of Native Women's Mass Incarceration." *American Indian Culture and Research Journal* 40, no. 1 (January 1, 2016): 19–32. https://doi.org/10.17953/aicrj.40.1.teran.

Theobald, Brianna. *Reproduction on the Reservation: Pregnancy, Childbirth, and Colonialism in the Long Twentieth Century*. Illustrated edition. Chapel Hill: University of North Carolina Press, 2019.

Thrush, Coll. *Indigenous London: Native Travelers at the Heart of Empire*. New Haven, CT: Yale University Press, 2016.

Thrush, Coll. *Native Seattle: Histories from the Crossing-Over Place*. 2nd ed. Seattle: University of Washington Press, 2017.

Trennert, Robert A. "Educating Indian Girls at Nonreservation Boarding Schools, 1878–1920." *Western Historical Quarterly* 13, no. 3 (July 1, 1982): 271–90. https://doi.org/10.2307/969414.

———. "From Carlisle to Phoenix: The Rise and Fall of the Indian Outing System, 1878–1930." *Pacific Historical Review* 52, no. 3 (August 1, 1983): 267–91. https://doi.org/10.2307/3639003.

———. *The Phoenix Indian School: Forced Assimilation in Arizona, 1891–1935*. Norman: University of Oklahoma Press, 1988.

———. "Victorian Morality and the Supervision of Indian Women Working in Phoenix, 1906–1930." *Journal of Social History* 22, no. 1 (1988): 113–28.

Trouillot, Michel-Rolph. *Silencing the Past: Power and the Production of History*. Boston: Beacon Press, 1997.

Tucker, Susan. *Telling Memories among Southern Women: Domestic Workers and Their Employers in the Segregated South*. Baton Rouge: Louisiana State University Press, 2002.

Ullah, Akm Ahsan. "Abuse and Violence against Foreign Domestic Workers: A Case from Hong Kong." *International Journal of Area Studies* 10, no. 2 (December 2015): 221–38.

United States. *Contagious and Infectious Diseases among the Indians*. 62d Cong., 3d Sess. Senate. Doc. No. 1038. Washington, DC, 1913. https://catalog.hathitrust.org/Record/102782523.

United States. Congress, House. *Annual Reports of the Department of the Interior for the Fiscal Year Ended June 30, 1900. Indian Affairs. Report of the Commissioner and Appendixes*. United States Congressional Serial Set; Serial Set No. 4101. Washington, DC, 1900.

United States Census. 1920 United States Federal Census. https://www.ancestry.com.

———. 1920 United States Federal Census. Records of the Bureau of the Census, RG 29, National Archives, Washington, DC.

———. 1930 United States Federal Census. https://www.ancestry.com.

———. 1940 United States Federal Census. https://www.ancestry.com.

Valoma, Deborah. *Scrape the Willow until It Sings: The Words and Work of Basket Maker Julia Parker*. Berkeley, California: Heyday, 2013.

Veracini, Lorenzo. *Settler Colonialism: A Theoretical Overview*. Houndmills, Basingstoke: Palgrave Macmillan, 2010.

Vučković, Myriam. *Voices from Haskell: Indian Students between Two Worlds, 1884–1928*. Lawrence: University Press of Kansas, 2008.

Weiss, Catherine. "Absent Men: Paid Domestic Work, Sexual Exploitation and Male Domination in the Family in the USA." *International Feminist Journal of Politics* 19, no. 3 (July 3, 2017): 342–56. https://doi.org/10.1080/14616742.2017.1293941.

Whalen, Kevin. "Labored Learning: The Outing System at Sherman Institute, 1902–1930." *American Indian Culture and Research Journal* 36, no. 1 (2012): 151–75.

———. *Native Students at Work: American Indian Labor and Sherman Institute's Outing Program, 1900–1945*. Seattle: University of Washington Press, 2016.

Williams, Samantha M. *Assimilation, Resilience, and Survival: A History of the Stewart Indian School, 1890–2020*. Lincoln: University of Nebraska Press, 2022.

Wolfe, Patrick. "Land, Labor, and Difference: Elementary Structures of Race." *American Historical Review* 106, no. 3 (2001): 866–905. https://doi.org/10.2307/2692330.

———. "Settler Colonialism and the Elimination of the Native." *Journal of Genocide Research* 8, no. 4 (December 2006): 387–409. https://doi.org/10.1080/14623520601056240.

Wong, Sau-ling. "Diverted Mothering: Representations of Caregivers of Color in the Age of 'Multiculturalism.'" In *Mothering: Ideology, Experience, and Agency*, edited by Evelyn Nakano Glenn, Grace Chang, and Linda Rennie Forcey, 1st paperback edition, 67–91. New York: Routledge, 1994.

Zahreddine, Nada, Rima Talaat Hady, Rabih Chammai, François Kazour, Dory Hachem, and Sami Richa. "Psychiatric Morbidity, Phenomenology and Management in Hospitalized Female Foreign Domestic Workers in Lebanon." *Community Mental Health Journal* 50, 5 (2014): 619–28.

Ziibiwing Center of Anishinabe Culture & Lifeways. *American Indian Boarding Schools: An Exploration of Global Ethnic & Cultural Cleansing*. Mt. Pleasant, MI: Ziibiwing Center of Anishinabe Culture & Lifeways, 2011.

Index

Act for the Government and Protection of Indians (California, 1850), 32
adoption. *See* child removal
African Americans: and domestic work, xvii, 59, 112, 237n35, 241n2; education at Hampton Institute, 35; health care for, 247n10; interracial relationships with Native women, 130–31; relationship to labor, 26, 112, 241n2; residential enclaves, xv, xvii
Aguilar, Rose, 191–92
Allotment Act of 1887 (US), 68, 149, 178, 204
American Indian Progressive Association, 10
Associated Charities of San Francisco, 119, 126. *See also* Children's Agency
Associated Charities of the City of Oakland, 189

Babb, Esther, 79
Barber, Belma, 1–2, 214n1
Bay Area Outing Program, xi–xii, 3–5, 11–16, 43–46, 51–60, 204–7; and child removal, 111–12, 116–46; control of wages, 43, 71–72, 135, 162; and criminalization of sexuality, 86–89, 94–106, 109–10, 116–17, 157–76; invasive exams for sexually transmitted infections, 89, 103; matrons and assistants, 56–57; nature of labor in, 63–67; and participant fight for commensurate wages, 60, 75–77, 81–82, 129–30, 227n96; process of, 57–63; runaways from, 85–110, 229n1; sexual health clearances for, 60, 100, 116, 138, 154–58, 232n55, 235n15; and stigmatizing pregnancy, 116–46, 138, 158–62, 167–76; and stigmatizing STIs, 94, 151, 154–76; and surveillance through work contracts, 67–70; and tuberculosis, 139, 185–203, 247n10; and unpaid or docked wages, 61–64, 69, 73–75, 95–96; wage system, 69–77. *See also* Royce, Bonnie V.; Traxler, Jeannette; Van Every, Mildred
Bethel, Amy, 121–23
boarding schools: and child separation, 3–4, 26, 35–37, 115, 124–28; and control of sexuality, 152–54, 157; and

boarding schools (*continued*)
domestic training xii, 58, 63–64, 81, 218n41, 222n12; and health care, 149, 181–85, 243n42; runaways from, 84–86. *See also specific schools*
Boggess, O. M., 102, 105, 163, 171, 194, 197
Boone, Grace, 70–71
Bureau of Indian Affairs (BIA), 39, 208, 222n5. *See also* Office of Indian Affairs (OIA)

Carlisle Indian Industrial School: founding of, 35; and outing, 4, 37–38, 44, 46, 221n99, 222n7; and tuberculosis, 183
Carson Indian School. *See* Stewart Indian School
Chemawa Indian School, 4, 8, 53, 59, 103, 225n67
child care, Traxler's interference in, 167–73
child labor, 3–5, 13–14, 29–46
child removal, 26; through adoption or fostering, 128–44, 145–46, 238n49; Bay Area Outing Program and, 111–12, 116–46 (*see also* Royce, Bonnie V.; Van Every, Mildred); through boarding schools and infant boarding, 3–4, 26, 35–37, 115, 118–28, 145–46. *See also* Stewart Indian School
Children's Agency (San Francisco), 119, 126–27
Children's Home Society of California, 121, 133, 143, 169, 174, 239n62
Chinese labor, xvii, 151, 214n5, 242n19
Christianization, 3, 35
Cleveland, Harriet, 65–66, 72
Cleveland, Lottie, 97–98
Cooper, Vivian, 93–94, 96
Crabtree, Loretta, 98–100
criminalization: of outing participants (*see under* Royce, Bonnie V.; Traxler, Jeannette; Van Every, Mildred); of sexuality, 86–89, 94–106, 109–10, 116–17, 157–76; and sterilization, 89, 154, 164, 170–76; and STIs, 89, 151, 153, 158–76
cult of domesticity, 39
Cushman Indian School, 75

daʔawʔá·gaʔ, xi, 213n1
Daniels, Bertha, 75
Dat So La Lee, 22
Dawes Severalty Act. *See* Allotment Act of 1887
Daughters of the American Revolution, 195–96
Department of the Interior, 61
diverted mothering, 111–18: through adoption or fostering, 128–44, 145–46, 238n49; and boarding schools, 124–28, 145–46; through infant boarding, 118–24, 145–46 Dock, Minnie, 185–87, 191–93, 201–3
domestication, 7, 27–28, 41, 57, 65
domesticity, cult of, 39
domestic labor, 5–7, 214n11; in the Bay Area, xvii–xviii; and boarding schools, xii, 34–41, 63–64, 226n75; California history of, 22–23, 29–34, 41; and outing, 45–46, 50–51, 64–65; and settler colonialism, 7–9, 27–28, 44–45, 241n2

"domestic science," xii, 1, 7, 36, 41–42, 63–65
Donnely, Lena, 101
Dyer, Agnes, 118–20, 123, 236n19

Egan, Lucy, 62, 71–72, 79
Eleck, Freda, 60–61
Elliott, Rosita, 142, 158–59, 175
Emm, Hazel, 61–62, 155
enslavement: African, 112 ; Indigenous, 14, 23–24, 29–34, 38, 153, 217n4; outing compared to, 102–5; and sex trafficking, 31–32
eugenics movement: as framing accusations of moral degeneracy, 149–50, 161; mental tests, 94, 170–71, 176, 232n32; sterilization, 154, 157, 160, 171, 176; theories of disease, 149–50, 178, 183–84

Flandreau Indian School, 10
Ford (née Green), Josephine, 131–33, 145
Fort Marion, prisoners at, 4, 34–35
fostering. *See* child removal
Four Winds Club: creation of, 228n124, 78, 83; as means of control, 77–78, 80–81; as sustaining and creating community life, 77–81, 205, 207–8
Fred, Velma, 74–75
Friends of the Indian, 195

gendered violence. *See under* settler colonialism
Godawa, Leona, 76–77
Godawa, Lois, 58
Gold Rush, 32, 168, 224n46
Golden Gate International Exposition (1939), 73
Graham, Martha, 96–97, 100, 232n45
Great Depression, 44, 137; and health care, 150; as incentive for outing, 76; and urban employment availability, 50, 65, 168; and wages, 73, 101–2, 105, 168
Green, Josephine. *See* Ford, Josephine

Hampton Institute (Virginia), 35, 220n76
Haskell Institute (Kansas), 8, 46, 59, 83, 88
Healey, Stella, 42–43, 51, 70
health care: for African Americans, 247n10; boarding schools and, 94, 149, 181–85, 192–93, 195–97, 202, 243n42; in Great Depression, 150; and the "Indian Problem," 113, 116, 178. *See also* Indian Health and Medical Service
health clearances, 19, 60, 154–55, 157; sexual, 116, 155, 157, 232n55, 235n15
health conditions, and settler colonialism, 114–15. *See also* tuberculosis
heteropatriarchy, 25–26, 68
Holbrook, Delphine, 1–2, 73–75
Holbrook, Lydia, 58
Holland, Lettie, 62
Hooper, Avis, 79, 134–38, 143,
Hunt, Allen, 78
Hunter, Bernice, 94–96

Ince, Patricia, 156, 162–66, 175–76
Indian Defense Association of Central and Northern California, 52, 227n96

Indian Fellowship League, 10
Indian Health and Medical Service, 178–81, 184–85, 195, 203, 248n31
Indian "New Deal." *See* Indian Reorganization Act
the "Indian Problem": and health care, 113, 116, 178; and privatized labor labor, 53, 227n91; as solved through education, 3, 35; and white maternalism, 57
Indian Relocation Act of 1956 (US), 204, 207
Indian relocation policies: as creating community, xiii, 204, 207–8; and health clearances, 156; as intended assimilation, xiii, 10–12, 24, 204; and voluntary relocation, 10–11
Indian Reorganization Act of 1934 (US), 12, 44
Intertribal Friendship House (IFH), xii, 80, 83–84, 208–9
Ishi (Yana man), 51, 224n40

Jack, Frances, 80
Japanese labor, xvii, 5, 52, 59, 214n5
Joaquin, Evelyn, 98–100
Johnson, Elaine, 70, 78–79
Jones, Kathryn, 62

Keisner, Lila, 166–74, 176, 245n73, 245n86
Kibby, Helen, 59–60

labor: and boarding schools, xii, 58, 34–41, 63–64; as domestication, 22–23, 27–28; as element of settler colonialism, 9–14, 22–27, 29–34; Native history of, 47–51; and Native peoples in California, 22–23, 29–34, 41, 218n37; and outing, 45–46, 50–51, 64–65
Ladies' Relief Society, xvi, 130, 161, 166–67, 174
Lake Tahoe. *See* da?aw?á·ga?
Little Children's Aid Society of San Francisco, 141
Los Angeles Indian Center, 10

Marsh, Josephine, 62
Martin, Marcie, 155, 243n39
maternalism, white. *See* white maternalism
McCarthy, Persia, 72
Meriam Report (1928), 12, 36–37, 179–82, 215n21
Mitchell, Genny, 80–81, 228n124
Mitchell, Maude, 124–25, 128, 146
Mitchell, Thana Thompson. *See* Thompson, Thana
Moore, Ida, 95–96
Morgan, Sue Andrews, 75–76
motherhood: and outing, 111–12, 118–46; stigmatization of Native practices of, 112–15. *See also* diverted mothering

Natchez, Josephine, 67–70
Nelson, Bernice, 8, 105–6
Nelson, Ivora, 7–8, 106–7
Nelson, Winifred, 79, 101–6, 233n73
Nix, Alice Marshall, 155
Nixon, Blanche, 193–203, 249n64
Nixon, Lucy, 79

Office of Indian Affairs (OIA), 222n5; and boarding schools, xii, 7, 42,

220n78; and outing programs, 37, 43–44, 153, 224n44, 229n1; and wage discrimination, 47–48. *See also* Bureau of Indian Affairs (BIA)
Ohlone peoples, xii–xiii, 22, 206
outing, 3–4, 34–35, 37–41, 44–46, 222n7; matrons, 56–57; as settler colonial structure, 9, 44–45; and sexual surveillance, 151–54. *See also* Bay Area Outing Program

Paradice, Ruby, 1–2, 66–67
Patterson, Rosalie, 70, 227n98
Penrose, Lillian, 138–41, 240n88
Penrose, Marie, 7, 78–79
Pensotti, Frances, 141, 144
Pete, Rose "Rosie," 1–2, 58
Peters, Marjorie, 79, 100–101, 233n57
Phoenix Indian School, 38–40, 46, 152–53, 225n54, 226n78
Plummer, Daisy, 129–31, 143, 146
Pratt, Richard Henry: and boarding schools, 34–35, 220n76, 226n77; controversy around, 220n78; design of outing, 4, 34–35, 37–38, 44, 214n2, 222n7; and other outing programs, 40, 46
"The Problem of Indian Administration." *See* Meriam Report (1928)
Puyallup Indian School. *See* Cushman Indian School

Reel, Estelle, 36, 44, 65
Rodriguez, Tony, 79
Rook, Minnie, 51
Royce, Bonnie V.: amicable relationship with families and outing participants, 107–8; controlling dispersal of wages, 43, 71–74, 120, 135, 162, 227n96; criminalization and disciplining of outing participants, 85, 90–94, 97–98, 101–4, 131, 159–61; and eugenics, 94; health provision, 155, 185–94; justifying low wages, 73, 96, 169; and maternalism in outing, 1–3, 53, 57 112; pressure for participants to adopt or foster their children, 128–32; pressure for participants to board their children, 119–21, 125–28, 134–36, 141–43, 159–61, 166–69; as unresponsive, 76–77, 92, 166–69, 188–90, 202
runaways: from boarding school, 84–85, 87–88, 222n113; from outing, 51–52, 85–110, 120, 229n1, 231n24

Sam, Ivy, 185–93, 201–3, 248n38
Sam, Sadie, 101, 120–21, 123
Save the Babies campaign. *See under* Sells, Cato
"scientific motherhood," 113–15
Scott, Savina, 79
Sells, Cato: and outing, 53–56, 112, 224n46; and Save the Babies campaign, 112–15, 145, 235n5, 235n7, 235n12
settler colonialism, 9, 17–18, 24–28, 217n16, 217n18, 230n8; and boarding schools, 86, 230n4; in California, xi–xii, 22–23, 25–34, 41, 224n46; and gendered violence, 25–26, 32, 117; and health conditions, 114–15; and Indigenous enslavement, 31–34, 217n4; and labor, 26–27, 47–51, 217n18;

settler colonialism (*continued*)
outing program as enduring, 7–8, 12, 34–41, 118, 147–48, 174–76; resistance to, 81–82, 85–86, 110; and settler domesticity, xii, 7–9, 27–28, 44–45, 50, 241n2; and white women, 56, 215n23, 219n69
sexuality: control of, in boarding schools, 152–54, 157; criminalization of, in Bay Area Outing Program, 86–89, 94–106, 109–10, 116–17, 157–76. *See also* health clearances: sexual
sexually transmitted infections (STIs): and detention or criminalization, 89, 151, 153, 158–76; and Indian health, 148–50; and outing programs, 100, 116, 138, 151–76, 232n55; as pathologizing, 89, 149–58, 242n19; and "Wassermann test," 138, 150, 155, 163, 242n38, 243n38
Shaw, Clara, 74–75
Sherman Institute: control of outing wages, 94; and gendered labor, 7, 40, 46, 58, 223n37; and health clearances, 155; and transfer to outing, 4, 7–8, 38, 59, 225n67
Smart, Della, 97–98
Snapp, Catherine, 97–98
Snyder, Frederic: communication concerning outing, 74, 94, 101, 127, 142, 192–93; managing outing logistics, 69, 97, 142, 188
Spencer, Carrie, 159–62, 171, 175, 244n48, 244n59
Srk, Mary, 79
sterilization: and criminalization, 89, 154, 164, 170–76; eugenic, 154, 157, 160–61, 170–76; and sexually transmitted infections, 149, 154, 164
Stewart Indian School: and beginning of Bay Area Outing Program, xii, xvii, 1, 16, 51–52, 206; control of outing wages, 97; and gendered labor, xii, 20–21, 42–43, 51, 63, 226n75; and health care, 94, 192–93, 195–97, 202; and punishment for perceived delinquency, 97–98, 101, 124, 129, 138–39; as raising children of outing participants, 119–20, 123–24, 127, 141–46, 188–92; and runaways, 51, 83–84, 88, 120; student experiences at 58, 63; and transfer to outing, 16, 38, 71, 225n67
stigmatization: of Native practices of motherhood, 112–15; of pregnancy, 116–46, 138, 158–62, 167–76; of STIs, 94, 151, 154–76;
surveillance: sexual, 151–54; use of social clubs as, 77–78, 81, 228n124; through work contracts, 67–70

Termination policy, 207
Thompson, Thana, 8, 73, 106–8
Traxler, Jeannette, 57, 94; criminalization of outing participants, 97; and health provision, 155, 162–63, 166; interference in child care, 167–73
tuberculosis: in the Bay Area, 179–80, 247n12; in boarding schools, 181–85; and eugenic or racialized explanations, 183–84; in Indian Country, 149, 177–79, 182–85, 194–95; and outing participants, 139, 152, 177, 185–203, 247n10
Tungate, Irene, 58, 225n55

Urban Indian communities, xii–xiii, 10–11, 83, 193, 204–10

Van Every, Mildred, 57, 240n89; contrasted with Royce, 14, 94; criminalization and disciplining of outing participants, 98–101, 164–66, 170–71; health provision, 155–56, 163–66, 194–203, 232n55, 243n42; justifying low wages, 73, 95; pressure for outing participants to give up/board their children, 124–25, 128, 133, 136–39, 143, 146, 240n89; recruiting from boarding schools, 59–60; as a social worker, 14–15, 66, 73, 158, 163–64; use of social clubs as surveillance, 77–78, 81, 228n124
venereal disease. *See* sexually transmitted infections (STIs)
Victorian morality, 39, 56–57, 63, 81, 116
violence, gendered. *See under* settler colonialism
Voluntary Relocation Program, 10–11

wages: control of, in Bay Area Outing Program, 43, 71–72, 135, 162 (*see also* Royce, Bonnie V.); Great Depression and, 73, 101–2, 105, 168; low, justified by outing matrons, 73, 95–96, 169; outing participant fight for commensurate, 60, 75–77, 81–82, 129–30, 227n96
Washoe, Phyllis, 73–74
"Wassermann test," 138, 150, 155, 163, 242n38, 243n38
Wasson, Esther, 16, 21, 63
Wasson, Gertrude, 125–28, 145–46
Whipple, Mabel, 73
white maternalism, 28, 33–34, 56–57, 81, 91, 215n23
white women, meddling. *See* Royce, Bonnie V.; Traxler, Jeannette; Van Every, Mildred
Wilder, Ruby, 1–2
Williams, Helen, 66
Williams, Theresa, 72
World War I, 150, 206, 242n13
World War II, 21, 50, 80, 206–7, 241n98

Young Women's Christian Association (YWCA): affiliation with Bay Area Outing Program, xviii, 2, 52, 78, 81; and Four Winds Club, 78–81, 83, 207–8, 228n124

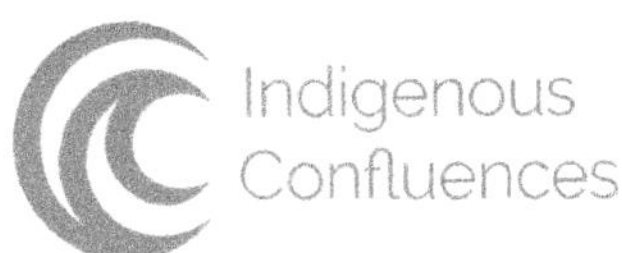

CHARLOTTE COTÉ AND COLL THRUSH *Series Editors*

Indigenous Confluences publishes innovative works that use decolonizing perspectives and transnational approaches to explore the experiences of Indigenous peoples across North America, with a special emphasis on the Pacific Coast.

Refusing Settler Domesticity: Native Women's Labor and Resistance in the Bay Area Outing Program, by Caitlin Keliiaa

Unrecognized in California: Federal Acknowledgment and the San Luis Rey Band of Mission Indians, by Olivia M. Chilcote

Alaska Native Resilience: Voices from World War II, by Holly Miowak Guise

Settler Cannabis: From Gold Rush to Green Rush in Indigenous Northern California, by Kaitlin Reed

A Drum in One Hand, a Sockeye in the Other: Stories of Indigenous Food Sovereignty from the Northwest Coast, by Charlotte Coté

A Chemehuevi Song: The Resilience of a Southern Paiute Tribe, by Clifford E. Trafzer

Education at the Edge of Empire: Negotiating Pueblo Identity in New Mexico's Indian Boarding Schools, by John R. Gram

Indian Blood: HIV and Colonial Trauma in San Francisco's Two-Spirit Community, by Andrew J. Jolivette

Native Students at Work: American Indian Labor and Sherman Institute's Outing Program, 1900–1945, by Kevin Whalen

California through Native Eyes: Reclaiming History, by William J. Bauer Jr.

Unlikely Alliances: Native Nations and White Communities Join to Defend Rural Lands, by Zoltán Grossman

Dismembered: Native Disenrollment and the Battle for Human Rights, by David E. Wilkins and Shelly Hulse Wilkins

Network Sovereignty: Building the Internet across Indian Country, by Marisa Elena Duarte

Chinook Resilience: Heritage and Cultural Revitalization on the Lower Columbia River, by Jon Daehnke

Power in the Telling: Grand Ronde, Warm Springs, and Intertribal Relations in the Casino Era, by Brook Colley

We Are Dancing for You: Native Feminisms and the Revitalization of Women's Coming-of-Age Ceremonies, by Cutcha Risling Baldy